GHOST FLEET AWAKENED

GHOST FLEET AWAKENED

Lake George's
Sunken Bateaux of 1758

Joseph W. Zarzynski

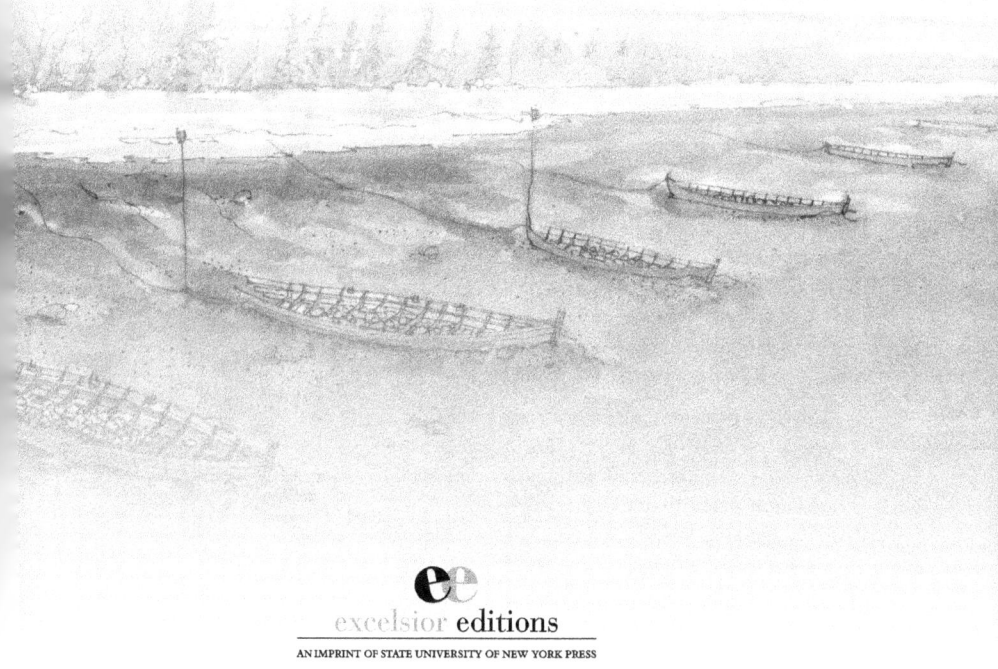

excelsior editions
AN IMPRINT OF STATE UNIVERSITY OF NEW YORK PRESS

Cover art: Mark L. Peckham, Colonial troops sinking bateaux at Lake George in the autumn of 1758, ink and watercolor. Image courtesy of the artist.

Published by State University of New York Press, Albany

© 2019 State University of New York

All rights reserved

No part of this book may be used or reproduced in any manner whatsoever without written permission. No part of this book may be stored in a retrieval system or transmitted in any form or by any means including electronic, electrostatic, magnetic tape, mechanical, photocopying, recording, or otherwise without the prior permission in writing of the publisher.

Excelsior Editions is an imprint of
STATE UNIVERSITY OF NEW YORK PRESS.

For information, contact State University of New York Press, Albany, NY
www.sunypress.edu

Library of Congress Cataloging-in-Publication Data
Names: Zarzynski, Joseph W., author.
Title: Ghost fleet awakened : Lake George's sunken bateaux of 1758 / Joseph W. Zarzynski.
Other titles: Lake George's sunken bateaux of 1758
Description: Albany, NY : State University of New York Press, [2019]
|
    Series: Excelsior editions | Includes bibliographical references and index.
Identifiers: LCCN 2018056833 | ISBN 9781438476728 (pbk. : alk. paper) | ISBN 9781438476742 (e-book)
Subjects: LCSH: Bateaux—New York (State)—George, Lake (Lake)
| Shipwrecks—New York (State)—George, Lake (Lake) | George, Lake (N.Y. : Lake)—Antiquities. | Excavations (Archaeology)—New York (State)—George, Lake (Lake) | United States—History—French and Indian War, 1754-1763—Naval operations, British.
Classification: LCC VM354 .Z37 2019 | DDC 973.2/6—dc23 LC record available at https://lccn.loc.gov/2018056833

10 9 8 7 6 5 4 3 2 1

Foremost, this book is dedicated
to Mary Patram Meaney, my wife,
and Lisa (Randesi) Melena, my goddaughter.
It is also dedicated to those who helped most
with Bateaux Below's archaeological study
of Lake George's Sunken Bateaux of 1758:
Dr. Russell P. Bellico, Bob Benway, John Farrell,
Terry Crandall, Vince Capone, Dr. D.K. (Kathy) Abbass,
Peter Pepe, Mark L. Peckham, Paul Cornell,
Scott Padeni, David Van Aken, Bill Appling,
Dr. Samuel Bowser, and Steve Resler.

Contents

List of Illustrations / ix
Preface / xiii
Acknowledgments / xvii

1 Early History of Bateaux / 1
2 The Bateau Watercraft / 11
3 Building Techniques / 21
4 Discovery of Lake George's Sunken Bateaux of 1758 / 27
5 The 1950s and Early 1960s: "Rediscovery" / 35
6 Toward Better Management / 41
7 Underwater Archaeology / 51
8 A Renaissance of Interest / 73
9 The "Mortar Bateau" / 93
10 What Lies Beneath: An Inventory / 105
11 Missing Bateau Shipwrecks / 113
12 Lake George's *Baby Whale* Submarine / 121
13 Wiawaka Bateaux and the National Register of Historic Places / 127
14 Submerged Heritage Preserves / 131
15 Stabilizing a Bateau Shipwreck Site / 143
16 Students Build Underwater Archaeology Equipment and Replica Bateaux / 147

17 "Raising the Fleet": An Art/Science Initiative / 155
18 Documentary Filmmaking, Bateaux, and Archaeologists / 159
19 Public Education Programs / 163

Conclusion / 183
Appendix I. "Operation Bateaux" Revisited Twenty-Four Years Later—Part 1 / 187
Appendix II. "Operation Bateaux" Revisited Twenty-Four Years Later—Part 2 / 191
Appendix III. Insights Gained from a Replica Lake George Bateau / 195
Appendix IV. A List of Some of the Dive Teams, Underwater Archaeology Teams, and Scuba Divers Who Dived Lake George's Sunken Bateaux of 1758 During Rediscovery and Study / 201
Glossary / 203
Notes / 209
Bibliography / 229
Index / 243
About the Author / 262

List of Illustrations

P.1. Scuba diver at Wiawaka bateaux site. / xiv
P.2. Scuba divers descending to Wiawaka bateaux, September 13, 1987. / xv
1.1. Map of the Hudson River, Lake George, and Lake Champlain corridor. / 2
1.2. Peckham drawing of a typical eighteenth-century bateau. / 3
1.3. Illustration by Yohn, Battle of Lake George, September 8, 1755. / 4
1.4. Drone shot of Fort William Henry Museum, Lake George. / 4
1.5. Cordell drawing of vessels on the lake, Abercromby campaign, July 1758. / 7
1.6. Whitesel image depicting submerged British bateaux, autumn of 1758. / 8
1.7. Peckham painting of Lake George sunken bateaux, winter of 1758–1759. / 8
2.1. Whitesel image of bateau "factories" in Schenectady, New York, 1758. / 12
2.2. Lake George bateau at the Adirondack Museum. / 13
2.3. An excavated sunken bateau, from 1963–1964 fieldwork. / 14
2.4. Lake George bateau exhibited in the New York State Museum. / 15
2.5. Thole pin pad and thole pins (oarlock). / 16
2.6. Crisman drawing, a reconstructed cross-section of Bateau 2626. / 16
2.7. Sample of a 1758 Lake George bateau bottom board. / 16
2.8. Crisman drawings, profile and plan views, Bateau 2626. / 18
2.9. Crandall drawing (plan view) of a Lake George military bateau. / 20
3.1. Hager drawing of the likeness of a Mohawk River bateau. / 22
3.2. Sample Lake George bateau batten. / 24
3.3. Sample Lake George bateau stem. / 24
3.4. Sample Lake George bateau frame. / 24
3.5. Sample Lake George bateau strake. / 24
3.6. Hager drawing: two men "poling" a bateau in shallow water. / 26
4.1. Sunken timbers from reputed Lake George floating gun battery. / 29
4.2. British sloop of 1757 raised from Lake George in 1903. / 30
4.3. Thompson photograph of recovered March 1757 British sloop, 1903. / 30

4.4. Several timbers of a 1903-raised British sloop. / 32
5.1. Scuba diver Carl Dunn emerges from Lake George. / 36
5.2. Fort William Henry archaeologist Stanley M. Gifford, early 1950s. / 37
6.1. A young Dr. Robert Bruce Inverarity, director of the Adirondack Museum. / 42
6.2. "Top Deck of Submarine," a World War II painting by Inverarity. / 45
6.3. Bow of 1758 *Land Tortoise* radeau that sank in Lake George. / 48
7.1. Early underwater camera system used in 1960 to help raise a bateau. / 52
7.2. One of three 1758 bateaux being raised at Lake George, early 1960s. / 52
7.3. One of three bateaux recovered from Lake George, early 1960s. / 56
7.4. One of an early 1960s-raised colonial bateaux being buried on a beach. / 58
7.5. Inverarity examines PEG vat. / 58
7.6. Following conservation in the 1960s, the bateaux were reassembled. / 59
7.7. Archaeological diver Terry Crandall. / 63
7.8. Perry-Link *Deep Diver* submarine on display in Fort Pierce, Florida. / 65
7.9. Harold Veeder, head of the Fort William Henry Corporation. / 66
7.10. Archaeological diver Terry Crandall at a colonial bateau shipwreck. / 67
7.11. State of New York booklet, a primer on underwater archaeology, 1969. / 70
8.1. People with PVC archaeology grid for training, September 12, 1987. / 74
8.2. Capone readies ROV for a training seminar, September 12, 1987. / 74
8.3. Capone piloting ROV at Wiawaka bateaux, September 13, 1987. / 74
8.4. Four archaeological divers plan a scuba dive at sunken bateaux, 1988. / 76
8.5. Klein 595 side-scan sonar during field tests off New England. / 76
8.6. Autonomous underwater vehicle (AUV) being deployed from a ship. / 76
8.7. Martin Klein, founder of Klein Associates, prepares side-scan sonar. / 77
8.8. Bateau C shipwreck at the Wiawaka bateaux site. / 78
8.9. Bateau C's bottom boards, battens, and frames. / 79
8.10. Drawing (plan view) of Bateau A at Wiawaka bateaux site. / 80
8.11. Drawing (plan view) of Bateau B at Wiawaka bateaux site. / 80
8.12. Drawing (plan view) of Bateau C at Wiawaka bateaux site. / 81
8.13. Drawing (plan view) of Bateau D at Wiawaka bateaux site. / 82
8.14. Drawing (plan view) of Bateau E at Wiawaka bateaux site. / 82
8.15. Drawing (plan view) of Bateau F at Wiawaka bateaux site. / 83
8.16. Drawing (plan view) of Bateau G at Wiawaka bateaux site. / 83
8.17. Caldwell's students built this twenty-three-foot replica bateau. / 84
8.18. Map of seven Wiawaka bateaux, circa 1758, created by Bateaux Below. / 86
8.19. Klein, Capone, Kozak, and the author examine lake charts. / 89

8.20. Peckham painting of a 1758-built British wharf at Lake George. / 91
9.1. Parker sketch of Lake George "mortar bateau" shipwreck. / 95
9.2. Crandall on a boat with two thirteen-inch mortar bombs raised from the lake. / 96
9.3. CAD illustration of a thirteen-inch diameter "mortar bomb" from the lake. / 103
10.1. Author diving Site VI, a cluster of nine sunken bateaux, July 27, 1988. / 108
10.2. Klein side scan sonar image of Site VIII showing two to four sunken bateaux. / 108
11.1. Map of hull pieces at Wiawaka bateaux, possibly from 1965 salvage. / 114
11.2. Lennan next to two anchors recovered from a shipwreck in 1954. / 116
11.3. Lennan next to a French siege cannon after being raised from the lake in 1954. / 118
12.1. *Baby Whale* research submarine during 1960 construction. / 121
12.2. *Baby Whale* submarine being attached to a concrete keel in 1960. / 122
12.3. Interpretive illustration of the 1960-built *Baby Whale* sunken submarine. / 123
12.4. Photograph of the sunken *Baby Whale* submarine after being found in 1995. / 125
13.1. Drawing of the 1758 *Land Tortoise* radeau shipwreck. / 128
13.2. Appling, a Bateaux Below volunteer diver, holding two signs. / 128
14.1. Lake historian's vision, an "underwater museum" of shipwrecks, 1964. / 132
14.2. Map of "The Sunken Fleet of 1758" shipwreck preserve at the lake. / 134
14.3. Cornell holding a sign for a Lake George shipwreck preserve. / 135
14.4. Brochure cover of one of the 1993-established shipwreck preserves. / 136
14.5. Map of locations of Lake George's three shipwreck preserves. / 137
14.6. Benway and Appling examine a twenty-three-foot replica bateau in the lake's shallows. / 139
14.7. National award for preservation of the lake's Submerged Heritage Preserves. / 142
15.1. Map of debris moved by divers from the sunken bateaux. / 144
15.2. Map of manmade debris removed by divers from the sunken bateaux. / 145
16.1. Two of Caldwell's replica bateaux being rowed by local school students. / 149
16.2. Bateaux Below divers sinking replica bateau, September 7, 1997. / 150
16.3. Two middle-school students tracing an eighteenth-century bateau stem. / 152
16.4. A replica bateau shipwreck on a walkway prior to being sunk, 2008. / 152
17.1. Lake George Arts Project's postcard promoting its 2009 exhibit. / 156
17.2. A painting in "Raising the Fleet: An Art/Science Initiative" exhibit, 2009. / 157
17.3. A diver views an underwater art exhibit at a shipwreck, 2009. / 157
18.1. DVD case, "Wooden Bones: The Sunken Fleet of 1758" documentary. / 160

19.1. McMahan at "Shipwreck Weekend at Lake George" conference. / 165
19.2. Cover page of an issue of *The Lake George Nautical Newsletter*. / 166
19.3. Blue and yellow metal historic marker about the "Sunken Fleet." / 169
19.4. Poster from a Fort William Henry Museum shipwreck exhibit. / 173
19.5. The author teaching a class on underwater archaeology, 2008. / 175
19.6. Boat modeler station with a scale model of the *Baby Whale* sub. / 178
19.7. Peckham sketch of the War of 1812 bateau found in Lake Champlain. / 180
19.8. Cordell painting, "Sinking of the Radeau," October 22, 1758. / 180
C.1. Signage to be installed at one of Lake George's shipwreck sites. / 183
A.1.1. An undisturbed 1758 sunken bateau, from 1963–1964 fieldwork. / 190
A.2.1. A lift bag recovering a thirteen-inch diameter iron mortar bomb, 1960s. / 193
A.2.2. Sunken colonial bateau showing a thole pin pad (oarlock). / 194
A.3.1. Drawing of a bateau, similar to a Delmar, New York, scout troop boat. / 197

Preface

On July 10, 1982, just thirteen months after getting certified to scuba dive, I made my first underwater foray to examine several of Lake George's sunken colonial bateaux (**bateau**[i] in the singular). These wooden vessels were arguably the most popular and versatile watercraft of their era for inland waterways. I was first shown one of the sunken bateaux by veteran scuba instructor Jack Sullivan, who had dived on these shipwrecks back in the early 1960s.

Several years later, on September 13, 1987, I made two scuba dives with other neoprene-clad **frogmen** off the Wiawaka Holiday House, an historic women's retreat on the shores of Lake George; recently the facility was renamed the Wiawaka Center for Women. The Wiawaka bateaux are located off the east side of Lake George, about a mile north of Million Dollar Beach, at the head of the waterway. At the time of my September 13, 1987, dives I was unaware that those scuba explorations would have such a dramatic and longstanding impact on my life.

September 13, 1987, was the final day of a three-day training session, called the "Archaeological Research Assistant Workshop." The program was sponsored by a not-for-profit corporation, the Atlantic Alliance for Maritime Heritage Conservation. The workshop, organized by Dr. Russell P. Bellico, Vince Capone, Jack Sullivan, and myself, took two years to plan as there were several delays scheduling the principal instructor, marine archaeologist R. Duncan Mathewson III. Since the 1985 discovery of the 1622 Spanish treasure galleon *Atocha*, found off Key West, Florida, Mathewson, the project's lead archaeologist, had been busy presenting lectures, teaching **underwater archaeology** workshops, and coordinating fieldwork at the seventeenth-century Spanish shipwreck. Mathewson, a lower Hudson River Valley, New York native, was somewhat controversial within the professional underwater archaeology community. Mathewson worked with Mel Fisher, a well-known Florida Keys treasure hunter. However, for scuba enthusiasts like myself who were interested in becoming archaeological divers to assist professional underwater archaeologists,

---

[i] For terms in bold text, see the glossary for more information.

Figure P.1 Scuba diver at one of the Wiawaka sunken bateaux in Lake George in 1987. (Credit: Dr. Russell P. Bellico)

training opportunities such as this 1987 workshop were scarce and thus were much appreciated. Furthermore, Mathewson did a fine job introducing recreational scuba divers to the field of underwater archaeology.

The September 13, 1987, workshop's practicum dives included three boatloads of energetic scuba enthusiasts that numbered over twenty people. A light rain that day kept vessel traffic on the lake to a minimum. Vince Capone, from New Jersey, with his company's Benthos Mini-Rover MkII **remotely-operated-vehicle (ROV)**, the workshop instructor R. Duncan Mathewson III, and New York State Museum senior archaeologist Phil Lord were all aboard the largest boat in our small flotilla, a pontoon watercraft loaned to us by the Lake George Volunteer Fire Department.

My two dives that day were my second and third scuba visits to the cluster of several colonial bateaux, lying in twenty to forty feet of water off the Wiawaka Holiday House. Those plunges into the waterway were plagued at times by low visibility due to the many scuba divers spread out over a few hundred feet. Nonetheless, we perused several colonial shipwrecks and also made noninvasive measurements of some of those sunken British warships. I wrote in my dive log that evening that those two scuba visitations were "tough dives," as I swam back and forth supporting other underwater explorers with their assigned tasks. Nonetheless, it was an exhilarating experience albeit an exhausting one. Though I had made numerous scuba visits to shipwrecks in several waterways since started diving in 1981, the September 13, 1987, dives were essentially my formal introduction into the field of underwater archaeology. And so began my fascination with shipwreck archaeology that would result in over three decades researching, studying, and writing about **"Lake George's Sunken Bateaux of 1758."** This book tells the story of these historic eighteenth-century British shipwrecks, and especially the archaeological investigation conducted by Bateaux Below and its forerunner organization, the Lake George Bateaux Research Team. I had the distinct pleasure of directing those two groups. Fundamental to our bateaux study was an eagerness to collaborate with other individuals and groups toward common goals—protecting and preserving these iconic shipwrecks and developing programs to interpret the results of our research for both scuba buffs and the non-diving public. In a figurative sense, we were "awakening the fleet," trying to bring a greater awareness to the public about these historic watercrafts. I hope this book will encourage local residents, as well as visitors to Lake George, to become stewards of these finite **submerged cultural resources**.

Figure P.2 September 13, 1987: Sport divers preparing to descend to the sunken Wiawaka bateaux during day three of an underwater archaeology training workshop. This was the genesis project that began Bateaux Below's twenty-four-year study of Lake George's sunken bateaux of 1758. (Credit: Joseph W. Zarzynski)

Acknowledgments

The genesis for this book, *Ghost Fleet Awakened: Lake George's Sunken Bateaux of 1758*, was my MA thesis in archaeology and heritage from the University of Leicester, School of Archaeological Studies (Leicester, UK). In 1975, I received a Master of Arts in Teaching degree from Binghamton University (Binghamton, New York) that prepared me for a thirty-one-year career teaching Social Studies to junior high and middle-school students in the Saratoga Springs City School District in Saratoga Springs, New York (1974–2005). However, nearly two-thirds of the way into that profession I yearned to expand my horizons into another field, that of underwater archaeology. So, after several years pondering my future, I decided to return to graduate school; after over two years of university studies, I submitted my MA thesis at the University of Leicester (Leicester, UK) in 2001. My thesis was entitled "Cultural Resource Management of Lake George's Sunken Bateaux of 1758: How History, Underwater Archaeology, Public Education Programs, and Shipwreck Preserves Promote Site Protection." Over the past several years, I have rewritten that document, added new information, and penned several additional chapters. Thus, this book nearly quadruples the length of the original graduate thesis manuscript.

Further, I adopted the term "Ghost Fleet," incorporating it into the title of the book. In the early 1960s, "Ghost Fleet" was an expression frequently employed by the print media to describe the rediscovery of "Lake George's Sunken Bateaux of 1758," the British warships that were unexpectedly located in the waterway by two teenage scuba divers in July 1960. The moniker "Ghost Fleet" was a popular appellation for these eighteenth-century shipwrecks. Newspaper reporters and the general public were surprised that the "Queen of American Lakes" (Lake George's nickname) was suddenly revealing its hidden history, a submerged squadron of French and Indian War (1755–1763) battle crafts.

The field operations at Lake George conducted in the early 1960s by the Adirondack Museum, now known as the Adirondack Experience—The Museum on Blue Mountain Lake, marked the beginning of applying some of the principles of an exciting and emerging scientific discipline, underwater archaeology.

This book begins with the history of these colonial military watercraft, and then explores the archaeological study of "Lake George's Sunken Bateaux of 1758" over the past six decades. Finally, the book reviews the management and **public outreach** programs designed to inform people about these submerged cultural resources. The four appendices that complement the book are valuable additions to this publication. The ultimate goal of *Ghost Fleet Awakened* is to inform the Lake George regional populace and visitors alike about these little-known but historic colonial shipwrecks. My hope is that readers will become advocates for programs to preserve for future generations what is left of these iconic sunken warships.

From 1987 to 2011, I had the privilege of directing Bateaux Below, an underwater archaeology research team, and its predecessor organization, the Lake George Bateaux Research Team (initially called the Atlantic Alliance Lake George Bateaux Research Team). Our dedicated volunteers had no or little funding, yet we were able to undertake and complete an impressive study of the bateau-class shipwrecks in Lake George. We also assisted state and local government agencies in their submerged cultural resources management of this significant but frequently overlooked sunken armada. In the course of this work, I spent 373 days scuba diving on Lake George's sunken bateaux, making a total of 443 dives; since 1981, I have made nearly 2,800 scuba dives with over 2,000 of those in Lake George waters, participating in a variety of cultural and natural science projects. Each dive on a bateau shipwreck has been an absolute thrill. Therefore, it is with great pleasure that I share with you the fascinating story of Lake George's "Ghost Fleet," an underappreciated underwater heritage resource of the Adirondack Mountains region.

Since this was a team endeavor with numerous participants and many supporters, I have many people, groups, and government agencies to acknowledge. First, I would like to thank my colleagues at Bateaux Below—Dr. Russell P. Bellico, Bob Benway, Vince Capone, Terry Crandall, and John Farrell. Sadly, as I've been putting the finishing touches on this book, John Farrell and Terry Crandall, two dear friends and key members of Bateaux Below, have passed away. They are truly missed.

Bill Appling, Dr. Samuel Bowser, Paul Cornell, Scott Padeni, and Steve Resler, all very accomplished scuba divers; Peter Pepe, a documentary filmmaker extraordinaire; and John Whitesel, a talented digital animator; likewise deserve special acknowledgment. Carl Dunn, a 1950s-era scuba diver worked for the Fort William Henry Corporation. Carl gladly shared his memories of delving into the depths of the lake during the early and mid-1950s, the formative years of scuba diving at the waterway. The Fund for Lake George, Inc., was generous, too, awarding Bateaux Below several small grants that primarily paid for some of our expenditures such as dive boat fuel, scuba tank fills, camera film, videotape, and other sundries.

I wish to acknowledge the fabulous support I received from my wife, Mary Patram Meaney (aka M.P. Meaney). Pat's constructive criticism has always been appreciated, and her assistance has seemed unlimited. Also, I certainly would be remiss if I did not recognize my mentor, Dr. D.K. (Kathy) Abbass. For over a quarter of a century, Kathy has been a sounding board for my underwater archaeology projects at Lake George and in other waterways, too. In addition, Dr. Russell P. Bellico's superb books on Lake George history, *Sails and Steam in the Mountains: A Maritime and Military History of Lake George and Lake Champlain*, *Chronicles of Lake George: Journeys in War and Peace* and *Empires in the Mountains: French and Indian War Campaigns and Forts in the Lake Champlain, Lake George, and Hudson River Corridor*, were constant references during my years of research. Russ is the foremost Lake George/Lake Champlain maritime and military historian. He is also a wonderful friend, gentleman, and the consummate professional.

Bob Benway's CAD (computer-aided design) drawings and underwater photography and videography, and John Farrell's excellent illustrations and scale boat and shipwreck models were greatly admired and much appreciated. Terry Crandall provided me with details about his 1963–1964 archaeological survey fieldwork on Adirondack Museum's "Operation Bateaux" (1960–1965). Terry's wife, Barbara Crandall, was likewise gracious, sharing Terry's papers, which proved insightful. Bateaux Below trustee Vince Capone, today the principal in his marine remote sensing firm called Black Laser Learning, was always available to answer my numerous sonar questions and to offer expert advice. Furthermore, whenever Bateaux Below was lucky enough to acquire the loan of a Klein side scan sonar or to have sufficient funding to rent one for shipwreck sleuthing at Lake George, Vince somehow found time from a hectic work schedule to journey from the lower Mid-Atlantic region to Lake George to operate that sophisticated sonar and navigation equipment. Besides being our primary side scan sonar technician, Vince also did most of our remotely-operated-vehicle (ROV) operation. Martin Klein and Garry Kozak of Klein Associates in Salem, New Hampshire, were extremely generous with frequent loans of one of the company's Klein side scan sonar units. That greatly advanced our submerged cultural resources inventory program. Simply stated, not enough credit and thanks have been given to the trio of Capone, Klein, and Kozak.

Several researchers over the past three decades also shared historical documents about colonial bateaux. Foremost among them were Dr. Russell P. Bellico,

Bob Benway, Scott Padeni, Mark L. Peckham, Dr. D.K. (Kathy) Abbass, and Bruce Terrell. I am also very grateful for the wonderful drawings done by Skidmore College graduate Maddy Cucuteanu, now a talented professional artist. Maddy redrew several of John Farrell's bateau shipwreck illustrations, and those drawings are included in this book. The staff at the New York State Museum in Albany, New York, was immensely helpful arranging time for me to examine and acquire photographs of the Lake George bateau shipwrecks and other related vessel pieces in their collection. I am also indebted for the guidance and support I received from everyone at SUNY Press, especially Amanda Lanne-Camilli, Chelsea R. Miller, Jenn Bennett-Genthner, and Fran Keneston. Likewise, I wish to thank Dr. Tim Runyan at East Carolina University for his invaluable advice and support over the past two decades. Shawn T. May, my knowledgeable attorney, kindly reviewed the book contract and other documents, providing me with excellent professional advice.

Several organizations, businesses, local municipalities, state agencies, and colleges deserve recognition for their assistance and support: Atlantic Alliance Lake George Bateaux Research Team (later called the Lake George Bateaux Research Team), Bateaux Below, Pepe Productions, Lake George Historical Association, Fort William Henry Museum, the French and Indian War Society, Adirondack Experience—The Museum on Blue Mountain Lake (formerly Adirondack Museum), Fort Ticonderoga, Historical Society of the Town of Bolton, New York State Divers Association, Klein Associates, Kasalaan & D'Angelo Associates, Wiawaka Center for Women (formerly the Wiawaka Holiday House), *Lake George Mirror*, *The Saratogian*, *The Chronicle*, Left Coast Press, The History Press, Hall's Boat Corporation, Lake George Marine Equipment Company, One Day Signs, Miller Mechanical, AngioDynamics, Adirondack Trust Company, Darrin Fresh Water Institute, Helen V. Froehlich Foundation, Museum of Underwater Archaeology, Rich Morin's Professional Dive Centers, Victory Sports, Capitaland Scuba Center, Diver's World, Waterfront Diving Center, Speakman's Company (re-enactors), Lake George Arts Project, Basin Harbor Maritime Museum (later renamed—Lake Champlain Maritime Museum), Ithaca College, Edwin A. Link and Marion Clayton Link Collections/Binghamton University Libraries' Special Collections, The Link Foundation, University of Leicester, Saratoga Springs City School District, Northern Dean, Lake George Power Squadron, Cooper's Cave Ale Company, Lake George Steamboat Company, Lake George Volunteer Fire Department, America the Beautiful Fund, Rural New York Historic Preservation Grant Program, the Preservation League of New York State, the J.M. Kaplan Fund Village of Lake George, Town of Lake George, Lake George Park Commission

Lake George Association, Lake George Watershed Coalition, New York State Office of Parks, Recreation and Historic Preservation, New York State Department of Environmental Conservation, New York State Office of General Services, New York State Department of State, Naval History and Heritage Command, New York Sea Grant-Oswego, Smithsonian Institution, Texas A&M University, Canal Society of New York State, Hudson River Maritime Museum, Museum of International Folk Art, Ticonderoga Historical Society, and the Evans Library (Florida Institute of Technology).

A selection of government officials—true public servants—deserve special mention for their assistance: Mark L. Peckham, Alan C. Bauder, John Carstens, Phil Lord, Lake George Village Mayor Bob Blais, Dr. Michael Lucas, Dr. Christina Rieth, Town of Lake George Supervisor Lou Tessier, Mike White, Susan Winchell-Sweeney, Kristin O'Connell, and Andrea Lain.

Others from a variety of fields and professions whom I want to acknowledge include (in alphabetical order) Dr. Mitch Allen, Amanda Andreas, Bill Armstrong, Sandy Arnold, Dana Ashdown, Bob Baker, John Barber, Ken Bartkowski, Dave Beck, Jane Bellico, Pete Benway, Ed Bethel, Dan Bishop, Hallie Bond, Dr. Chuck Boylen, Dr. John Broadwater, Tim Butler, Ted Caldwell, Carolynn Raven Carpenter, Chris Carola, Karen Cavotta, Steve Cernak, Norm Channing, Tracey Clothier, Lee Coleman, Dr. Carol Collins, Steve Collyer, Bill Cooper, Tim Cordell, Jane Cornell, Dr. Kevin J. Crisman, Dale Currier, Chip D'Angelo, Dick Dean, Cathy DeDe, Dr. James Delgado, Richard Dickinson, David Diehl, Christine Dixon, Kerry Dixon, Bob Doheny, Bill Dow, John Earl, Marie Ellsworth, Karen Engelke, Dr. Jeremy Farrell, John Farrell, Jr., Dan Fisher, Bob Flacke, Sr., Ken Fortier, Will Fortin, Mark Frost, Bruce Fullem, Catt Gagnon, John Gardner, Bill Gates, Ivy Gocker, Elinor (Mossop) Gottschalk, Kip Grant, Claire Griffith, Don Hall, Lisa and Tony Hall, Bill Hammond, John Hart, Tim Hendricks, Keith Herkalo, Scott Heydrick, James Hood, John Illsley, Emmett Inserra, Dale Jenks, Art Jones, Dale R. Kelly, Dr. Thomas F. Kelly, Bill Key, Dr. Alexey Khodjakov, Dr. Kurt Knoerl, Dr. Mike Koonce, Charles Kuenzel, Dan Kumlander, Bill LaBarge, John Lefner, Doug Leininger, Jennifer Lemak, Bob Leombruno, Dr. Carla R. Lesh, Dr. Nate Leslie, Dennis Lewis, Laura Lee Linder, Paul Lord, Thomas Reeves Lord, Dr. Jonathan Lothrop, Stephen Loughman, Grace MacDonald, Maria Macri, Jeff Many, Rich Martin, Dr. R. Duncan Mathewson III, Mattison Family, Mark Matucci, Don Mayland, Marilyn Mazzeo, Chris McGuirk, Charles M. McKinney III, Kendrick McMahan, John Meaney, Dr. Joe Meany, David Miller, Elizabeth Miller, Michael J. Miller, Rich Morin, Kathy Flacke Muncil, Gale Munro, Marisa Muratori, Diane Newman, Dr. Robert Neyland, Dr. Sandra Nierzwicki-Bauer,

Aaron Noble, Brigid Nowlin, Gary Paine, Denny Pajak, Eugene Parker, Alex Parrott, James Parrott, Tim Pehl, Joe Pepe, Jerry Pepper, Hanna Person, Michele Phillips, Paul Post, David Ragule, Tom Rasbeck, Ralph Rataul, John Ray, Hanna Rhodes, Wit Richmond, LeRoy Rider, Kurt Riley, Dr. Michael "Bodhi" Rogers, Gerald Root, Dr. Julie Schablitsky, Linda Schmidt, Molly Scofield, Steve Scoville, James Sears, Brigid Shaw, Lauren Sheridan, Ted Smetana, Jon Smith, Bill Snyder, Jeff Sova, Joe Sporko, Dr. Megan Springate, Dr. David Starbuck, John Strong, John Strough, Jack Sullivan, Preston Sweeney, Bob Thompson, Jeff Tingle, Ray Tucker, Anne Tyrrell, Charles Vandrei, Melodie Viele, Laura Von Rosk, Brad Utter, Tom Wahl, Gary West, Nick Westbrook, David White, Ralph Wilbanks, Brian Wilcox, Joe Wiley, Meaghan Wilkins, John Wimbush, Susan Winchell-Sweeney, Dr. Khristaan D. Villela, Kal Wysokowski, Brian Yates, John Yost, Claudia Young, Gary Zaboly, Marian and Walter Zarzynski, and Dick Zielinski.

Chapter One

Early History of Bateaux

For much of the seventeenth and eighteenth centuries, the English[i] and French were bitter rivals for control of the eastern seaboard of North America and the lands of the Ohio River Valley region. At stake were the rich resources of this vast territory—forests for timber, furs, fertile lands for crops, and control of trade routes. This fierce competition resulted in several notable **colonial wars** known in the Western Hemisphere as King William's War (1689–1697); Queen Anne's War (1702–1713); King George's War (1744–1748); and the French and Indian War (1755–1763).[1, ii] With only a few major roads cut through the frontier woodlands of colonial North America, interior waterways became the principal transportation routes to move armies, supplies, and trade items. During these military conflicts, English regular and **provincial** (colonial) soldiers erected a series of fortifications along the Upper Hudson River, Lake George, and the Lake Champlain corridor. This strategic gateway ran from southern New York into New France (Canada). Thus, controlling the Hudson River, Lake George, and Lake Champlain corridor was key to winning these wars. Along this important passageway, English military outposts opposed their enemy, the French and their Native American (aka First Nation) allies. The bateau (also spelled batteau, batoe, and battoe) was the primary vessel used along this network of inland water routes.

Bateaux were the utilitarian vessels of their era and were mostly operated on lakes, rivers, creeks, and sometimes even along the protected waters of the Atlantic seaboard. Noted American naval architect and historian Howard I. Chapelle described the colonial vessel: "The French word 'bateau' meant no more than 'boat' in the first years of the French settlement in Canada, but early in the eighteenth century this word had become accepted as a type-name for a double-ended,

---

i In 1707, England and Scotland joined and became Great Britain. After 1707, these people were referred to as British.

ii Some historians claim the French and Indian War started in 1754, whereas others say it began in 1753. Scholars often refer to this military conflict as the Seven Years' War (1756–1763).

Figure 1.1 A map showing the region of the Hudson River, Lake George, and Lake Champlain corridor with some of its colonial fortification sites. (Credit: Peter Pepe)

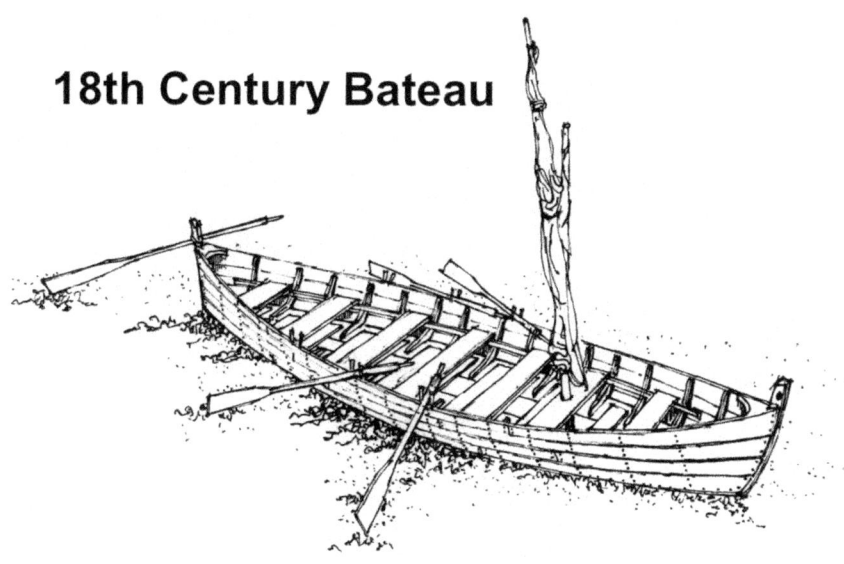

Figure 1.2 Drawing of a typical eighteenth-century bateau. (Credit: Mark L. Peckham)

flat-bottomed, chine-built small boat much used along the St. Lawrence and on the American lakes."[2]

Possibly the earliest reference to military bateaux in the colony of New York was in 1666. Three hundred light bateaux and bark canoes were put into service for a French incursion into English-held northern New York.[3] During Queen Anne's War (1702–1713), English colonial boat builders and carpenters constructed military bateaux along the Mohawk River in New York. In 1711, the British built six hundred bateaux on the shores of the Hudson River at Albany, New York.[4] However, it was not until the French and Indian War (1755–1763) that the bateau provided a decided advantage for the British military.

During the French and Indian War, bateaux were arguably as important to the British and provincial soldiers as their muskets. Bateaux played a crucial role at Lake George as early as 1755, the year when the British and provincials first established an encampment at the south end of the strategic thirty-two-mile waterway. On September 8, 1755, French regulars, Canadians, and their Native American allies attacked a British military column as those soldiers and their Haudenosaunee (Iroquois) allies trekked south from their base camp at the head of the lake along the military road to Fort Lyman (later named Fort Edward).

Figure 1.3 Illustration by Frederick Coffay Yohn showing British and provincial soldiers fighting the French and their Native American allies during the Battle of Lake George (September 8, 1755). Yohn's painting appeared in the 1905 Glens Falls Insurance Company calendar. (Credit: Frederick Coffay Yohn and Dr. Russell P. Bellico)

Figure 1.4 A drone shot of Fort William Henry Museum located on the south shore of Lake George, New York. The replica fortification was finished in 1954 and is a reproduction of historic Fort William Henry, a British military installation from 1755–1757. (Credit: Peter Pepe)

A series of fierce skirmishes fought that day would later become known as the Battle of Lake George. The British and provincials were victorious in part because they were able to create a makeshift defensive "wall" near their position at the head of the lake. That **redoubt** was fashioned from felled trees, wagons, and even some overturned bateaux that were likely pulled up on shore for cover. Behind this odd, but effective, defensive line, William Johnson's British and provincial soldiers and artillerymen decimated the enemy with musket balls, cannon shot, grapeshot, and canister shot. The French-led army and their Native American allies were defeated, one of the few British victories early in the French and Indian War.[5]

The British and provincial military, fresh from their triumph over their rivals, then began building Fort William Henry, completing it by late 1755. The military installation, a **Vauban-style earth-and-wooden fortification**, was erected at the south end of Lake George. It posed a direct threat to the French who controlled the 110-mile Lake Champlain, a major waterway located just to the north of Lake George. There was no major British offensive from Fort William Henry launched into the French-held Champlain Valley in 1756. However, in mid-March 1757, a force of French regulars, Canadians, and Native Americans attacked Fort William Henry at Lake George. The wilderness waterway was located about sixty miles north of Albany, New York, a British city in the interior of the thirteen colonies. After several days laying siege to the British fortification, the French-led forces succeeded in burning all the outbuildings, but they could not seize the sturdy frontier fortress.[6] A *Schenectady Reflector* (Schenectady, New York) newspaper account, published April 1, 1842, provides us with details about the March 1757 French raid on Fort William Henry. The 1842 story was from a letter dated March 26, 1757, published in the *Boston Gazette*. The newspaper narrative reported that before the French retreated to their strongholds in the Champlain Valley they burned two **sloops** and most of the British bateaux that had been pulled up on shore.[7] The French may have destroyed as many as three hundred bateaux lying along the shoreline in that late winter raid.

Later in 1757, in early August, a more imposing French, Canadian, and Native American expeditionary force attacked Fort William Henry. This time, the British and provincials, positioned inside Fort William Henry and in nearby encampments, surrendered to the French after several days of intense siege warfare. The vastly superior French-directed legion captured many supplies and armaments. They then torched Fort William Henry before retreating north to their two forts located in the Champlain Valley. James Fenimore Cooper immortalized this August 1757 event in his famous 1826 historical novel *The Last of the Mohicans*.

These early events of the French and Indian War showed the British the necessity of building bateaux to transport their regular and provincial troops into the Lake George/Lake Champlain theater and also westward along the Mohawk River toward the Great Lakes. Colonel John Bradstreet, considered today to have been a British military logistics genius, formed the "Battoe Service" to address the need for a massive boat-building campaign at Albany and Schenectady, New York.[8]

One of Bradstreet's junior officers in the Battoe Service, who would go on to have a noteworthy career in the American army during the American Revolution (1775–1783), was Philip Schuyler. The young Schuyler assisted Bradstreet during the French and Indian War by helping to coordinate the movement of military materials, foodstuffs, and soldiers into the hinterlands. Among his many tasks, Schuyler purchased lumber and other maritime supplies for the carpenters and boat builders who constructed bateaux for the war effort. For his labor and diligence, Philip Schuyler was well paid: 255£ 10s (in 1758), 242£ 18s (in 1759), and 255£ 10s (in 1760).[9]

Following an unsuccessful July 1758 British military incursion into the Champlain Valley by a colossal British military force directed by General James Abercromby, the British leadership made a daring decision because they had no fortification at Lake George—Fort William Henry had been destroyed in August 1757. Without a stronghold to house troops to protect their Lake George fleet over the winter months of 1758 and 1759, the British decided they would deliberately sink many of the vessels of their formidable Lake George squadron. The wooden warships were sunk in the shallows of the lake to protect them over the wintertime from marauding French and their Native American allies. It was intended that the submerged watercraft would be relocated by the British the following year, and then raised, repaired, and placed back into action for the 1759 campaign against the French military fortresses in the Champlain Valley. Among the British vessels sunk in the autumn of 1758 were the sloop *Earl of Halifax*, two **radeaux**, several **row galleys**, an unspecified number of **whaleboats**,[10] and 260 bateaux.[11] This "wet storage" (aka "cold storage") of wooden warships would later become known as "The Sunken Fleet of 1758."

In the late spring and early summer of 1759, many of those submerged battle crafts were successfully salvaged from the lake bottom for British General Jeffery Amherst's 1759 expedition against the French forts along the shores of Lake Champlain. Amherst had replaced Abercromby as the commander of the British army at Lake George. However, some submerged bateaux were not recovered, as Amherst's military unit quickly departed their encampment at the head of Lake George to engage the enemy to the north. Amherst's eleven thousand soldiers and

Figure 1.5 A drawing depicting bateaux and whaleboats, part of the formidable armada of British warships on Lake George during the July 1758 Abercromby campaign against the French in the Champlain Valley. (Credit: Tim Cordell)

eight hundred warships traveled over Lake George using some of the very vessels that had been sunk in the lake in 1758 and raised from the bottom of Lake George in 1759. Amherst's substantial martial contingent promptly occupied the two French fortifications at the south end of Lake Champlain—Fort Carillon (later called Fort Ticonderoga) and Fort St. Frédéric (later known as Crown Point). Both fortifications had been abandoned and deliberately destroyed by the retreating French.[12]

Bateaux showed their versatility, too. During the 1759 Amherst campaign, British artillery officer, Captain-Lieutenant Henry Skinner, who served under General Amherst, reported on the bateaux and their adaptability. In his 1759 journal, Skinner noted that "cannon, **mortars**, and **howitzers**" were mounted upon rafts crafted "by building a stage on three battoes."[13]

By 1760, fighting in North America had pretty much ended. The war formally concluded with a French surrender at the Treaty of Paris in 1763.[14] John Gardner, a prominent twentieth-century naval architect and boat builder, wrote of this colonial conflict in North America: "This war was won in boats, and for the greater part, in a particular kind of boat, the bateau."[15]

Bateaux were likewise employed in the American Revolution. According to Howard I. Chapelle, a naval architect at the Smithsonian Institution, in 1776 the British Admiralty drafted plans for a standard bateau. That design was later discovered in the Admiralty Collection of Draughts.[16] The 1776 British bateau plan depicted a wooden watercraft that was a little over thirty feet long. Its length,

Figure 1.6 A computer-generated image depicting a cluster of submerged British bateaux with sinking rocks inside them. Some of these shipwrecks later became known as "Lake George's sunken bateaux of 1758." (Credit: John Whitesel & Pepe Productions)

Figure 1.7 This illustration depicts what some sunken bateaux of 1758 might have looked like over the winter of 1758–1759. Mark L. Peckham, a maritime artist, shows how each of the submerged boats were filled with hundreds of pounds of sinking rocks, marked by crude floating buoys for relocating the vessels in the spring of 1759, and lines running from the submerged bateaux back to shore. (Credit: Mark L. Peckham)

size, and shape were rather comparable to those bateau shipwrecks found in Lake George that dated to the French and Indian War.

In 1775, thirty bateaux were constructed at Lake George for the American patriots. In April 1776, Benjamin Franklin was one of several Americans sent by the Continental Congress on a diplomatic mission to Canada. Franklin and his entourage traversed Lake George in a sizeable bateau.

During British General John Burgoyne's unsuccessful 1777 campaign to seize Albany, New York, and thus split the rebellious colonies in two, **German auxiliary** and British troops operated bateaux on Lake Champlain, Lake George, and the Hudson River.[17]

In the War of 1812 (1812–1815), bateaux were also deployed in a midsummer 1813 British incursion from Canada into the United States that resulted in attacks on American military installations and private property in Plattsburgh, New York, and Swanton, Vermont. Britain's attempt to claim hegemony over the Champlain Valley culminated the following year during the Battle of Plattsburgh, fought on Lake Champlain on September 6 through 11, 1814. However, Commodore Thomas Macdonough's American fleet defeated a larger British squadron on Lake Champlain, thus ending the threat of a British victory in the strategic Champlain Valley.[18] During that war, Richard Eggleston, a shipwright from Essex, New York, a small village along the western shore of Lake Champlain, constructed over 250 bateaux for the Americans.[19]

In 1999, residents of Plattsburgh, New York, were reminded of the significance of bateau vessels to their local heritage. Two bateaux from the War of 1812, sunk in the shallows of Lake Champlain, were discovered off the city of Plattsburgh during a severe drought.[20] Thus, the bateau watercraft played an integral role in several military conflicts in the Lake George–Lake Champlain region.

Small wooden vessels of the colonial era, like the bateau, often had a short life span because they quickly wore out, were casualties of mishap or armed conflict, and were biodegradable. However, many of the sunken bateaux in Lake George, some with intact bottom boards, a few **battens** (aka cleats), and with several **frames** (aka ribs) and **garboard strakes** (aka lowest side planks), survived in their watery graves for over 250 years. These are significant to an American culture with deep ties to our British ancestry. The scarcity of these types of colonial vessels in American waters makes the **assemblage** of Lake George's sunken bateaux even more important. East Carolina University–trained underwater archaeologist Bruce G. Terrell, now with the **NOAA** National Marine Sanctuaries program, clearly recognized this when he wrote in 1991: "There are few images and fewer extant remains of [colonial] mountain boats."[21]

Chapter Two

The Bateau Watercraft

The origin of the bateau in New York waterways is somewhat a mystery. This is largely because bateau builders generally did not require drawn boat lines from which to construct these boats.[1] It is therefore difficult to sort out the lineage of this class of watercraft, a vessel that had such an integral role as a commercial and military boat in North America during the colonial era and into the early nineteenth century.

Bateaux played a special part in the history of the English colonies and French-controlled New France (Canada), especially along the Hudson River–Lake George–Lake Champlain water corridor and the Richelieu River. Unfortunately, although bateaux are mentioned in the chronicles of this region, very little was devoted to providing details about their construction and the capabilities of this transportation form.[2]

Three of the most eminent authorities on colonial bateau construction—Howard I. Chapelle, John Gardner, and Dr. Kevin J. Crisman—differ somewhat on the origins of the watercraft type. Chapelle was a naval architect who several decades ago worked for the Smithsonian Institution in Washington, DC, becoming the museum's Historian of Naval Architecture. He believed that the bateau of the seventeenth and eighteenth centuries "had become accepted as a type-name for a double-ended, flat-bottomed, chine-built small boat much used along the St. Lawrence and on the American lakes."[3] Chapelle gave the upper length of colonial bateaux at about forty-five feet.[4] He considered the hull type to be common with some medieval crafts from England. Furthermore, Chapelle suggested that the hull shape of the bateau was "little different from that of some of the Dutch and Baltic **prams** of more recent times, and the construction was basically the same."[5] He thought that the colonists in New France used the bateau form along the St. Lawrence River that was an adaptation of "one of the many French flat-bottomed small craft."[6] Nathan A. Gallagher, a graduate student in the Nautical Archaeology program at Texas A&M University and a student of Crisman, referred to one class of these vessels as the "batteaux plats," meaning "flat boats."[7] Chapelle believed the colonial French and English adopted the word "bateau" to describe this class of flat-bottomed vessel.[8]

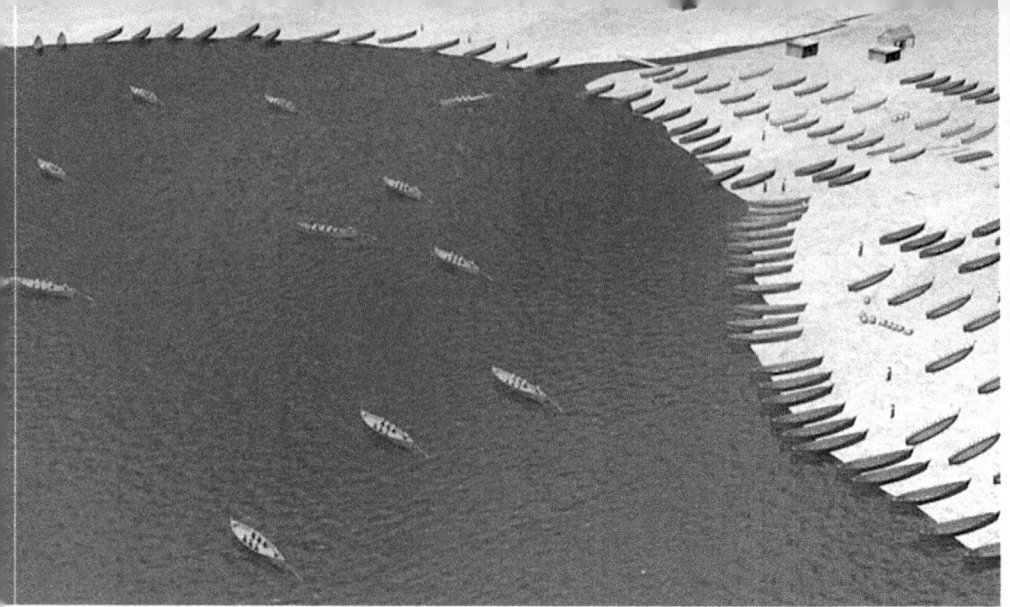

Figure 2.1 A computer-generated image of the bateau "factories" in Schenectady, New York, during the French and Indian War. Bateaux were mass-produced here, not by a few boatbuilders, but by teams of many marine craftsmen and laborers, construction probably somewhat similar to modern-day assembly line production. (Credit: John Whitesel and Pepe Productions)

John Gardner was a venerated expert on wooden boat building. For years he was an associate curator of small craft at the Mystic Seaport Museum in Mystic, Connecticut. A coastal New Englander, Gardner died in 1995 at the age of ninety and was until the time of his death very active in small-craft boat building and related studies.[9] In the 1960s, he labored on the reconstruction of a few eighteenth-century bateaux that had been raised from Lake George in the early 1960s. Gardner believed that the flat-bottom small boat design of the bateau class did not come from English colonists in America.[10] Rather, John Gardner hypothesized that the bateaux found on the rivers around Albany, New York, and at Lake George came from "the New York Dutch, who certainly would have been familiar with flat craft, in use for centuries on the rivers of Germany and the Low countries."[11] The Mystic Seaport Museum small boat authority thought that the descendants of Dutch boat builders in Albany, originally an early seventeenth-century Dutch settlement called Fort Orange, probably worked at the British **bateau "factories"** in Albany and Schenectady, New York, during the French and Indian War. Therefore, Gardner claimed the Dutch most likely influenced the construction form of colonial bateaux.[12]

Dr. Kevin J. Crisman is a Vermonter and a renowned nautical archaeologist and professor at Texas A&M University's Nautical Archaeology Program. In August 1985, Crisman, fellow underwater archaeologist Arthur Cohn, and boat

Figure 2.2 This photograph shows a 1758 Lake George bateau shipwreck that for years was exhibited at the Adirondack Museum in Blue Mountain Lake, New York. In August 1985, underwater archaeologists Dr. Kevin J. Crisman and Arthur Cohn measured and recorded the historic vessel. (Credit: Dr. Russell P. Bellico)

builder Dexter Cooper, all working with the Basin Harbor Maritime Museum (today known as the Lake Champlain Maritime Museum), studied the remains of a colonial bateau shipwreck that had been retrieved from Lake George;[i] the vessel was later designated Bateau 2626 by the New York State Museum. It was one of three bateaux recovered from the waterway in the early 1960s by the Adirondack Museum in Blue Mountain Lake, New York. The bateau was conserved and later exhibited at the Adirondack Museum. The Basin Harbor Maritime Museum team measured and photographed the historic bateau shipwreck's surviving hull structure, which consisted of bottom planks, battens, and garboard strakes.

The Adirondack Museum's restored colonial bateau also included a **stem** and **sternpost** with their accompanying **knees**, as well as many frames fashioned from hardwood, probably oak. Following Crisman's recording of that eighteenth-century colonial bateau in the Adirondack Museum, boat builders and carpenters at the Basin Harbor Maritime Museum in Vergennes, Vermont, fashioned a replica colonial

---

i Crisman cites the date for the actual recording of Bateau 2626 as August 1985. Gallagher gives a date of 1986. The latter date may be when post–data collection analysis was completed.

military bateau, called *Perseverance*,[13] based on the Adirondack Museum's French and Indian War–era bateau recovered from Lake George. Crisman was amazed that the hull timbers of the 1758 bateau (Bateau 2626) that once was embedded in Lake George's muddy lake bottom still showed evidence of tool marks and even tar stains; the top of the frames, stem, and sternpost that stood proud above the lake bottom were somewhat eroded.

Crisman's analysis of the Lake George bateau that was displayed at the Adirondack Museum suggests that British colonial bateaux "appear to have been entirely a New World invention."[14] In 2015, Gallagher wrote an informative master's thesis ("The Lake George Bateaux: British Colonial Utility Craft in The French and Indian War") that examined the nautical design of the three Lake George bateaux recovered from the waterway in the early 1960s.[15] The three bateau shipwrecks and various hull timber pieces from other Lake George bateaux recovered in the early 1960s are now in the collection of the New York State Museum. The three Lake George colonial bateaux are known as Bateau 2626 (32 feet long), Bateau 4560 (31 feet, 9-3/4 inches), and Bateau 4566 (31 feet, 10 inches).[16] The state museum also has a related assemblage that consists of miscellaneous bateau pieces retrieved from other bateau shipwrecks in the lake, as well as other unidentified non-bateau hull structure. That assemblage is known as Bateaux Collection 4530.[17]

Figure 2.3 One of the excavated sunken bateaux from 1963-1964 fieldwork conducted by the Adirondack Museum. The image shows part of the colonial boat's bottom boards, two frames, and a side hull plank known as a garboard strake. (Credit: Terry Crandall)

One of the best contemporary descriptions of a colonial bateau comes from Swedish naturalist Peter Kalm. In the mid–eighteenth century, Kalm traveled through parts of North America. In 1749, he visited Albany, New York, and Kalm described the bateau vessels he observed:

> Battoes are another kind of boats which are much in use in Albany: they are made of boards of white pine; the bottom is flat, that they may row the better in shallow water. They are sharp at both ends, and somewhat higher towards the end than in the middle. They have seats in them, and are rowed as common boats. They are long, yet not all alike. Usually they

are three and sometimes four fathoms [twenty-four feet] long. The height from the bottom to the top of the board (for the sides stand almost perpendicular) is from twenty inches to two feet, and the breadth in the middle about a yard and six inches.[18]

Furthermore, Kalm noted that there was no similar type of boat in Sweden or other regions of Europe.[19]

Dr. Kevin J. Crisman stated that bateaux were generally equipped with four to six oars for propulsion, with an oar or paddle tied off the stern to steer.[20] There was no rudder. According to archaeological diver Terry Crandall, who worked in 1963–1964 for Adirondack Museum's "Operation Bateaux" in Lake George, wooden thole pins and thole pin pads were found on several sunken bateaux. These pieces were employed on bateaux before the introduction of metal oarlocks (rowlocks), that became common fixtures later on in history on small wooden rowboat-type vessels. Crandall discovered extra thole pins and thole pin pads at some of the bateau wrecks, suggesting that when the originals broke or wore down, they were easily replaced.[21]

In shallow waters, such as rivers and streams, a long pole was wielded by a bateauman to push and power a bateau. On a lake, the watercraft might also have been rigged with a crude mast and sail, permitting the bateau to sail with the wind.[22] This is supported by a mast step found in Lake George Bateaux Collection 4530.[23]

Dr. Caleb Rea was a colonist who participated in the 1758 British offensive against the French forts in the Champlain Valley. Over nine hundred bateaux and dozens of other warships participated in British General James Abercromby's campaign. In 1758, Dr. Caleb Rea wrote in his journal about the bateaux in that British fleet, stating ". . . we made Sails of Blankets and Tents."[24]

Colonial bateaux were relatively easy to build, one of the reasons they were so

Figure 2.4 A photograph of one-half of a 1758 Lake George bateau shipwreck recovered by the Adirondack Museum in the early 1960s. The bateau shipwreck is part of an exhibit entitled "Enterprising Waters: New York's Erie Canal" that opened in 2017 at the New York State Museum in Albany, New York. (Credit: M.P. Meaney and New York State Museum, Albany, New York. Courtesy New York State Museum)

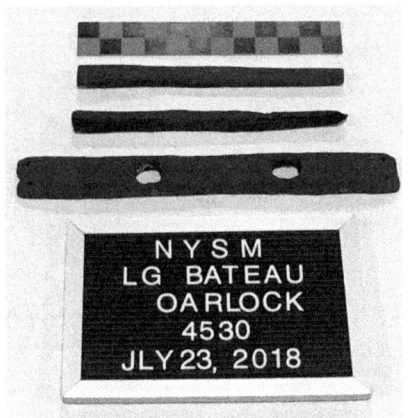

Figure 2.5 A 2018 photograph of a "thole pin wear block" (thole pin pad) and thole pins in the collection of the New York State Museum. These conserved bateau pieces are from the "Operation Bateaux" fieldwork conducted by the Adirondack Museum from 1960 to 1965. (Credit: M.P. Meaney and New York State Museum, Albany, New York. Courtesy New York State Museum)

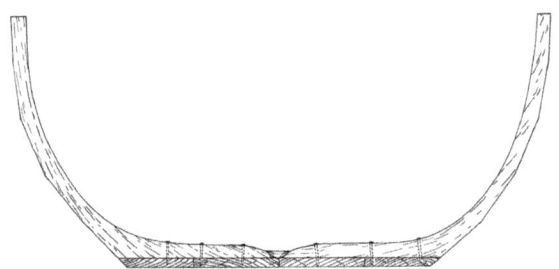

Figure 2.6 A drawing, reconstructed cross-section, of the Adirondack Museum–exhibited Lake George bateau shipwreck, also known as Bateau 2626. (Credit: Dr. Kevin J. Crisman)

Figure 2.7 A 1758 bateau bottom board recovered from Lake George in the early 1960s during Adirondack Museum fieldwork. This hull structure is one plank from an end of a bateau of a multi-plank bottom board assembly. The ranging rod, four-feet long with one-foot increments, is for scale. (Credit: M.P. Meaney and New York State Museum, Albany, New York. Courtesy New York State Museum)

plentiful and popular. They were three or four bottom planks wide, boards generally of pine. The pine was readily available from the abundant forests of the region. Crisman noted that the bateau that he and others from the Basin Harbor Maritime Museum studied at the Adirondack Museum in August 1985[25] measured thirty-one feet, ten inches along the bottom and thirty-three feet, two inches overall length[26]; reconstructed dimensions suggest thirty-two feet for length over the posts.[27] The vessel (Bateau 2626) was four feet wide on the bottom[28] with reconstructed dimensions for the beam of the watercraft at six feet, six inches.[29] Bateau 2626 was four bottom boards or planks wide. These bottom boards were 1 to 1-1/2 inches thick with one bottom board having a maximum width of 12-3/4 inches. The outside edges of these bottom boards were beveled. This allowed the garboard strakes, the lower side planks, to fit over the bottom boards.[30]

Battens, the cross pieces made of pine that were hammered over the tops of the bottom boards, were about one inch thick and eleven inches wide. Crisman recorded that the battens on the bateau exhibited in the Adirondack Museum were nailed to the bottom boards about every two feet or so from bow to stern. Crisman noted about twenty nails were used per batten as fasteners.[31] From what I have observed inspecting many Lake George bateau shipwrecks lying on the lake bottom, I can certainly attest to that high number of wrought iron nails pounded into each batten. Many of these iron nails appear to have been pounded over (clenched) to prevent them from backing out.

Crisman wrote that the Lake George bateau that his archaeology team examined in 1985 had a stem, sometimes called a stempost, that was slightly curved and was probably oak or another hardwood. The bottom of the stem was triangular in shape, and the stem bottom was notched to allow it to fit over the forward ends of the bottom boards that came to a point at the bow. A small knee was nailed to the after end of the stem. This bow assembly protected the bottom boards when the watercraft was beached.[32] John Gardner believed the stem for a three-plank bottomed bateau, compared to a four-plank bottomed bateau, had a greater curvature.[33]

In the aft end of the Adirondack Museum bateau was the sternpost, made of a hardwood, most likely oak. The sternpost was a straight piece that angled a bit aft. It was nailed to the bottom planking and supported by a small knee.

The after ends of the **strakes**, the side planking, overlapped the sternpost and were affixed with wrought nails. The Lake George sunken bateaux were probably three or four strakes (side planks) in height.

The frames for the bateau were also hardwood, mostly oak, and about two inches wide. Each frame was attached to the bottom boards using three or four wrought iron nails.[34]

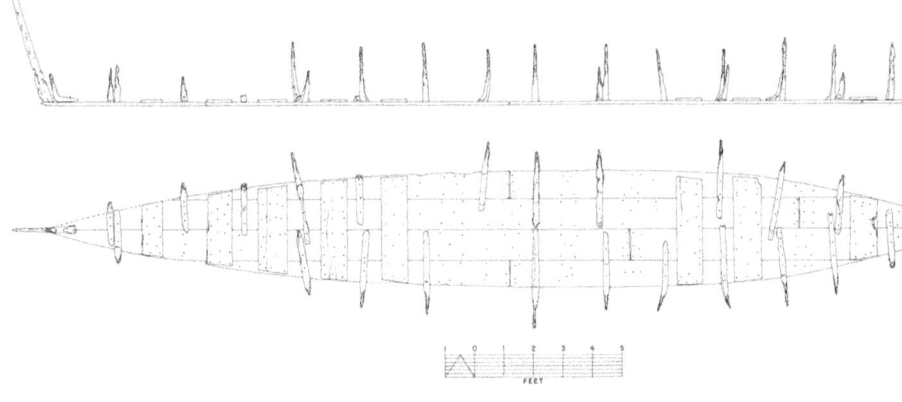

Figure 2.8 Dr. Kevin J. Crisman's drawings, profile and plan views (vessel's stern at left and bow at right) of a 1758 Lake George bateau shipwreck (Bateau 2626) once exhibited at Adirondack Museum in Blue Mountain Lake, New York. (Credit: Dr. Kevin J. Crisman)

Bateaux were generally made with thirteen frames per side, for a total of twenty-six frames per vessel.[35] The strakes (side planks) were about one foot or more in width (the maximum width of Bateaux 2626 was 12-3/4 inches), and their outside edges were beveled to fit the overlapping garboard strakes.[36]

Gardner wrote that it is uncertain if Lake George's bateaux "were **clinker** or **carvel** planked."[37] Clinker or **lapstrake** planked meant a vessel's outer hull planking overlapped, reminiscent of a Viking ship. Carvel planked meant a vessel's outer planking was affixed side by side. Terry Crandall, the archaeological diver for the Adirondack Museum during the summers of 1963 and 1964, worked on many Lake George colonial bateau shipwreck sites. He had the advantage of perusing these shipwrecks not long after their discovery in the early 1960s, when their structural integrity was more articulated then years later, after many sunken bateaux had been damaged by souvenir-seeking scuba divers. Crandall claimed that the sunken bateaux he observed in Lake George over 1963 and 1964 were predominantly carvel planked.[38]

The seams between the planking of the bottom boards and strakes of bateaux were **caulked** with tar or another substance to make the watercrafts as watertight as possible.[39] Nonetheless, bateaux frequently leaked. So bailing scoops, probably carved from basswood, a common tree in the colony of New York, were employed to remove water from inside the vessels.[40] In August 1961, Stan Zeccolo, a scuba diver who often dived in Lake George, reported to the Adirondack Museum that he discovered and photographed a wooden scoop at a sunken bateau site.[41] During the 1759 General Jeffery Amherst military campaign into the Champlain

Valley, Massachusetts-born soldier Lemuel Wood wrote in his journal, "... we had orders [that] every company should prepare a sufficient number of scoops for bailing bateaux."[42]

Though most bateaux were not armed with artillery, some reportedly carried light cannon. Bateaux were used primarily to transport troops and supplies and thus were generally not armed for combat. Nevertheless, in some situations during the French and Indian War, British bateaux did mount artillery armament. British General Jeffery Amherst reportedly armed some bateaux with a cannon, three-pounders.[43] These artillery-carrying bateaux probably had to be reinforced to carry the heavy weight and because of cannon recoil.[44] Furthermore, to identify the individual bateaux during the 1758 British campaign against the French in the Champlain Valley, each boat was generally marked with a regimental designation.[45]

Dennis Lewis, a "North Country" military historian from upstate New York, believed that colonial bateaux were constructed in a "variety of sizes depending on the job to be done." Also, Lewis postulated that French-built colonial bateaux were likely larger than those used by the English.[46] Gallagher concurs. However, he also believes the Lake George bateaux were shorter, but probably were wider and with higher sides.[47] Additionally, some French bateaux incorporated oak bottom boards into their construction, especially the outside hull bottom planks since they were susceptible to more wear and tear along the numerous rapids of French waterways in the St. Lawrence River Basin.[48]

Dr. Joseph Meany, at the time Senior Historian at the New York State Museum, wrote that there were basically two sizes for British bateaux in the mid-eighteenth century. The smaller bateaux were about twenty-four feet in length and sometimes called "Albany boats" because they were constructed in Albany, New York, along the Hudson River. These had a "beam" of about three feet.[49] On May 19, 1755, Colonel Jacob Wendell, a British officer, wrote that the "common Battoes" were about twenty-four feet in length and that for the purposes of a forthcoming military incursion against Crown Point (aka Fort St. Frédéric), larger bateaux, thirty feet long, must be built.[50] Meany's research also indicated that the British constructed longer bateaux that were commonly called "Schenectady Bateaux" or "Schenectady boats" because these were assembled in boatyards along the Mohawk River in Schenectady, New York.[51] These vessels appear to have been longer, up to forty-five feet, the length Chapelle gave for the upper limit size of British bateaux. However, the bateaux on Lake George appear to be more in the thirty- to thirty-five-foot range, with most of those studied in the lake by Bateaux Below measuring twenty-five to thirty-six feet in length along the bottom boards.

During the French and Indian War, bateaux sometimes had to be moved overland from one lake, river, or stream to another waterway. If the **portage** was a short distance, this was often accomplished by a team of men that carried the watercraft. Obviously, this was a laborious task, especially if the wooden vessel was heavy after recently being in water and having absorbed moisture into the wooden hull. If the boat had been out of the water for a time, it would be relatively dry, and thus lighter in weight. Sometimes bateaux were portaged using wagons, especially if the "carry" was a long distance and wagon transportation was available.[52]

The colonial bateau was certainly ideal for water transportation along the Upper Hudson River, Lake George, and Lake Champlain corridor. Bateaux were vessels that carried large numbers of men and cargo, and they were easy to maintain and deploy in the interior waterways of the North American wilderness.

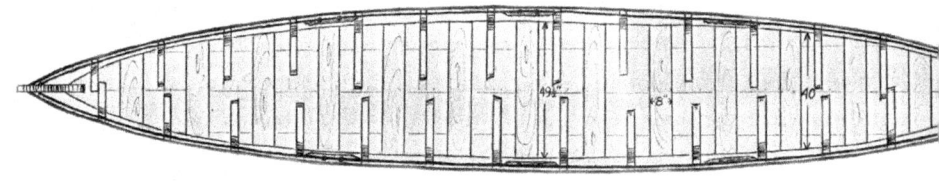

Figure 2.9 Archaeological diver Terry Crandall's drawing (plan view) of a Lake George military bateau based on his fieldwork conducted for Adirondack Museum over 1963–1964. (Credit: Terry Crandall)

Chapter Three

Building Techniques

Since the colonial bateau was a **vernacular watercraft**, built according to specific traditions of a place or culture, construction techniques sometimes varied from place to place. This chapter gives a description of how some colonial-era bateaux might have been assembled, but this is not the only construction method that could have been used. Bateau building did not require a master shipwright to oversee the construction of these commonplace vessels. Rather, carpenters and even lesser skilled laborers could produce these utility boats.

As previously mentioned, one of the reasons that the Dutch, English (after 1707 known as the British), and the French used bateaux in colonial North America was not just their utility as a small workhorse vessel for inland waterways, but because the crafts were relatively easy to construct. Furthermore, the forests of colonial New York were abundant in the raw materials required to construct bateaux. Trees had to be felled, trimmed into logs, and then squared. The wood was then sawed into boards and dried. The planks, generally pine, provided the bottom boards, strakes (side boards), and transverse cross boards known as battens (cleats). Other bateau pieces, such as frames (ribs), stem, and sternpost, were then cut from the natural crooks of hardwood trees, principally oak. Bateau oars and paddles, the latter used in lieu of a rudder, were also tooled. Since some bateaux might be rigged with a single mast upon which a crude sail could be affixed for sailing, masts frequently had to also be cut. Wooden scoops for bailing water from a leaky boat were also carved. Pine pitch was likewise required as a bateau building material for patching and even possibly as a type of **sheathing** for covering the bottoms and sides of vessels.

The bateaux at Lake George were either three or four boards in width along the bottom. Lake George Bateau 2626 was four planks wide, and Lake George Bateaux 4560 and 4566 were each three planks wide.[1] The Lake George bateaux studied *in situ* (in their original place) and in museums had bottom boards that were generally pine. It is believed that if bottom boards were single planks, these could be twenty-eight feet long or greater. If that length could not be acquired for

Figure 3.1 Robert E. Hager's interpretation of the likeness of a Mohawk River bateau, rigged with mast and sail. (Credit: Robert E. Hager)

bottom boards, two or more shorter pieces would have been joined together by either a **butt joint** or **scarf joint** to form a single bottom board. Bottom boards were about twelve inches wide and one inch or slightly greater in thickness. Hand wrought iron nails or spikes, often about three inches long, were required to fasten the vessel together. As previously mentioned, when wrought iron nails were hammered through planking, these metal fasteners were sometimes clenched or crimped for better holding effectiveness. There are photographs of wrought iron nails collected during the Adirondack Museum's 1960–1965 "Operation Bateaux" that show both straight and clenched nails. **Treenails (trunnels)**, a type of wooden peg, were not used as fasteners for bateau construction, but were common fasteners in constructing larger vessels such as sloops (single-mast sailing vessels) or **floating gun batteries** (large unconventional warships whose main purpose was to carry heavy artillery for bombardment).

Robert E. Hager, a graduate of Syracuse University, was an authority on late eighteenth-and early nineteenth-century inland watercraft in New York. He believed that during bateau construction, the boat's bottom boards often were placed on a small platform, a type of **ways**, a support structure upon which the watercraft was built. This wooden platform aided in the ease of a bateau's assembly. Hager was especially interested in Mohawk River bateaux. Hager suggested that the bottom boards probably lay in place on the narrow platform with the outside edge of each side of the vessel, port and starboard, tapered to the bow and stern to form the teardrop shape or pointed ends of the bateau.[2] The bateau was generally fuller (broader) at the bow, with a narrower pointed stern.

Once the bottom boards were in place, transverse planks called battens were nailed over the top of the bottom boards. However, the bateau's bottom had to have a longitudinal curve or **rocker**. In 1967, small boat expert John Gardner described the rocker as the "fore-and-after convexity of the bottom."[3] Gardner's analysis of the bateaux that were raised from Lake George and that he studied at the Adirondack Museum was they had a twelve-foot bottom that was flat in the amidships (center or middle). The rocker curve started approximately nine or ten feet equally from each end of the bateau, rising up to four inches at bow and stern.[4]

According to Hager, one way of creating this rocker when constructing a bateau may have been accomplished by lashing down the center of the bateau bottom boards to the small building platform (ways) and then employing blocks underneath the boat to create the curvature at both the bow and stern.[5]

The stem, the forward vertical piece of the bateau, was a single piece of wood that was curved, normally cut from hardwood, probably oak. The slightly curved

Figure 3.2 This 2018 photograph shows a batten from one of the Lake George bateaux recovered from the waterway in the early 1960s by the Adirondack Museum. These transverse boards were nailed over the bottom boards. This batten is somewhat narrower on top than on the bottom, an indication that this piece came from near one of the two ends of the boat rather than from the amidships section. The scale is twelve inches long with one-inch increments. (Credit: M.P. Meaney and New York State Museum, Albany, New York. Courtesy New York State Museum)

Figure 3.3 Photograph of a stem, the forward-most timber of a colonial bateau. From the collection of Fort William Henry Museum. (Credit: Joseph W. Zarzynski and Fort William Henry Museum)

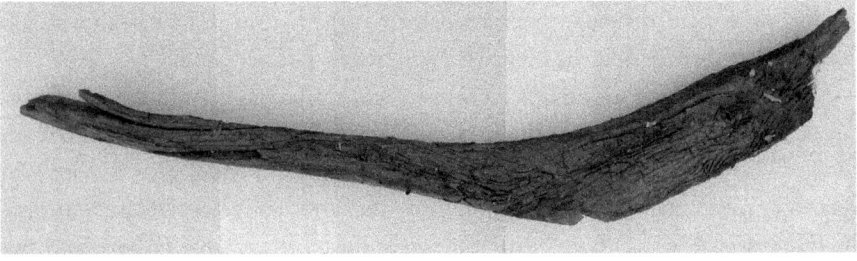

Figure 3.4 Photograph of a frame from a Lake George colonial bateau shipwreck in the Fort William Henry Museum collection. (Credit: Joseph W. Zarzynski and Fort William Henry Museum)

Figure 3.5 A 2018 photograph of one of the strakes recovered from a 1758 bateau shipwreck (Bateau 2626) during Adirondack Museum fieldwork in the early 1960s. The strake shows signs of wastage as it was undoubtedly exposed above the lake bottom sediment for many decades, thus contributing to its deterioration. The ranging rod, four feet long with one-foot increments, is for scale. (Credit: M.P. Meaney and New York State Museum, Albany, New York. Courtesy New York State Museum)

stem timber, that **raked** slightly forward, was fitted to the forward end of the center plank or planks that came to a point at the bow.

According to John Gardner, the stem would have been supported by an inner piece called an **apron** that lined the aft part of the stem.[6] Dr. Kevin J. Crisman, however, described this assembly as the stem being reinforced with a small knee that was spiked to both the after end of the stem and the bottom boards.[7]

The sternpost, a multiple-piece wooden component, was attached to the rear or stern of the bateau watercraft. This straight piece was not plumb (vertical) but angled slightly aft. It was nailed to the bateau's bottom boards and reinforced by a small knee nailed to both the sternpost and vessel's bottom boards.

Frames, sometimes called ribs, were each a single piece of wood, but generally cut from two sections of hardwood trees, that is, the crooks of trees. This section would be the junction of a limb and trunk or a limb and limb so that the grain of the wood follows the curve. As previously mentioned, each bateau generally had thirteen frames per side, port and starboard, for a total of twenty-six frames per bateau. Frames were about two inches in thickness. Frame angles were very important to ensure proper curvature of a bateau's sides.[8]

Once the bottom boards, stem, sternpost, and frames were fitted into place, it was time to add the strakes (side planking) to the wooden bateau skeleton. Special care must have been taken when attaching the strakes so they would help make the boat as watertight as possible. The first side plank attached was the garboard strake, the lowest side plank, followed by the remaining upper strakes. Strakes were probably attached on alternating sides, one strake on one side, and the corresponding strake on the other. In some bateaux, a small triangular piece of wood was inserted into the bow and stern peaks that, when fitted into place, resembled a small forward and aft "deck."[9]

Gunwales (gunnels), the upper or top part of a watercraft's hull, were attached, too. These could be both the outer and inner gunwales, the latter sometimes called inwales. Then any excesses of frames protruding above the gunwales were trimmed away. So that boat leakage would be minimal, caulking was then done.

Seats, made up of planks running transverse (across) the centerline of the bateau, would have also been added for the rowers and other occupants. The rowlocks, made up of wooden thole pads and thole pins, would have then been attached to the gunwales of the vessel. Oars, a stern paddle for steerage, possibly some long wooden poles for "poling" in shallow water, and one or more wooden scoops for bailing water would have been crafted, too.[10]

Figure 3.6 Robert E. Hager's drawing of a colonial bateau. Note the two men "poling" the boat along the shallow water of a river. (Credit: Robert E. Hager)

Chapter Four

Discovery of Lake George's Sunken Bateaux of 1758

About a century and a half after the British military leadership deliberately sank their Lake George squadron in a "wet storage" over the winter of 1758 to 1759, residents and visitors to Lake George revisited this sunken fleet. Over a period of several decades from the late nineteenth century and well into the mid-twentieth century, local newspapers such as the *Lake George Mirror* published news stories about Lake George's sunken French and Indian War bateaux.

The June 10, 1893, issue of the *Lake George Mirror* newspaper published an article entitled "The Sunken Batteaux of Lake George." The weekly seasonal newspaper reported that four bateaux (aka batteaux) were visible in the shallows of the lake. One was near Hill View on the west side of the waterway, about five miles from the south end of Lake George. A second sunken bateau was located off the Old Fort George Hotel on the southeast corner of the lake. A third bateau formed "part of the Crosbyside hotel [sic] pier," a property later known as the Wiawaka Holiday House. A fourth bateau was found "in the open lake, not very far from the pier in front of the Fort William Henry hotel [sic] grounds." This article clearly showed the late nineteenth-century media's and public's fascination with the lake's history, especially its sunken heritage.[1]

A few weeks later, on July 8, 1893, the *Lake George Mirror* recorded that Henry L. Sherman "has in his possession a small piece of one of the sunken bateaux, sunk in the broad lake off the Fort William Henry pier. Some winters ago, a piece of plank was pulled from the side of the craft, and it is from this plank that the relic was secured."[2]

Two years later, on August 3, 1895, the *Lake George Mirror* recorded the salvage of part of a bateau. In an article entitled "A Relic of By-Gone Days: A Forty-foot Plank from the Hull of a Sunken Batteaux," the newspaper gave details on the recovery of a bateau plank from the west side of the lake. On July 18, 1895, five men used two boats to pull the bateau plank from the lake bottom. That piece was "40 feet long, 15 inches wide and 2 inches thick with an estimated weight of from 300 to 1500 pounds." The article described the plank as coming from a vessel "used for the transportation of troops or provisions from one end of the lake to the other, during the memorable French and Indian War." The forty-foot long plank was "hauled by horse power" from the shore to Coolidge's Diamond Point House where it was "visited by residents and visitors, all anxious to obtain a view of this relic of a past century, rescued from its home beneath the waves."[3]

The *Lake George Mirror* newspaper's reference to a forty-foot bateau plank is somewhat long for an average colonial bateau. Forty feet was around the upper end for the length of a Lake George colonial bateau. However, historic preservationist Mark L. Peckham hypothesized that the British-led forces sank the larger and longer bateaux in the lake in 1758 and hid the shorter bateaux inland. These smaller bateaux were lighter and easier to transport overland, in the woods around Lake George, and elsewhere.[4] Or the so-called bateau plank recovered in 1895 came from a different type of colonial watercraft, possibly a sloop, a flat-bottomed barge, or a row galley, and not from a bateau.

Furthermore, the 1895 newspaper account reported that there were also two bateaux sunk off Fort William Henry Hotel. The enthusiasm of this newspaper article writer shows that over a century ago there certainly was significant interest in Lake George's sunken colonial warships.

One hundred and twenty years ago, the *Lake George Mirror* published another colonial bateau-related article on September 10, 1898. The news story proposed that a "Lake George Museum" should be established at the south end of the waterway. The newspaper article suggested that the historical facility should include boats "taken from the water and brought on shore" so that the "thousands of summer visitors who flock to the lake every year, will have the pleasure of looking at crafts built more than one hundred and forty years ago . . ." In retrospect, this article heralded one of the first attempts calling for cultural tourism at Lake George related to the waterway's submerged heritage resources.[5]

On June 24, 1899, the *Lake George Mirror* again reported on sunken bateaux in Lake George in their news story entitled, "French and Indian War: Timbers from the Colonial Batteaux in the Caldwell Station."[i] An oak knee, possibly a bateau frame, and another piece from a bateau were on display at the Delaware & Hudson Company's train station at the head of the lake. The writer of this *Lake*

---

i Today's Village of Lake George and the Town of Lake George were originally known as Caldwell, named after James Caldwell, an owner of much of the land at the south end of Lake George in the late eighteenth century and early nineteenth century. Today, the Village of Lake George is a small municipality lying within the larger Town of Lake George.

George Mirror news story then debated whether these "valuable relics of the French and Indian War" came from French vessels or British bateaux.[6]

The June 9, 1900, issue of the *Lake George Mirror* printed another article that highlighted the public's growing interest in Lake George's sunken colonial bateaux. The newspaper reported that Commodore John Boulton Simpson, one of the founders of the Sagamore Hotel in the Town of Bolton, "has another [bateau] piece" and there is "one [bateau] in Dunham's bay [*sic*] and one or two in the bay at the north end of [Floating] Battery Island."[7] Historian Dr. Russell P. Bellico believes the reported "one or two" bateaux sunk off Floating Battery Island probably are the disarticulated remains of a small floating gun battery and might not be typical bateau remnants.[8] It may be that the submerged site was indeed a large bateau, but a military watercraft more heavily constructed than a typical bateau. It may also have been modified, possibly even with an upper wooden casemate added to protect the crew.

Terry Crandall reported that during his 1963–1964 archaeological diving for the Adirondack Museum that he was sent by Dr. Robert Bruce Inverarity to inspect the waters around Floating Battery Island. Crandall later wrote that the "floating battery ... was unique, but badly scattered and strewn about, several major sections (ribs) were removed [by me] for analysis" by the museum staff.[9]

Jack Sullivan and I made a scuba dive off Floating Battery Island on July 8, 1983, but we did not find any remnants of the reputed floating gun battery shipwreck, as we were too far from the island. However, a decade later, on October 10, 1993, Bob Benway and I made the long boat ride from the Bateaux Below dock behind the Old Courthouse in the Town of Lake George north to Floating Battery Island, where we dived near the picturesque isle. Benway and I located several frames and planks, found in shallower water than where Sullivan and I had dived a decade earlier. I took underwater videography of three shipwreck frames, vessel timbers that appeared larger in size than the average colonial bateau shipwreck resting in Lake George.[10]

Figure 4.1 Underwater photograph of hull timbers from a reputed sunken floating gun battery in Lake George. This warship had a sturdy hull, possibly even bateau-like. (Credit: Dr. Russell P. Bellico)

Figure 4.2 Photograph of the March 1757-sunk British sloop raised from Lake George in July 1903. (Credit: Joseph W. Zarzynski Collection)

Figure 4.3 This 1903 photograph by A.N. Thompson shows another view of the March 1757-sunk British sloop. The vessel's stern is up on shore and its bow further out on the lake. After being recovered from the lake in July 1903, the iconic warship was cut up for souvenirs. (Credit: Joseph W. Zarzynski Collection)

On July 2, 1903, a forty-four-foot long, fourteen-foot wide, and seven-foot deep sunken sloop was raised from about fifteen to twenty feet of water from east of the old steamboat dock at the south end of Lake George.[11] A newspaper article published months later, however, reported the date at "about" July 3, 1903.[12] William H. Tuttle of Glens Falls, New York, directed the project that according to a newspaper account was "Empowered by an act of the Legislature of the State of New York . . ."[13] The historic eighteenth-century warship was raised from Lake George with the aid of locomotive Engine 444 of the Delaware & Hudson Company and its railroad crew. Though clearly not a bateau, the British warship was one of the sloops burned and then sunk during the March 1757 French raid on Fort William Henry. According to newspaper stories in 1903, the submerged hulk had been loaded with about ten tons of cobble (rock) that had to be removed by the early twentieth-century salvors before the sunken vessel could be pulled to shore. After the French and Indian War shipwreck was retrieved, the recovery crew found a "peck of musket balls and about fifty round shot or cannon balls ranging from two pounds to five pounds in weight." Also gathered from the skeletal wooden hull were a Spanish coin with the date 1743 and two pewter forks. One of the forks had the initials "F.M" on the handle.[14] The July 29, 1891, issue of *The Chatham Courier* (Chatham, New York) newspaper reported that the "blackened wreck" in shallow water off the site of the 1755–1757 Fort William Henry had been partially salvaged "at different times" of its cannonballs and that "in 1820 two small cannon [aka cannons] were removed from the wreck."[15] Tragically, the sloop, pointed at bow and stern and fashioned of white oak with black oak frames, was reportedly cut up for souvenirs shortly after it was raised in 1903.[16] Several of these cut-up hull timbers from the 1903-raised 1757 sloop shipwreck have surprisingly survived. In the early 1990s, the Lake George Historical Association received a donation of pieces of this sloop, each sawed away from either **floor timbers**, the central parts of frame timbers that lay across the keel and upon which the floor of the vessel is laid, or **futtocks**, the top sections of hull timber that form the compound frames on a larger vessel.

Fort William Henry Museum has a few pieces, too, similar in size and shape to those in the Lake George Historical Association collection. In 2008, Cleverdale, New York, antique dealer John Lefner purchased several wooden pieces of this sloop from a person who was "weeding" his personal collection. Steve Resler, at the time a volunteer diver with Bateaux Below, and I inspected Lefner's 1757 sloop-related assemblage. I arranged for Lefner to donate the sloop remnants to the New York State Museum in Albany, New York, where today they are in that repository. There are also two wooden gavels, repurposed from timbers of the 1757 Lake

George sloop, that are exhibited at the Warrensburgh (archaic spelling) Museum of Local History in Warrensburg, New York.[17] Now over a century after these shipwreck timbers were raised from the lake and because they had no professional conservation at that time, they continue to slowly degrade. Fortunately, in the autumn of 2017, an archaeology colleague, Brigid Shaw, and I persuaded Ithaca College professor Michael "Bodhi" Rogers to use the college's two Artec structured light 3-D scanners, called Eva and Spider, to laser scan the three Fort William Henry Museum sloop timbers. Thus, even if these original vessel timbers disintegrate, they are now fully documented using this state-of-the-art laser technology. Artec's Eva was the same kind of laser scanner that imaged Barack Obama to produce the first 3-D portrait of a United States president.[18]

Figure 4.4 Several hull timbers from the 1903-raised British sloop in the Lefner Collection at the New York State Museum. (Credit: New York State Museum, Albany, New York. Courtesy New York State Museum)

One wonders what happened to the fragments of the remaining historic 1903-raised hulk that were not cut up and sold as souvenirs. In 1920, *The Warrensburgh News* reported in an article entitled "Improvements of Beach at Lake George" about a recent cleanup frenzy conducted at the south end of the waterway to collect "drift wood and other refuse litter" laying on the shore. The article then provided news coverage that the "old boat which for a number of years has been going to decay on the beach has been removed and burned."[19] It is quite probable that the "old boat" mentioned in this 1920 newspaper account was none other than the remaining hull structure of the 1757 British sloop that had been removed from the lake in 1903.

The 1903 recovery of the sunken French and Indian War sloop certainly contributed to a growing public sentiment for relic hunting on both land and underwater searching for colonial artifacts. The July 24, 1915, issue of the *Glens Falls Post-Star* (Glens Falls, New York) published an article entitled "Relic Hunters Are Numerous." The story's subtitle was "Shores and Water of Historic Lake George Favorite Hunting Grounds." The account reflected on the expanding interest by treasure hunters to free-dive underwater seeking historical treasures in the lake.

The 1915 newspaper story also mentioned how, "By diving, several iron rings and pieces of chain, which had rotted away from the hulks" of lake shipwrecks, "were brought to the surface."[20] Regrettably, at that time there were no public or government outcries against this uncontrolled relic hunting.

The April 10, 1919, issue of *The Saratogian* (Saratoga Springs, New York) newspaper published a news story reporting that W.L. Adee of Saratoga Springs, New York, made a "clock case and a pair of wooden candlesticks" crafted from timbers from the 1903-raised 1757 sloop. The items were exhibited at the F.C. Maynard jewelry store in Saratoga Springs.[21] Crafting such items as canes, candlesticks, chairs, and other household necessities from shipwrecks was common around the world before cultural mores and historic preservation laws discouraged such repurposing.

Fortunately, an emerging local historical preservation ethic toward Lake George's shipwrecks began in 1934. On August 18, 1934, the *Lake George Mirror* published an editorial entitled "Preserve Historical Relics." In the short essay, the newspaper's editorial staff commended a suggestion made a week earlier by James L. MacDonald, the manager of the Fort William Henry Hotel. MacDonald stated that a French and Indian War bateau seen in the shallows of the waterway at the head of the lake should be raised and exhibited in a building specifically constructed for the shipwreck at Fort George Park near the southeastern corner of Lake George. The pro-historical preservationist editorial went on to announce that several sunken bateaux had been seen on the lake bottom when the water was calm and visibility good.[22] Today, it is refreshing to read that rather than cut up an historic vessel, as was done with the 1757 British sloop raised from the lake in 1903, some Lake George citizens in 1934 were articulating a shipwreck preservation mentality.

Chapter Five

The 1950s and Early 1960s

"Rediscovery"

Shipwrecks of Lake George's sunken bateaux of 1758 were discovered in the nineteenth century when residents, as well as inquisitive visitors to the waterway, noticed vestiges of the submerged squadron resting in the shallows of the lake's clear waters. Decades later, the 1950s brought new possibilities for underwater exploration as scuba (self-contained underwater breathing apparatus) was slowly growing in popularity.

Circa 1953, while diving with early scuba equipment, but without a wet suit to keep warm, Carl Dunn, a Warren County, New York resident, spotted a ballast pile or what might have been a mound of sinking rocks atop a sunken bateau at the south end of the lake.[1] This was one of the earliest, if not the first, sighting by a scuba diver of a bateau shipwreck in Lake George. This type of underwater exploration—scuba (also written SCUBA)—was only about a decade old. In the early 1940s, Jacques Cousteau and Emile Gagnan, two Frenchmen, invented scuba.[2] Within a few years, the use of the aqualung gained in popularity in Europe and North America. Several years after Dunn's pioneering scuba investigation of a colonial shipwreck at Lake George in the early 1950s, scuba divers would be regularly visiting the Adirondack waterway, and more shipwreck discoveries would be made.

While Dunn was scuba diving in the lake off the site of Fort William Henry in the early 1950s, an archaeological investigation on the 1755–1757 fortification grounds was being conducted under the direction of archaeologist Stanley M. Gifford. The terrestrial excavation was part of an effort funded by a group of businessmen building a replica of the British and provincial fort to attract tourists.[3] To advertise the archaeological excavation and the construction of replica Fort William Henry, Gifford presented numerous talks around the region to civic organizations. During one such lecture to the Albany Kiwanis given on April 20, 1954, Gifford told Kiwanis members that if they were swimming in the lake to

Figure 5.1 Early 1950s scuba diver Carl Dunn emerges from Lake George holding a colonial-era kettle. Dunn dived in the waterway for Fort William Henry Corporation. He might have been one of the first scuba explorers to see an eighteenth-century sunken bateau in the lake. (Credit: Fort William Henry Museum)

keep an eye out for "cannon and other relics" sunk during the 1758 Abercromby military operation at the head of Lake George. Gifford believed that submerged colonial artifacts lying in the shallows of the waterway might possibly be found by observant swimmers.[4]

By the year 1958, scuba diving around the Empire State was becoming a trendy recreational sport. In the Atlantic Ocean, Long Island Sound, and some eight thousand lakes, rivers, and ponds, scuba divers were beginning to explore the inviting depths of the state's abundant waterways. In 1958, the state government estimated that 1,500 scuba enthusiasts were diving around the Empire State. This period also saw growth in the state's scuba clubs, with thirty-six dive clubs totaling about eight hundred members in 1958. The YMCA and other indoor pools around New York were being used to train more and more people to become scuba divers, especially during the wintertime.[5] Thus, it was not surprising that these underwater adventurers would be attracted to the relatively pristine waters and submerged history of the "Queen of American Lakes."

In 1959, four scuba divers from the "Mechanicville-Stillwater-Greenwich" area of New York recovered a two-hundred-pound "English cannon" from the bottomlands of Lake George. According to the August 13, 1959, issue of the *Troy*

Times Record (Troy, New York), the sport divers thought the iron cannon was from a "British patrol boat on Lake George during the French and Indian War."[6] One of the cannon's two trunnions, the cylindrical protrusions off the tube on the artillery piece whose purpose was for mounting the weapon on a gun carriage, was missing.[7]

Knocking off a trunnion was one way to disable a cannon, making it useless during combat. The dive group theorized the light cannon they discovered in Lake George in 1959 would have fired a "shot weighing between one and two pounds." An article in the August 12, 1959, issue of *The Troy Record* newspaper described the English cannon as a **falconet** and reported that it was cast at a Philadelphia foundry, possibly during the early 1740s. Colonial vessels sometime carried falconet **ordnance**, a type of small caliber artillery piece, frequently employed as anti-boarding armament. The small iron cannon found in Lake George in 1959 was reportedly discovered in about twenty-two feet of water.[8] The artillery piece mentioned in the 1959 *Troy Record* article was 2 feet, 6-1/2 inches in length and weighed approximately two hundred pounds.[9] It is not known if this was armament aboard a bateau watercraft, from a more substantial vessel such as a

Figure 5.2 In the early 1950s, archaeologist Stanley M. Gifford was excavating the grounds of Fort William Henry (1755–1757) while Carl Dunn was scuba diving for the museum in nearby Lake George. In 1954, Gifford asked the Albany Kiwanis organization to alert members swimming at Lake George to look for sunken colonial artifacts for the museum. (Credit: Fort William Henry Museum)

row galley or a sloop, or if the cannon was jettisoned over the side of a colonial warship to abandon the ordnance. Except for the missing trunnion, the 1959-raised cannon was described as being in "excellent" condition.[10]

In 1961, one of these four divers gave a talk before a church group in Mechanicville, New York. According to the January 24, 1961, issue of *The Saratogian* newspaper, the scuba explorer "also had on display many of his underwater finds including several sections from some of the bateaux which received so much publicity last summer [1960]" as well as "pictures" (i.e., photographs) of the cannon they found in 1959.[11]

In July 1960, two teenage scuba divers made a dramatic find off the east shore of Lake George, not far from Million Dollar Beach. The teenagers, Fred Bolt, reported as being seventeen years old, and Robert (Bob) LaVoy (some newspapers incorrectly called him Dick LaVoy), age eighteen, located a cluster of several sunken bateaux.[12] However, an article in *The Saratogian*, dated April 25, 1961, reported on an April 18, 1961, lecture presentation made by Robert Lord, at the time the former curator of Fort William Henry Museum. Lord's program was given to members of the Saratoga Historical Society. Lord commented during the lecture that the Lake George bateau fleet, noticed in Lake George in 1960 by scuba divers Bolt and LaVoy, may have been actually first observed in 1954. Lord said that in 1954 little attention was paid to the shipwrecks since they were initially believed to be coal barges.[13] That said, Bolt and LaVoy are generally credited with making the spectacular find, the rediscovery of Lake George's sunken bateaux of 1758.

Shortly after this development, Robert Flacke, a U.S. Navy reservist and one of the principals of Fort William Henry Corporation, authenticated the find. Flacke said that about ten to fifteen sunken bateaux rested embedded in the lake bottom. The shipwrecks were "some 30 to 80 yards from shore" appearing to have been "deliberately sunk."[14] Robert Lord, at the time the curator of replica Fort William Henry, said after the 1960 rediscovery of the bateau-class shipwrecks that each sunken boat was "pointed toward shore and was loaded with rocks, indicating the flotilla was scuttled."[15]

Shortly after the announcement of the Bolt-LaVoy shipwrecks revelation, the *Glens Falls Times* newspaper reported on July 26, 1960, that, "A team of expert divers and representatives of the Smithsonian Institution of Washington, DC, will arrive in Lake George within the next few days to inspect discoveries of ancient sunken vessels and artifacts..."[16] In the meantime, Bob LaVoy said shortly after the Bolt-LaVoy find that he and other divers had recently returned to the site and uncovered "ancient bottles, a pistol and other artifacts."[17]

Later that month, the July 30, 1960, issue of the *New York Times* reported that the sunken bateaux were "in perfect formation, parallel to each other, and perpendicular with the shore line [*sic*]." That same article quoted Robert Lord, Fort William Henry Museum's curator at the time, speculating that the warships "were ordered scuttled during the winter to prevent damage by ice, beavers and [French] raiding parties."[18]

An article entitled "Find Naval Relics At Bottom Of Lake" in the July 28, 1960, issue of the *Amsterdam Evening Recorder* (Amsterdam, New York) stated that since the rediscovery of the sunken lake squadron, LaVoy and others had been "working eight hours a day" recovering artifacts from the sunken vessels.[19]

In 1993, I interviewed Bob LaVoy for an article in *The Lake George Nautical Newsletter*, a publication produced by Bateaux Below. During the interview, LaVoy said that the spatial pattern of distribution of the sunken bateaux clearly showed that the British intended to retrieve the vessels. He said the bow stems were in place, the shipwrecks were covered with stones, and the sunken bateaux's frames protruded from the soft sediment that covered the wooden shipwrecks. LaVoy commented that he even discovered evidence on a few of the sunken bateaux that they had some type of rigging for sailing. He also added that while diving on one bateau shipwreck he found a pair of "old eyeglasses" and even some "paper on a bateau, possibly from a *Bible*."[20]

Also, beginning in late July 1960, some local newspapers reported on another important discovery made by two Saratoga Springs, New York divers Walter Stroup (age thirty-one) and Fred Tarrant (thirty-two). The two Saratogians located an unusual eighteenth-century shipwreck off the south end of the lake. The sunken vessel was loaded with about forty colonial-era mortar bombs, each weighing over 150 pounds.[21] The shipwreck soon became known as the "mortar bateau" or "mortar bomb bateau." I have devoted a full chapter (chapter 9, The "Mortar Bateau") to this unconventional boat and its military cargo as well as the debate over who actually first found the ordnance-laden shipwreck.

The rediscovery of the lake's sunken colonial bateaux in 1960 was not just newsworthy and exciting for the Adirondacks/Lake George region, it likewise ushered in a new era—the birth of cultural resources management of Lake George's underwater heritage.

Chapter Six
Toward Better Management

No sooner did the newspaper ink dry announcing the 1960 Bolt-LaVoy underwater detection, then the authorities of the State of New York were suddenly confronted with ownership issues of these historic shipwrecks and what to do with the sunken British and provincial warships lying in Lake George. After all, the lake bottom was property of the State of New York. At first, the media was even unclear about who "owned" the sunken bateaux.[1] Robert Lord, curator of Fort William Henry Museum, initially announced that "the find, which is of historic, not monetary value, legally belonged to Mr. LaVoy."[2]

An article in the *The Knickerbocker News*, dated August 2, 1960, reported that the State Education Department ordered law enforcement officials to seal off the area where the sunken bateaux were located. State officials feared that private exploration by recreational divers could lead to these bateaux being damaged. Further, the state agency granted the Adirondack Museum the sole authority to investigate the shipwrecks and recover any objects of archaeological significance.[3]

Since the sunken bateaux were on state bottomlands, the State of New York eventually assumed control of these cultural remains. In an article in the August 2, 1960, issue of the *Glens Falls Times* newspaper, it was reported that LaVoy and Bolt agreed to cooperate with the Adirondack Museum, the historical organization that was granted permission by the state government to raise some of these sunken warships.[4] Documents in the Adirondack Museum's collection show that LaVoy soon developed a cooperative spirit with the Blue Mountain Lake historical facility. LaVoy and Dr. Robert Bruce Inverarity (director of the Adirondack Museum) corresponded, and Inverarity received important information about the two teenagers' scuba inspections of the sunken fleet of bateaux.

The New York State Education Department's decision to grant the Adirondack Museum and its host organization, the Adirondack Historical Association, a permit was based upon authority granted to the agency by Section 233 of New York Education Law that went into effect on March 6, 1958. Specifically, two points of that statute relate directly to the sunken colonial bateaux. First, Section 233

Figure 6.1 Dr. Robert Bruce Inverarity before he came to the Adirondack Museum in the mid-1950s. (Credit: Archives of American Art)

states that "no person shall appropriate, excavate, injure or destroy any object of archaeological and paleontological interest, situated on or under lands owned by the state of New York, without the written permission of the commissioner of education," and second, that

> [p]ermits for the examination, excavation or gathering of archaeological and paleontological objects upon the lands under their respective jurisdictions may be granted by the heads of state departments or other state agencies to persons authorized by the commissioner of education for the purposes of the state museum and state science service, with a view to preservation of any such objects worthy of permanent preservation and, in all cases, to the acquisition and dissemination of knowledge relating thereto.[5]

In many respects, the spirit of the 1958 New York Education Law is based on the American Antiquities Act of 1906, a groundbreaking federal law that protected "any historic or prehistoric ruin or monument, or any object of antiquity, situated on lands owned or controlled by the Government of the United States..."

The 1906 federal law also provided for "permits for the examination of ruins, the excavation of archaeological sites and the gathering of objects of antiquity" upon designated federal lands.⁶

Though the New York State Education Department had the right to grant archaeological permits, the state's award of a permit to the Adirondack Museum and its governing body, the Adirondack Historical Association, for the archaeological study of Lake George's sunken bateaux in the early 1960s was not well received by some in the Lake George area. The Adirondack Museum was not located along the shoreline of Lake George. Although Lake George lies within the Adirondack Mountains and the Adirondack Park, the thirty-two-mile long waterway actually is located along the southeastern corner of the mountain range. Thus, the Adirondack Museum, located in the rural hamlet of Blue Mountain Lake, New York, in the heart of the Adirondack Mountains, was over an hour away by automobile from the south end of Lake George. Inverarity countered, stating that the historical association's charter authorized them to "pursue and encourage historical study and research relating to . . . the Adirondack Park," a geographical entity that included Lake George.⁷

However, residents along the banks of Lake George have long referred to themselves as "Lake Georgians" and infrequently as citizens of the Adirondacks. Therefore, it was not surprising that some people living around Lake George were surprised by the State Education Department's decision that granted the Adirondack Museum an archaeological permit to study Lake George's sunken bateaux of 1758. The *Lake George Mirror* newspaper published an editorial on August 12, 1960, entitled "Shall Historic Objects Found in Lake George Go to Museums Elsewhere?" The editorial asked the local "Chambers of Commerce and other organizations" to take a stand against removing artifacts from the lake and sending them to the Adirondack Museum. Further, the newspaper editorial suggested that the Lake George Association, a local not-for-profit environmental watchdog group, "should supersede any Adirondack association in supervising or directing the disposition of objects recovered from the lake."⁸

Though the newspaper editorial was well received by Lake George-area historic preservationists, ironically, that same day that the *Lake George Mirror* also published a small advertisement entitled "Fortune Beneath The Waves!" The advertisement from an entrepreneur in Hague, New York, announced the sale of metal detectors for underwater use to find "sunken boats, equipment, and treasure."⁹

On August 20, 1960, the *Albany Times-Union* newspaper printed an article entitled "Ticonderoga Opposes State Action: 2 Forts Join in Bateau Battle." The two reconstructed colonial military installations, Fort Ticonderoga, once a French stronghold called Fort Carillon, and Fort William Henry, a former British and provincial fortress, had opposed one another during the French and Indian War. The decision by the state agency to grant the Adirondack Museum the right to manage the recovery of sunken bateaux from Lake George brought the management of the once two opposing forts together in a somewhat unfamiliar alliance.[10]

In a *Lake George Mirror* article published on August 26, 1960, Edward P. Hamilton, Director of Fort Ticonderoga, explained his views in a letter he sent to the New York State Education Department commissioner that was published in some regional newspapers. Hamilton stated: "The Adirondack Museum, at least hitherto, has been interested only in the history of the resorts, logging and transportation within the Adirondacks, and all this only in the 19th Century and later." Hamilton suggested that the Fort William Henry Corporation should raise some of the sunken bateau-class boats. Hamilton also reminded local citizens of the rarity of the bateaux when he exclaimed: "It is amazing how little is known about the vehicle that was the work horse of colonial North America." The Fort Ticonderoga Museum director went on to declare that a state permit to conduct studies and raise one or more sunken colonial bateaux "should not be given by the State to the first one that asks for them."[11]

Nonetheless, the State of New York's Education Department stood by its original decision. The Adirondack Museum, under the guidance of Inverarity, would conduct the archaeological survey and excavation of Lake George's sunken colonial bateaux.

However, the pressure put upon the Adirondack Museum must have been convincing because by midsummer of 1961, Inverarity was quoted in the *Lake George Mirror* newspaper as stating that Adirondack Museum, Fort Ticonderoga, and Fort William Henry would each get bateaux should enough be raised, conserved, and be available to go around. Inverarity said, "You can't cut pieces of a pie until you have the whole pie first. Wait until we have raised as many of these boats as we can find." He went on to comment that the State of New York would decide what museums would get bateaux recovered from Lake George.[12]

Eventually, the early 1960s disagreement between these museums died down. Moreover, Lake George's hometown newspaper, the *Lake George Mirror*, would become—and still is today—one of the staunchest supporters of historic preservation issues concerning the "Queen of American Lakes."

Seattle, Washington-born Inverarity (1909–1999), who would direct the study of Lake George's sunken bateaux, was an intriguing and talented person with a diversified and accomplished professional career. That certainly prepared him for his administrative job with the Adirondack Museum. Early in his professional life, the six-foot, six-inch Inverarity studied Pacific Coast Native American tribes and also became an expert in the field of puppetry.[13] During the height of the Great Depression in the mid-1930s, Inverarity was appointed the director of the State of Washington's Federal Art Project, a program formed by the Works Progress Administration.[14] Inverarity also penned several books on a variety of cultural topics, clearly illustrating his talents as a "Renaissance Man." A superb artist, one of Inverarity's jobs during World War II (1941–1945) was that of administrator of naval camouflage design for the U.S. Navy (1941–1943), and from 1943 to 1945 he was an official artist of with the U.S. Navy. The *Watertown Daily Times* newspaper in Watertown, New York, reported in 1965 that Inverarity received a meritorious civil service award for his service as a war artist during World War II.[15] After the war, Robert Bruce Inverarity was awarded a bachelor's degree in art and anthropology from the University of Washington. He then received his Master and PhD degrees from the Fremont School in Los Angeles.[16]

Before coming east to take over the administration of the Adirondack Museum in the mid-1950s, Inverarity was the director of the Museum of International Folk Art in Santa Fe, New Mexico from 1949 to 1954.[17] The institution was

Figure 6.2 Dr. Robert Bruce Inverarity directed Adirondack Museum's "Operation Bateaux" (1960–1965). During World War II, Inverarity was a naval camouflage designer and an artist for the U.S. Navy. Here is one of his pieces of navy art, an oil painting, date unknown, entitled "Top Deck of Submarine." (Credit: Naval History and Heritage Command)

founded by Florence Dibell Bartlett of Chicago, an art collector and a patron of folk art. She had a ranch near Santa Fe, and Inverarity was tasked with creating the museum complex from the ground up. To prepare for that challenging task, he reportedly visited forty-five museums, studying these institutions' structures, exhibits, and administrative hierarchies. Inverarity's expenses for that travel and museum research were funded by a 1951 grant from the Axel Wenner-Gren Foundation for Anthropological Research. The official groundbreaking for the Museum of International Folk Art was held in August 1950, and the museum opened in 1953.[18]

Inverarity's vast experience with administrative museum work in his home state of Washington before World War II and later in Santa Fe certainly prepared him for his next challenge, to help establish the Adirondack Museum in Blue Mountain Lake, New York. From the mid-1950s until 1965, Inverarity served as the director of the Adirondack Museum. He held various administrative posts after his stint at the Adirondack Museum, including serving as the director of the Philadelphia Maritime Museum from 1969 to 1976.[19]

Two months after retiring from the Philadelphia Maritime Museum in 1976, Inverarity excited the art and archaeological worlds by selling his noteworthy collection of Native American artifacts and artwork to the British Museum in London. These were incredible cultural objects he'd acquired over a lifetime as an anthropologist and art aficionado. At the time, an art specialist at the Sotheby's Parke-Bernet auction house in New York City called Inverarity's Native American cultural acquisitions "one of the finest in America ... it could be worth up to $900,000 on the open market. It is among the top five or 10 collections in America and Canada."[20] Inverarity, a Fellow of the Royal Academy of Arts in London,[21] reportedly did not break up his collection to sell it piece meal for more money. Rather, the tall and scholarly Washington native kept the rare assemblage intact, thus making it much more intrinsically valuable for academic analysis and interpretation. Additionally, Inverarity took far less than the monetary worth of the unique collection, and in so doing made it affordable for purchase by the British Museum, a world-class institution dedicated to the study and exhibit of human art, culture, and history.

Several years ago, an art scholar from Seattle, Washington, revealed a bit of professional football trivia associated with the late Dr. Inverarity. A January 28, 2014, story written by Dr. Robin K. Wright, the Curator of Native American Art with Seattle's Burke Museum of Natural History and Culture, University of Washington, presented an unknown aspect about the multitalented anthropologist. Wright's article announced that Inverarity's 1950 book, *Art of the Northwest*

Coast Indians, included a photograph of a picturesque regional Native American mask. That image was used by a design artist in the mid-1970s as the inspiration and model for the Seattle Seahawks' team logo. The football team's emblem depicts a profile likeness of a "sea hawk."[22]

In the early 1960s, besides dealing with various museum staffs arguing over who had the right to excavate the lake's sunken colonial bateaux, a formidable test that faced the State of New York, the custodial caretakers of Lake George's sunken heritage, was shipwreck vandalism. The quick and strong stand taken by the New York State Education Department toward Lake George's sunken bateaux of 1758, based on the 1958 State Education Law, Section 233, probably prevented a scheduled "treasure hunt" at the lake that was scheduled for the summer of 1960. A news story in the August 23, 1960, issue of the *Albany Times-Union* newspaper described how the Lake George Chamber of Commerce and the Fort William Henry Corporation announced the cancellation of a "skin diving treasure hunt" they intended to co-sponsor on September 17 and 18, 1960. In the article, "Hunt Called Off at Lake George," the event's organizers rescinded the scheduled scuba treasure search "in order to cooperate with the State" and be historically preservation minded.[23] The unexpected rediscovery of sunken French and Indian War-era bateaux at Lake George in the year 1960 tested the authority of the State of New York government to protect and manage submerged cultural resources in state waterways. However, unlike the incidents in the late 1800s and early 1900s when some of Lake George's sunken warships were removed from the waterway, in 1960, the state government took firm steps to protect this finite and fragile colonial fleet. This might have been the first time that the protection of and the archaeological study of underwater cultural resources in the Empire State were interpreted under Section 233 of the 1958 New York State Education Law.

The August 30, 1960, issue of the *Glens Falls Times* published an article that detailed the collective strategy of the late summer 1960 to protect the sunken bateaux. First, the Adirondack Museum used local and regional media outlets to appeal to scuba divers to not disturb the recently rediscovered bateau shipwrecks and to report any historical finds to Warren County Sheriff Carl K. McCoy. The museum's plea attempted to inform divers that any wood removed from these sunken boats, if not "scientifically processed for preservation" using knowledgeable and trained personnel, "will slowly fall to pieces." Second, the Adirondack Museum informed recreational divers that state law makes it a misdemeanor to excavate or remove any objects of archaeological interest that could lead to a fine and other possible punishment. Sheriff McCoy reportedly oversaw the application of this law. Third, scuba divers were encouraged to enjoy their sport in the lake and were asked to report any shipwreck finds without removing objects. Fourth, the Adirondack Museum asked the Lake George Chamber of Commerce for assistance in acting as a liaison between their museum and the people of Lake George. Charles Jefts, president of the local chamber of commerce and also an avid scuba diver, graciously supported this public information campaign.[24]

The next major impact on submerged cultural resources management of shipwrecks in New York state, including Lake George's sunken bateaux, came years later in 1988 when President Ronald Reagan signed the **Abandoned Shipwreck Act of 1987 (ASA)** into law. The statute, proposed in 1987, affirms the authority of American states to claim and manage abandoned shipwrecks on state submerged lands. A shipwreck is defined in the law as the vessel or wreck and also all of its contents (artifacts). As dictated by this law, Native Americans have title to shipwrecks on tribal lands, that is, in tribal waters. Under the ASA, the U.S. Government retains title to sunken American warships. Further, the U.S. respects the sovereignty of foreign warships sunk in American waters. Thus, it can be interpreted that these British shipwrecks in Lake George from 1758 are the property of the British government (United Kingdom) and the federal and state governments are administering these for that country. An important provision of the ASA pertains to public access to shipwrecks. Shipwrecks are perceived as cultural resources with multiple uses and values. Thus, not only are shipwrecks important to archaeologists and historians, they likewise have value to fishermen (who fish around shipwrecks), recreational scuba divers, and the tourism sector, too. Therefore, the ASA's guidelines directed states to provide reasonable public access to shipwrecks and the states were encouraged to create shipwreck parks for scuba divers.[25]

Figure 6.3 This photograph shows the bow of the 1758 *Land Tortoise* radeau, a type of British floating gun battery that was sunk in Lake George. The vessel was discovered on June 26, 1990, by members of the group that later became known as Bateaux Below. The Abandoned Shipwreck Act of 1987 (ASA), signed into law in 1988, changed how shipwrecks like this would be managed and protected in American waters. (Credit: Dr. Russell P. Bellico)

The ASA had a profound impact, too, on how the State of New York would manage its submerged cultural resources. According to Alan C. Bauder, the Submerged Lands and Natural

Resources Manager for the New York State Office of General Services, the state's "ad-hoc Committee for Submerged Cultural Resources was convened around 1987 to address the issues of management of the shipwrecks in New York waters that were subject to the Federal Statute known as the Abandoned Shipwreck Act."[26] The ad-hoc committee has generally consisted of representatives from several state agencies, including the Education Department, Department of Environmental Conservation, Office of Parks, Recreation and Historic Preservation, Department of State, Law Department, Office of General Services, and the Canal Corporation/Thruway Authority. Over the years, other agencies were added. The committee tried to meet four times annually, but with the introduction of electronic mail (e-mail), this type of communication frequently made face-to-face sessions unnecessary. The agendas for these meetings varied but often included issues of current interest, permit approval under Section 233, enforcement legislation, policy development, data base design, and status reviews of agencies' activities.[27]

Though well intended, there has been a critical component missing in the ad-hoc Committee for Submerged Cultural Resources in that it had no formal and official representation from the recreational dive community, dive store and scuba charter sector, and non-state employed underwater archaeologists, the three groups that did the scuba diving on shipwrecks in the Empire State. Further, there has been no "effective" mechanism for these three stakeholder entities to have a "viable and continued dialogue" with state officials to voice their concerns, grievances, and suggestions. Sadly, this sometimes resulted in distrust among some of these stakeholders (dive community, dive store and scuba charter sector, and underwater archaeologists) toward some agency representatives.

In 1998, ten years after the ASA became law, Anne G. Giesecke, one of the principal proponents of the ASA, commented on the first decade of the ASA in a paper she presented at the 1998 Society for Historical Archaeology Conference in Atlanta, Georgia. I attended that conference and heard Giesecke's erudite review of the ASA:

> We cannot legislate values. We can legislate rules which direct behavior. Environmental and archaeological resources are managed at the most local level.... The Abandoned Shipwreck Act and state laws implementing management programs protect many sites and expand the public's understanding of the value of these resources. The Abandoned Shipwreck Act is not an end point but an important success in the process of governance.[28]

It is quite obvious that Section 233 of New York Education Law and the ASA set a foundation for the better management of New York's submerged cultural resources. There are several government agencies that have worked cooperatively to manage New York's submerged heritage. The Office of General Services is the custodial caretaker of submerged lands and issues permits for a vast variety of activities. The State Museum (State Education Department) oversees permits for archaeology conducted at shipwreck and other underwater cultural sites. The Office of Parks, Recreation and Historic Preservation oversees the **National Register of Historic Places** program in the state and helps to coordinate archaeological surveys. The Department of Environmental Conservation protects the state's natural resources, and at Lake George this agency oversees the Submerged Heritage Preserves program. The Department of State is the manager of coastal waterways. Finally, the Office of Attorney General protects the cultural resources of the Empire State, including submerged heritage sites.[29]

The remaining chapters examine how archaeological and educational programs, **shipwreck preserves**, site stabilization projects, and other strategies have complemented the management, preservation, and protection of Lake George's sunken bateaux of 1758.

Chapter Seven
Underwater Archaeology

The first underwater archaeology project at one site of Lake George's sunken bateaux of 1758 occurred in September of 1960, two months after the shipwrecks' rediscovery by teenage scuba divers Fred Bolt and Bob LaVoy. During that month, scuba divers under the direction of the Adirondack Museum's Dr. Robert Bruce Inverarity raised one or more bateaux from the lake. Eventually, a total of three bateaux were successfully recovered from the lake during the early 1960s. The September 22, 1960, *Watertown Times* newspaper reported that there appeared to be some archaeology involved in that 1960 shipwreck recovery operation, that is, "charting the position of the fleet" before their "salvage."[1]

Inverarity, the Adirondack Museum director, outlined the need to recover one or more colonial bateaux from the depths of Lake George: "No colonial bateaux have been preserved; there are only two known drawings in existence, and we are not certain whether they truly reflect colonial bateaux. So, it becomes extremely important to determine the lines and the construction of these boats, which had a great deal to do with the whole growth of boat building in America."[2]

It should be noted that underwater archaeology as a science was still very much in its infancy in the early 1960s. During the decade of the 1950s, French and Italian crews studied Roman shipwrecks lying in the Mediterranean Sea off France and Italy, as well as by the French off Tunisia. However, today many scholars maintain that the first so-called underwater archaeological study of a shipwreck really began in 1960 on a Late Bronze Age sunken vessel lying off the west coast of Turkey in the eastern Mediterranean Sea. Over 1958 and 1959, American photojournalist Peter Throckmorton lived aboard Turkish workboats in the eastern Mediterranean Sea, and he learned from deep-sea sponge divers of an ancient shipwreck. Throckmorton was instrumental in getting a young graduate student of **classical archaeology** from the University of Pennsylvania named George F. Bass to come to Turkey to apply archaeological principles to excavate what is now known as the Cape Gelidonya shipwreck.[3]

51

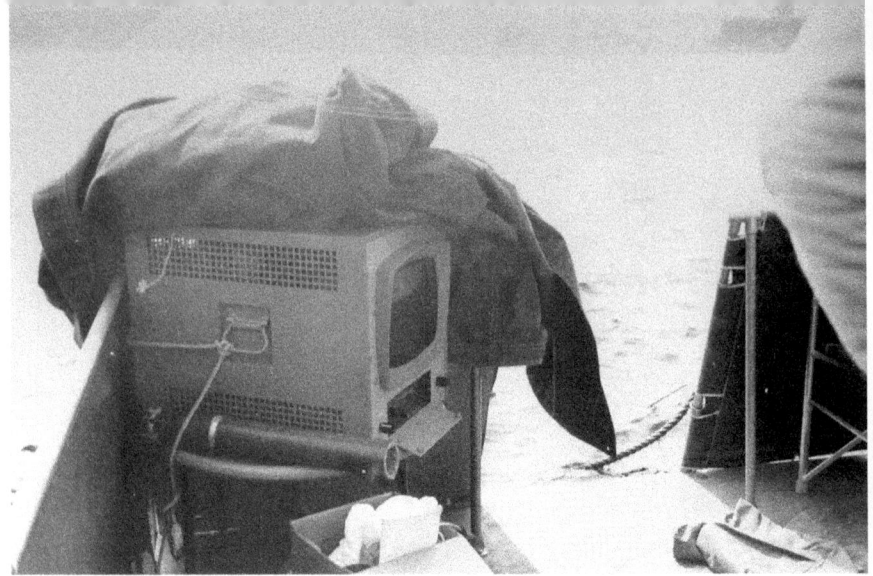

Figure 7.1 In 1960, this early underwater camera system was provided by General Electric (Schenectady, New York) to the Adirondack Museum for operation to aid in raising a 1758 bateau shipwreck from Lake George. (Credit: Adirondack Experience)

Figure 7.2 One of the three 1758 bateau shipwrecks raised from Lake George by the Adirondack Museum during the early 1960s. Note the tire inner tubes used for flotation. (Credit: Adirondack Experience)

Bass, considered one of the earliest pioneers in the field of underwater archaeology and the author of one of the first books on the subject, *Archaeology Under Water* (1966), knew Inverarity and described him as the "perfect choice for the job" to study Lake George's sunken colonial bateaux. Bass wrote that Inverarity was already involved in researching small watercraft in America and, though the Adirondack Museum director was not a scuba diver, he was particularly intrigued with colonial bateaux. According to Bass, Inverarity acquired the use of an underwater television camera in 1960. The underwater camera system, emerging technology for underwater archaeology projects, was deployed from a catamaran (pontoon boat) during the September 1960 recovery of the first bateau shipwreck from Lake George. Inverarity had scuba divers train the camera on the sunken bateaux so he could view the sunken vessels *in situ*. Then Inverarity made decisions for the execution of underwater fieldwork based on his observations via camera.[4] The General Engineering Laboratory of General Electric (Schenectady, New York) designed this underwater camera, its waterproof housing, and the subsurface lights. The business corporation provided the high-tech equipment to Inverarity's team.[5]

The *Albany Times-Union* newspaper published the article—"Bateau Raised In Lake George"—in their September 24, 1960, issue. The story reported on the recovery of a bateau shipwreck, raised from about thirty feet of water "after divers rigged slings and air-filled inner tubes under [it]."[6] The retrieval of this historic colonial vessel was reportedly accomplished by a team of three Navy divers from Washington, DC, and three local divers. The Navy frogmen were on special assignment and under the direction of Navy Commander N.E. Nickerson, chief of the Navy's Experimental Diving Unit in Washington, DC. Following the Navy's involvement in the underwater recovery of the first bateau, Nickerson prepared a short report on his team's work during the project. The Navy divers worked at Lake George from September 18 to 23, 1960. Also, reportedly, the federal government did not pay for providing the elite military scuba squad to the bateau fieldwork. Rather, the initial bateau vessel recovery was funded by the Adirondack Museum.[7]

The underwater camera equipment provided by General Electric met with mixed results. U.S. Navy Commander Nickerson summarized the success of the underwater camera system that permitted Inverarity and other non-divers to view the sunken bateaux: "Due to inexperience with the equipment and the generally poor visibility conditions prevailing, good underwater TV results were not obtained. A brief suitable presentation was obtained, however, sufficiently clear, for the topside observers to view the area and see the remains of the boats."[8] Nevertheless, the application of the underwater camera system with subsurface lighting was indeed revolutionary. It was believed at the time to be the very first use of a closed-circuit television camera system at an inland waterway for an underwater archaeology excavation.[9] The *Albany Times-Union* published an article on the underwater television camera deployment. The story described the high-tech device as a "television camera, mounted on a surface-controlled under-water [*sic*] sled bearing batteries of powered lights." The October 28, 1960, story went on to state that Inverarity hoped to employ the camera unit again in the summer of 1961 for "full use along the 32-mile long lake."[10] However, it does not appear, based on the archival record, that Inverarity had the luxury of deploying the underwater camera system after 1960.

Following the successful recovery of that sunken British warship in 1960, Inverarity announced that "it was the first time a Colonial bateau ever had been recovered intact." According to the *Albany Times-Union*, during that endeavor, divers located a total of eleven bateau shipwrecks.[11]

The *Albany Times-Union* article also reported that the scuba team had even discovered a "two centuries" old grappling hook from the mud under one of the bateaux.[12] Nickerson described the colonial iron artifact: "In the early afternoon [September 22, 1960] an anchor of the grapnel type was located and brought to the surface. From its appearance and configuration, it appeared to be of a type used by the British on Lake George in the late 1750's."[13] The unearthing of that artifact hints at how, in 1759, British regular and provincial troops probably located and then attempted to recover some of their submerged warships deliberately sunk the previous year, vessels put into "wet storage" in 1758 for retrieval the following year. There is also the possibility that the recovered grapnel anchor was from French salvage attempts during the French and Indian War.

U.S. Navy Commander N.E. Nickerson's report stated that his dive team was involved in the raising of only one bateau, that taken from the southeastern part of the lake on September 23, 1960. He described the sunken vessel, which was filled with stones and also covered with sediment: "After stones were removed and the silt cleared away it was found that the bottom boards were all still intact with most of the lower rib [aka frame] sections in place and the garboard strakes still intack [*sic*]. The colonial boat was in approximately 30' of water and was brought to the surface with inner tubes lashed in place thruout [*sic*] its length." Nickerson went on to report that the eighteenth-century bateau was "towed without incident" to "a gently sloping sandy beach" where the sunken bateau was "beached at approximately 8:15 p.m."[14]

In the September 24, 1960, issue of the *Glens Falls Times*, Inverarity provided more information, declaring that the recovery of the sunken bateau was a "laborious task" because his divers had to remove rocks from inside the boat, rocks that had been used by the British in 1758 to help sink it.[15] After removing the rocks from the sunken bateau, two ropes were then run under the historic watercraft to help in lifting the warship off the lake bottom so that several slings could be attached from stem to stern. Deflated automobile inner tubes were then attached to the slings and were inflated using an air tank. The eighteenth-century warship quickly came to the surface and was then towed to a sandy beach on the west side of the lake.

The September 24, 1960, issue of the *Plattsburgh Press-Republican* (Plattsburgh, New York) also reported on the bateau recovery. It announced that six divers were involved in the operation, which took three hours to run ropes around the bateau, fasten deflated inner tubes, attach pumps to inflate the inner tubes, and finally slowly raise the historic warship to the surface.[16]

Media accounts from the 1960s do not record how many sunken bateaux were raised by the Adirondack Museum project in 1960. Though documentation about this project is scarce, it is nonetheless now believed that a total of three bateaux were raised in the early 1960s. Probably only one bateau was recovered from the lake in 1960.

During this lengthy preparation by project divers to ready the bateau for the recovery, one shipwreck in this cluster of originally fourteen or fifteen bateaux was severely vandalized by unscrupulous divers who had observed the location of the bateau shipwrecks. Inverarity stated, "This was terribly disappointing to us. The people who did this are nothing but underwater delinquents."[17] An October 29, 1960, Associated Press article covering the vandalism ran the poignant headline, "Aquanaughties Wreck Bateau."[18]

On January 11, 1961, New York State Historian Albert B. Corey presented a talk on the sunken bateaux of Lake George to a group of Cohoes, New York Rotarians. In the presentation, Corey suggested the State of New York "licensing" scuba divers involved in shipwreck diving. "We need a systematic preservation of what are truly historical documents [sunken bateaux]," Corey exclaimed, "and skin [i.e., scuba] divers, no matter how expert they seem to be, just have to learn how to help preserve sunken historical material they may discover."[19] Corey added that hunters, fishermen, and drivers of automobile vehicles are licensed, so why not license scuba divers to train them in what to do when they find historic shipwrecks.[20] Unfortunately, no details were provided on how the State of New York might go about training and licensing interested scuba divers. Such a program would have minimized shipwreck vandalism and optimized how to direct scuba divers to assist in shipwreck preservation and historical and archaeological data recovery.

Figure 7.3 One of the three bateaux recovered from the depths of Lake George in the early 1960s. (Credit: Adirondack Experience)

Souvenir collecting of historic artifacts by scuba enthusiasts has been a problem at Lake George since the 1950s when divers first began reconnoitering the depths of the waterway. Unfortunately, the lake has had a longstanding reputation within the recreational scuba community as a good place to go to recover "goodies"—namely, historic artifacts. Either uninformed of historic preservation laws or simply not caring about destroying our underwater heritage, these unethical scuba divers, relatively few in number compared to the number of sport divers, have plundered historic shipwrecks. Relic-hunting divers have removed artifacts and, sadly, even torn apart submerged vessels in search of plunder. These "thieves of time"[21] remove the opportunity to study an archaeological site to document and interpret its history for both scholars and the general public. Fortunately, most recreational divers are not plunderers, but I have seen firsthand the aftermath of shipwreck vandalism.

In many respects, archaeologists are much like crime scene detectives and forensic scientists. They want the site undisturbed to study it in its original context. Luckily, over the past three decades a better preservation ethic has been exhibited by most scuba enthusiasts diving the waters of Lake George. These law-abiding divers should be praised for being mindful of historic preservation.

It was reported that some of the three sunken bateaux raised in the early 1960s were temporarily buried on a local beach as part of their opening conservation treatment. Then the bateaux were moved and conserved in a lab setting. It is somewhat unclear where the initial chemical conservation was done. According to an article in the July 21, 1961, issue of the *Lake George Mirror*, some of that early preservation work may have done at the Fort William Henry Hotel garage. Likewise, other conservation treatment was reportedly undertaken at the Adirondack Museum. The bateaux were put into spacious tanks, treated with Carbowax, a type of **polyethylene glycol (PEG)**, and following conservation treatment, the eighteenth-century warships were reassembled.[22]

Polyethylene glycol has frequently been employed to conserve wooden objects that have been underwater. PEG replaces the water in wooden artifacts and shipwreck timbers, making the wood more dimensionally stable. It also minimizes shrinkage and warping of the treated timber when the wood dries. Famous historic shipwrecks like the *Vasa*, a Swedish warship that sank in 1628 and was recovered in 1961,[23] and the English warship *Mary Rose*, lost in the English Channel in 1545 and raised in 1982,[24] were both initially conserved using a type of PEG.

The PEG preservation treatment selected by Inverarity's staff at the Adirondack Museum was reported to be a technique devised by personnel with the U.S. Forest Products Laboratory in Madison, Wisconsin. Inverarity spent a lot of time studying

Figure 7.4 One of the early 1960s-raised colonial bateaux being buried on a beach shortly after it was raised from the lake. This berming of the shipwreck in wet sawdust and sand kept the wooden watercraft from drying out as an initial step in the conservation of the vessel. (Credit: Adirondack Experience)

Figure 7.5 Dr. Robert Bruce Inverarity (right), director of the Adirondack Museum, examines the polyethylene glycol (PEG) solution used during the early 1960s for the preservation treatment of three 1758 bateaux recovered from Lake George. (Credit: Adirondack Experience)

this treatment, and folders found in the Adirondack Museum library with his correspondence attest to this. The PEG treatment chosen by Inverarity was designed to help preserve the wooden parts of the bateaux and minimize warping and shrinking of the wood. Tests conducted at the museum on untreated versus PEG-treated bateau pieces produced revealing results. An untreated piece of white pine that had been on the bottom of Lake George for over two centuries shrank 7.5 percent from its waterlogged condition. A test on a bateau piece, also of white pine, that was treated with polyethylene glycol for three weeks had minimal shrinkage—well under 1 percent. Further, the PEG-treated bateau wood had no visible checkerboard-like cracks, called checking, along the surface of the boat timber.[25] However, the last half-century has seen many advances in how to more effectively apply PEG conservation on shipwrecks. Unfortunately, in some earlier applications, this type of conservation treatment has met with mixed results.

Figure 7.6 Following polyethylene glycol (PEG) conservation treatment in the early 1960s, the bateau shipwrecks were assembled at the Adirondack Museum. (Credit: Adirondack Experience)

On April 26 and 27, 1963, Inverarity participated in a first in underwater archaeology. He presented two professional papers in St. Paul, Minnesota, at the Conference on Underwater Archaeology sponsored by the Minnesota Historical Society and the Council of Underwater Archaeology. This gathering of maritime historians and underwater archaeologists was billed as "the first international conference on underwater archaeology."[26] Inverarity's first paper was entitled "The Conservation of Wood from Fresh Water," in which he discussed the conservation treatment of the 1758 sunken bateaux recovered from Lake George.[27] In his second paper, "New York Report," Inverarity informed conference attendees about his archaeological work at Lake George and dealing with scuba divers and state law related to shipwrecks and historic preservation.[28] Among the other speakers at this conference were such luminaries in the emerging field of underwater archaeology as Dr. George F. Bass, Anders Franzen, Howard I. Chapelle, Edwin C. Bearss, and Mendel L. Peterson.[29]

Eventually, one of the 1758 bateaux raised in the early 1960s was exhibited at the Adirondack Museum, today called Adirondack Experience. Jerold (Jerry) Pepper, librarian at the Adirondack Museum, reported that the Lake George bateau was first exhibited at his museum in 1968. According to Pepper, a quarter-century later, in 1993, the colonial bateau was returned to the New York State Museum[30]; Nathan A. Gallagher cites the bateau's display at the Adirondack Museum as being from 1966 to 1993.[31] The three Lake George colonial bateaux (Bateaux 2626, 4560, and 4566) are now housed in a New York State Museum storage facility in the Rotterdam, New York, area. On September 9, 2005, Glens Falls, New York documentary filmmaker Peter Pepe (Pepe Productions) and I had the opportunity to tour the state museum storage facility where we perused the disassembled Lake George 1758 bateaux. On July 23, 2018, I again visited the state museum storage building to work with museum personnel to photograph several pieces of the Lake George bateaux recovered from the waterway in the early 1960s.

In some cases, the 1960s conservation process appears to have oversaturated some of the hull timbers. These wooden boat pieces have slightly "sweated" their PEG treatment as the chemical is migrating out of the wood cells. In so doing, it appears as if the vessel timbers have a distinct layer of wax-like coating. However, other boat pieces, likewise treated with PEG in the 1960s, seem to have held up fairly well from the conservation. Nevertheless, Gallagher has expressed some concern with the 1960s PEG conservation of the Lake George bateaux. He points out that since PEG is corrosive to iron, the wrought iron fasteners that are still in place in the bateaux are corroding because they were not conserved separately. Further, since PEG can reabsorb moisture, the storage of the three bateaux and other miscellaneous bateau hull structure pieces in the collection are vulnerable to deterioration because the museum's storage facility is not entirely climate controlled.[32] Nevertheless, museum personnel do monitor interior climate conditions, and these cultural scientists do everything they can to optimize the preservation of this rare colonial boat collection.

Certainly, the early 1960s saw tremendous interest in colonial bateau watercraft in the region. Beginning in the summer of 1961, Fort Ticonderoga Museum displayed a replica colonial bateau that they built for viewing by tourists who visited their facility. A photograph of this replica bateau was pictured in the July 7, 1961, issue of the *Lake George Mirror*. The replica showed a small wooden bateau much shorter in length than those found on the bottomlands of Lake George. The Fort Ticonderoga replica probably was more like the size of bateaux observed by Swedish traveler Peter Kalm during his visit to the region in the mid-eighteenth century.[33]

According to Nick Westbrook, the Director of the Fort Ticonderoga Museum in the 1990s, their replica bateau was 16 feet long, 4 feet wide, and 3 feet, 2-1/2 inches high. The watercraft was built after consulting with small boat authority John Gardner and other small boat experts. Westbrook wrote in 1993: "The [replica] bateau was displayed here [Fort Ticonderoga] . . . for a number of years, and then rejoined its relic mates at the Adirondack Museum." Westbrook added that in the early 1990s when the Adirondack Museum renovated an exhibit at their Blue Mountain Lake, New York facility, the replica half-scale bateau model was returned to the Fort Ticonderoga Museum.[34]

During 1960 and 1961, Inverarity relied on several sport divers from the area that he frequently corresponded with to provide him with information about the condition of Lake George's sunken bateaux. Among this cadre of scuba divers were Gene Parker, Stan Zeccolo, Charles Jefts, and several others.

In July 1961, Inverarity held a meeting at the Old Warren County Courthouse in the Town of Lake George at which he addressed a group of about forty interested scuba divers and others. Lake historian Harrison K. Bird Jr. from Huletts Landing, New York, and State Historian Dr. Albert B. Corey were also in attendance. Inverarity reported that the State of New York had no funding to hire scuba divers to work on the sunken bateaux. Any funds that might be acquired would have to go into the expensive "preservation process" of any recovered sunken bateaux. Moreover, Inverarity told those in attendance that this was not a single summer project, but that it could take ten years to complete. However, he thought that scuba manufacturers might be enticed to donate dive equipment and that any scuba divers involved in this important project would be awarded a certificate of merit from the Adirondack Museum for their volunteer diving.[35]

The scuba divers in attendance at the July 1961 meeting were from the Schenectady and Albany area, Long Island, Connecticut, New Jersey, and even Florida. The divers formed a short-lived organization called the Underwater Archaeological Research Association. In an article in the *Schenectady Gazette* dated several months later (February 7, 1962), the dive association desired to work with the state government in accordance with historic preservation law. These scuba enthusiasts were not only intrigued by Lake George's historical significance and diving in the waterway but were likewise interested in the underwater heritage resources found near Fort Ticonderoga at Lake Champlain. In 1962, the club president was Stan Zeccolo, one of the regional divers who in the late summer of 1960 located a colonial bateau shipwreck on the west side of the waterway near the mouth of English Brook.[36] Unfortunately, this well-intentioned organization's activities soon disappeared from the literature record.

During the early 1960s, Lake George's sunken bateaux of 1758 were often targeted by antiquity-stalking scuba divers. In one case, in the autumn of 1961, two divers from the Mechanicville, New York, area presented Boy Scouts with a wooden rib (frame) from one of the lake's sunken warships. The bateau piece was to be for "permanent display in the troop meeting room."[37] Though this donation was seemingly well intended, the bateau frame, yanked from a shipwreck site without state permission, actually contributed to the demise of the integrity of the underwater cultural site. This furthermore damaged the bateau frame since it would not undergo professional conservation.

In 1962, the *Lake George Mirror* was one of the regional newspapers supporting the pro-historic preservation ethic starting to emanate around the "Queen of American Lakes." In a short June 29, 1962, article entitled "Scuba Diving in Lake George," the local newspaper reminded scuba enthusiasts that "all finds of relics and artifacts in the lake must be reported to the office of Warren County Sheriff in the Village of Lake George."[38]

The following year, 1963, saw the beginning of a new and dynamic phase of the Adirondack Museum's "Operation Bateaux." Over the summers of 1963 and 1964, and as before in the early 1960s, the endeavor was executed under an archaeology permit issued by the State of New York's Education Department. Unlike the previous years of the early 1960s, this time a dedicated scuba diver, Terry Crandall, was contracted by the Adirondack Museum to conduct most of the underwater archaeological fieldwork. Terry Crandall later wrote of the reason for his hiring:

> In the spring of 1963 Dr. Inverarity chose a different course rather than dealing with a host of divers who had become quite competitive and jealously guarded their individual "finds" and location.[39]

It appears that one of the reasons for this 1963–1964 phase of Operation Bateaux was to get a clearer understanding of the vessel "lines," that is, hull form, of a typical 1758 bateau. On October 3, 1960, Inverarity wrote a letter to Colonel Edward P. Hamilton, Director of Fort Ticonderoga Museum, in which he addressed this issue: "We [Adirondack Museum] do not have enough ribs [frames] on the bateau we raised to get the lines. However, I still have hopes because there are more that I intend to get. I have learned a good many important things from the material we have already brought up and I think in time we will be able to produce the [bateau] lines."[40]

The successful two-summer endeavor (1963–1964) by Terry Crandall consisted of a bateau shipwreck inventory, a sampling of various pieces of sunken bateaux, and some excavation of bateaux to examine vessel structure and recover artifacts from the uncovered bateaux. Terry Crandall was an excellent choice for this new chapter of "Operation Bateaux." Besides being a sixth-grade public school teacher with additional administrative duties in a school system in the Mohawk Valley, Crandall was affiliated with a dive business called Otsego Divers based in Richfield Springs, New York. He was also a veteran of the U.S. Army with a background in military intelligence gathering. As a school instructor and administrator, he had his summers free and was a superb scuba diver. Terry Crandall later admitted that he was recommended for the job by Jere Hallenbeck, the operator of National Aquatic Services dive store in Syracuse, New York. Crandall went on to become a K–12 public school principal and a scuba instructor. Inverarity again directed the archaeology and diving project during the 1963 and 1964 years of "Operation Bateaux."[41] Though the term "Operation

Figure 7.7 Scuba diver Terry Crandall was the selection of Dr. Robert Bruce Inverarity to conduct the Adirondack Museum's 1963–1964 underwater archaeology fieldwork on the sunken bateaux of 1758. (Credit: Terry Crandall)

Bateaux" was used from 1960 to 1965, the appellation really became popular during the 1963 and 1964 fieldwork.

Just a couple of months before "Operation Bateaux" started up again for the 1963 field season, Inverarity became quite concerned about increased vandalism of the sunken bateaux by souvenir-seeking scuba divers. An April 29, 1963, *Sarasota Herald-Tribune* (Sarasota, Florida) article, "Scolded for Water Raids," quoted Inverarity as saying he was "sick to death of skindivers" (i.e., scuba divers) who disturbed shipwreck sites. What's more, Inverarity declared disappointment with two other factions, stating, "It's like fighting off the enemy, and we are also fighting off amateur historians and archaeologists who think they are experts."[42] Inverarity made these remarks at the 1963 underwater archaeology conference in St. Paul, Minnesota, a symposium that attracted professional archaeologists, historians, and museum curators. The Minnesota Historical Society and the Council of Underwater Archaeology co-sponsored the conference.[43] As previously mentioned, this academic conclave has the distinction of being one of the first national conferences on underwater archaeology, and it formalized the group, the Council of Underwater Archaeology, today known as the Advisory Council on Underwater Archaeology (ACUA).[44]

Inverarity's growing discouragement that some in the scuba-diving community were destroying the lake's sunken heritage was a reflection of the growth of historic preservation in the United States that really became prominent in the early 1960s. Historians and other cultural scientists had come to the conclusion that the post-World War II effort to modernize the country's buildings was at the same time destroying many of America's old and historic structures. So, suddenly in the 1960s, a ground swell realization occurred that the nation's historic infrastructure needed to be protected from this zeal of modernity. In the early 1960s, this emerging historic preservation ethic had not yet reached many in the scuba community. Further, a common belief among divers at the time was that archaeology was simply collecting artifacts, a longstanding antiquarian perspective that conflicted with the new standards of underwater archaeology being pioneered by Dr. George Bass in the eastern Mediterranean Sea. It would take years before a preservation ethic would take firm root in Lake George, but the Adirondack Museum's early 1960s fieldwork was undoubtedly a beginning to cultivating this mentality.

During 1963 and 1964, Terry Crandall used his scuba proficiency, teaching adroitness, and military training, combined with Inverarity's administrative and anthropological skills, to do admirable archaeology for the times. Crandall's experience derived from "Operation Bateaux" later helped him get elected president of the New York State Divers Association, a post he held from 1965 to 1967.[45]

Arguably, one of the earliest artifact recovery projects in American waters that began to employ some facets of underwater archaeology was the 1951 underwater excavation of the HMS *Looe* (1741–1744), directed by Mendel L. Peterson. At the time, Peterson was the Curator of the Division of Naval History, U.S. National Museum (aka Smithsonian Institution) in Washington, DC.[46] That project was also Edwin A. Link's introduction into the underwater world.[47] Link had earlier in his notable career established his professional reputation building aviation flight simulators known as "Link trainers," which helped teach potential pilots the basics of flying an aircraft. The compact flight simulator, nicknamed "Blue Box," was constructed at Link's production facility in Binghamton, New York. His business made him a considerable fortune and by the early 1950s he went into semi-retirement. After the early 1950s *Looe* project, Link and his wife Marion turned their undivided attention to the sea. They would go on to become accomplished amateur marine archaeologists. Ed Link would also broaden his interest in the underwater world to later become the leading innovator in submersible and sea lab design and fabrication.[48]

By the early 1960s, Bass was beginning to define and hone the principles and techniques of underwater archeology. He eventually turned the discipline into a bona fide science[49] taught in universities around the world, including Texas A&M, East Carolina, West Florida, Indiana, Southern Denmark, Flinders (Australia), Bristol (UK), Ulster (Northern Ireland), Haifa (Israel), and elsewhere. Additionally, a popular non-university instructional program that teaches underwater archaeology to sport divers in several countries around the world is the Nautical Archaeology Society. However, in the early 1960s, the field of underwater or maritime archaeology was still in its infancy, and Lake George was absolutely at the forefront for this maturing scientific discipline.

Figure 7.8 The Perry-Link *Deep Diver* research submarine, launched in 1966, is now exhibited in Fort Pierce, Florida. This pioneering undersea vehicle with lockout diver capability was designed by Edwin A. Link and John Perry. Link was an aviation simulation innovator who later turned his attention to marine archaeology and developing underwater craft for oceanic exploration and naval deep-sea rescue. Several years before "Operation Bateaux" at Lake George, Link participated in arguably the first underwater archaeological investigation of a shipwreck, the HMS *Looe*, lost off Florida in 1744. (Credit: M.P. Meaney)

Often making solo scuba dives without a dive buddy, generally for reasons of site security, Terry Crandall mostly "conducted raw search missions along the eastern shore" of the lake. Crandall described the essence of his 1963–1964 work:

> I like to think of the bateau as sort of the colonial counterpart of a combination of pick-up truck, family van and interstate hauler since it was the prime mover of personnel and supplies over distances both short and long in the absence of decent roads. Thus, the Adirondack Museum was a pioneer in illuminating the important contribution of this vessel in establishing our nation ... My [1963–1964] contribution was but a continuation of the original [1960] find to log new and additional bateaux sites for future consideration.[50]

Crandall said he was instructed by Inverarity to locate and examine sites in which there were known sunken bateaux or rumors of possible bateaux. Inverarity had a list of possible bateau and other colonial shipwreck sites. Harold Veeder, one of the co-founders of the Fort William Henry Corporation that oversaw the administration of Fort William Henry Museum, gave Inverarity a list of suspected bateau shipwreck sites. Inverarity used this checklist and other intelligence he gathered from a variety of sources to direct Crandall to several locations to search for colonial bateau shipwrecks. Overwhelmingly, most of Terry Crandall's reconnaissance dives were conducted in the lake's South Basin. Sometimes Crandall brought along one or more dive buddies whom he trusted to assist him with this scuba reconnaissance.

On some occasions, Crandall took what he called "a slow pontoon ride" north to check areas looking for colonial bateaux. One such location was off Dome Island near Bolton Landing, and Crandall reported he located no bateau shipwrecks near there. Another locale of interest was farther north into the waterway's Narrows, a mid-lake spot where the waterway's opposite shorelines compressed. There, Crandall reported he spotted one rather large "frame member" that

Figure 7.9 In the early 1960s, Harold Veeder, head of the Fort William Henry Corporation, provided Dr. Robert Bruce Inverarity (Adirondack Museum) with a list of locations around Lake George where there might be sunken colonial bateaux. (Credit: Fort William Henry Museum)

Figure 7.10 Archaeological diver Terry Crandall with his underwater camera at a colonial bateau shipwreck during 1963-1964 fieldwork for the Adirondack Museum. (Credit: Terry Crandall)

was "over six feet long" lying underwater on some rocks. He recovered that for the Adirondack Museum.[51]

Crandall employed a methodical search pattern during his reconnaissance scuba forays. Diving solo or with a team of reliable scuba divers, including Lee Couchman, Gene Parker, Tony George, Jack Sullivan, and others, Crandall found "a number of new bateaux sites" in Lake George.[52] Crandall kept daily notes during this fieldwork, which he forwarded regularly to the Adirondack Museum for Inverarity to review and use to provide feedback and directions on future fieldwork. According to a summary of Crandall's 1963-1964 diving for the Adirondack Museum, he investigated twenty-four sites, some which had bateaux, others that did not, and some that had non-bateau shipwrecks.[53] Crandall likewise annotated a map that showed thirty-one or thirty-two sunken bateaux in the South Basin of the lake.[54] However, that lake chart was not inclusive of all the sunken bateaux in this section of the waterway. Missing were several bateaux from the largest assemblage, the site of the original 1960 rediscovery, and other sunken bateaux as well. Crandall was once sent to investigate a locale in the lake where a reputed submerged cannon was rumored to be associated with a bateau shipwreck. Crandall described his subsequent reconnaissance dive this way: "False Report. Cylindrical log mistaken for cannon—1963."[55]

In the 2010 documentary "Wooden Bones: The Sunken Fleet of 1758" (Pepe Productions, 58 minutes), Crandall discussed evidence he discovered at bateau shipwrecks over 1963 and 1964 and how the British may have marked the bateaux they sank in 1758 for recovery the following year:

> What I did find on a couple of occasions were other objects that belied the fact that the British did indeed intend to refloat the vessels that were sunken ... I found a section of a log which had been pointed to some degree and then a hole drilled though it and it was sunk right along with the bateaux site itself as if it were a float where the rope had wasted away but then it too became waterlogged and sunk to the bottom ... more than one of these would have marked the particular spot where a cluster of bateaux were resting on the bottom.[56]

Crandall's fieldwork in 1963 and 1964 is especially noteworthy because, though he was not a trained archaeologist, he nevertheless employed some of the fundamentals of underwater archaeology to his bateau fieldwork tasks. Much of his knowledge about using archaeological principles came from the detailed instructions provided him by the project director, Inverarity. For more on the 1963–1964 "Operation Bateaux" fieldwork, see appendices I and II.

Anticipating he would continue working on "Operation Bateaux," in mid-April, Crandall attended the 1965 Council of Underwater Archaeology (CUA) conference in Toronto.[57] The CUA, formed in 1959, had been institutionalized by the organization's 1963 conference held in Minnesota,[58] which was attended by Inverarity.

Unfortunately, some of the data collected by Crandall for the Adirondack Museum are not easily available to researchers. After visiting the Adirondack Museum, a quarter-century after "Operation Bateaux," Crandall said he was surprised to discover that some of his daily notes and other field documentation appeared to be absent from the collection. Apparently, sometime after Operation Bateaux (1960–1965), Crandall's field notes and photographs and some of Inverarity's records were divided. Part of the collection might have been sent to the New York State Museum, while some of it remained at the Adirondack.[59] Further, Inverarity abruptly left the Adirondack Museum in 1965, which might have contributed to the dispersal of the collection. Inverarity might even have kept some personal documents associated with "Operation Bateaux."

For twenty-eight years, from 1988 to 2016, I had the pleasure and good fortune to interview Terry Crandall on numerous occasions during projects on Lake George and at his residence in the Mohawk Valley. Sadly, in July 2016, my good friend passed away. Thankfully, his 1963 and 1964 fieldwork activities for Adirondack Museum were featured in the 2010 Pepe Productions and Bateaux Below DVD documentary "Wooden Bones: The Sunken Fleet of 1758."

Following the end of the 1964 underwater archaeology fieldwork by the Adirondack Museum, the next diving on the sunken bateaux occurred in the summer of 1965 in a dual operation. A representative of the New York State Police contacted Inverarity requesting a joint project to conduct (1) a training session for state police divers and (2) fieldwork to raise one or more sunken bateaux. Inverarity agreed and secured the use of a pontoon boat for the dive team. He also provided instructions on how to undertake the bateau recovery using a lifting frame, an improvement over the use of inner tubes and a rope cradle as employed in the early 1960s. The endeavor also received major media exposure in a *New York Times* article entitled "Lake George Divers Find 1758 Battle Craft." The June 27, 1965, story reported on a New York State Police "summer-training program" that planned to recover "the remains of at least eight bateaux, scuttled at the end of the summer of 1758." In retrospect, a recovery of this number of bateaux sounds rather ambitious. The state police reportedly volunteered for the project, and their personnel included "15 veteran, qualified scuba divers and 17 trooper candidates." One of the two photographs in the *New York Times* shows scuba divers handing bateau pieces to personnel aboard a pontoon boat marked with a nameboard indicating it was an official New York State Police vessel.[60] Word has it that Inverarity became upset when he was not invited to be present during the Lake George fieldwork.[61] Years later, in 1988, Crandall interviewed a diver on the 1965 project. The *New York Times* reported in their news story that the State Police planned to recover many sunken bateaux. It appears, however, that pieces of only one bateau shipwreck were retrieved from the lake bottom.[62]

Effective September 1, 1965, Inverarity resigned his administrative position at the Adirondack Museum. At the time, Harold K. Hochschild was the president of the Adirondack Historical Association, the not-for-profit corporation that oversaw the operation of the Adirondack Museum.[63] Holman J. Swinney, who had been director of the Idaho Historical Society, replaced Inverarity. The Adirondack Museum's underwater study of Lake George's sunken bateaux of 1758 effectively ended with Inverarity's departure near the end of the summer of 1965. The lack of any follow-up on "Operation Bateaux" may have been because Swinney's research specialties were in other fields, regional and architectural history of central New York[64] and the history of gun making in the colony and later the state of New York.[65]

By 1967, a rift remained between many sport divers and dive clubs and the state officials tasked with managing and preserving shipwrecks in Empire State waterways. On November 9, 1967, *The Knickerbocker News* carried a story entitled "Historians, Divers Collide on Treasures." The thrust of the debate was that most historians were concerned that recreational divers were looting historical treasures from state waters, whereas divers were feeling they were being prevented from keeping artifacts they found.[66] Additionally, **cultural resources managers** were worried that the loss of these relics meant not knowing their history.

A Plattsburgh, New York diver called for state government support in the form of diving equipment, help, and money that would encourage dive clubs around the Empire State to collaborate with historians for the successful recovery of submerged artifacts. Other scuba divers wanted specialized training from scholars to inform them of the problems with amateur recovery of sunken historical objects.

During this time in the 1960s, Robert Flacke, President of the Fort William Henry Corporation, thought that the depths of Lake George should be completely surveyed to determine which areas should be for historical use, presumably meaning for archaeological study by professional archaeologists and historians.[67]

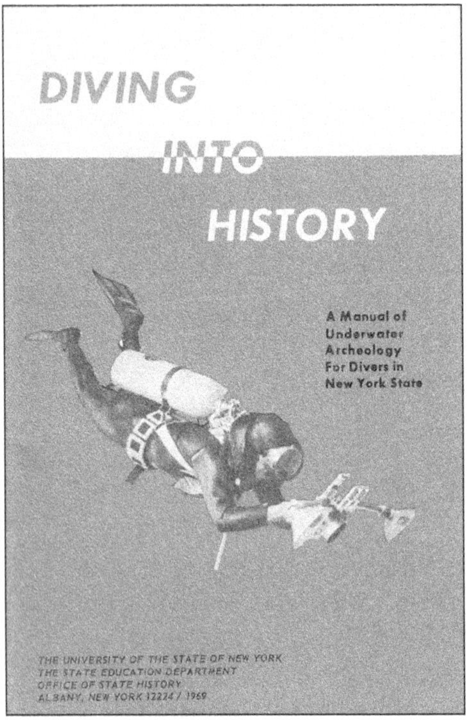

Following "Operation Bateaux," over two decades would pass before a serious renaissance of archaeological curiosity in Lake George's "Ghost Fleet" occurred. Ahead of this regeneration, three major publications mentioned Lake George's sunken bateaux, promoting shipwreck preservation. In 1969, the Office of State History in the New York State Education published a thirty-three-page booklet entitled *Diving into History: A Manual of Underwater Archaeology for Divers in New York State*. Several pages were devoted to Lake George's sunken bateaux.

The state publication described the colonial bateaux and the 1960 rediscovery of some of the vessels from Lake George. Likewise, the booklet addressed the Lake George bateaux: "The well preserved bateaux, under an agreement with the State of New York, were placed in the Adirondack Museum, where they now stand as a tribute

Figure 7.11 The cover of a 1969-published State of New York booklet designed not only as a primer on underwater archaeology for sport divers but also to promote historic preservation of shipwrecks in the Empire State. (Courtesy New York State Museum)

to the amateur divers who first found them, and the professional archaeologist and responsible divers who retrieved and preserved them."[68] It should be mentioned, however, that only one bateau was exhibited at the Adirondack Museum, not multiple bateaux, as described. Nonetheless, the publication was an ambitious attempt to encourage scuba divers to conform to the precepts of underwater archaeology and historic preservation.

The same year the *Diving into History* booklet was published by the State of New York, in July 1969, *Skin Diver* magazine, the most popular scuba periodical in the United States, published an article on scuba diving in Lake George. The story, entitled "Lake George" and written by Lud Wolf, included underwater photographs provided by two accomplished scuba divers, Gene Parker and Bernie Campoli. The article's writer reported on the "fourteen longboats" (aka bateaux) found in the lake in 1960. However, at the end of the article the author mentioned "two souvenirs" he recovered from Lake George: "an old navy anchor and what appeared to be the gear housing of a large boat."[69] Apparently, Wolf's motivation was not entirely historic preservation.

Another publication with a reference to Lake George's bateaux, released four years after the *Diving into History* booklet, was *Erving's World Wide Skindiver's Guide* (1973 edition). The publication actually gave the location of the Wiawaka bateaux. However, the book's author incorrectly called them "6 Indian bateau." The guide then correctly described them as being located on a "sloping bottom" in twenty-five feet of water off the Wiawaka property. To the publisher's credit, the book did an admirable job promoting scuba diving at Lake George, and the editorial staff did call for visiting divers to practice shipwreck preservation. Further, the author of the section on Lake George asked scuba enthusiasts who visited the Wiawaka bateau shipwrecks to "Don't disturb, just look."[70]

In the late 1970s and early 1980s, correspondence occurred between the New York State Education Department and the proprietors of a dive shop near Albany, New York, regarding Lake George's submerged cultural resources, including its sunken colonial bateaux.[71] However, no professional study of the lake's sunken bateaux, guided by an archaeologist, appears to have occurred as a result of this dialogue.

In 1986, the Basin Harbor Maritime Museum, today known as the Lake Champlain Maritime Museum, located in Vergennes, Vermont, constructed a full-scale replica colonial bateau. The design for the replica vessel was generated from a mid-1980s nautical survey of the Lake George colonial bateau shipwreck on exhibit at the Adirondack Museum. Staff at the Basin Harbor Maritime Museum then built a replica colonial bateau that they named *Perseverance*, based on one of the bateaux raised from Lake George in the early 1960s. The boat-building endeavor was supported by a grant from the Vermont Council on the Humanities—and by plenty of volunteer labor as well. The replica was an excellent example of a public outreach campaign to inform people about eighteenth-century bateaux.

On August 22, 1992, the New York State Museum launched a replica bateau built by museum personnel and others. The museum's construction program, "The Batteau Project," was allied with the Schenectady Urban Cultural Park's 1992 exhibit on colonial bateaux and Durham boats.[72]

Arthur Cohn, the Basin Harbor Maritime Museum director, recognized the importance of this type of **replica archaeology** and eloquently described one of the reasons for his museum's 1985–1986 replica bateau project: "This is the grandfather of troop transports. It was the first design brought to North America by the European settlers. The Indians used dugout and birch bark canoes."[73]

Chapter Eight

A Renaissance of Interest

Finally, over two decades after the Adirondack Museum's "Operation Bateaux" ended in 1965, in September 1987 a renewed interest began in the underwater archaeological field studies of Lake George's sunken bateaux. As I mentioned in the preface, on September 11 to 13, 1987, a group of about twenty scuba divers participated in a workshop at Lake George receiving instruction in the principles and techniques of underwater archaeology.

The goal of the workshop was to train recreational divers to become "archaeological divers" to work as technicians to assist professional archaeologists in shipwreck archaeology projects. The workshop was nearly two years in planning and was the collective effort of Dr. Russell P. Bellico, a Westfield State University (Westfield, Massachusetts) professor and a summer resident at Lake George; Vince Capone, a New Jersey remote sensing specialist; Jack Sullivan, a Saratoga County, New York scuba instructor; and myself. R. Duncan Mathewson III, a marine archaeologist from the Florida Keys, was contracted as the principal instructor for the workshop. Capone taught a primer in the use of a remotely-operated-vehicle (ROV) for shipwreck studies. The ROV workshop was conducted during pool work training on the second day of the workshop as well as deployed during the third day of the instructional program, a preliminary mapping exercise of several sunken bateaux in the lake. Phil Lord, a well-respected archaeologist with the New York State Education Department, was invited and attended the last day of the workshop to view the practicum fieldwork. The three-day seminar resulted in the founding of the Atlantic Alliance Lake George Bateaux Research Team, soon afterward renamed the Lake George Bateaux Research Team. I had the privilege of directing the organization.

Soon after the association was founded in mid-September 1987, we began a nonintrusive mapping of seven 1758 British and provincial shipwrecks commonly referred to as the Wiawaka bateaux. The shipwrecks were named after the nearby Wiawaka Holiday House, a not-for-profit summer vacation complex for women. Three years later, over the winter of 1990–1991, several principals of the

Figure 8.1 September 12, 1987: Day two of a three-day underwater archaeology workshop. Author (right) and several others prepare a PVC archaeology grid for a training session at a p in Queensbury, New York. (Credit: M.P. Meaney)

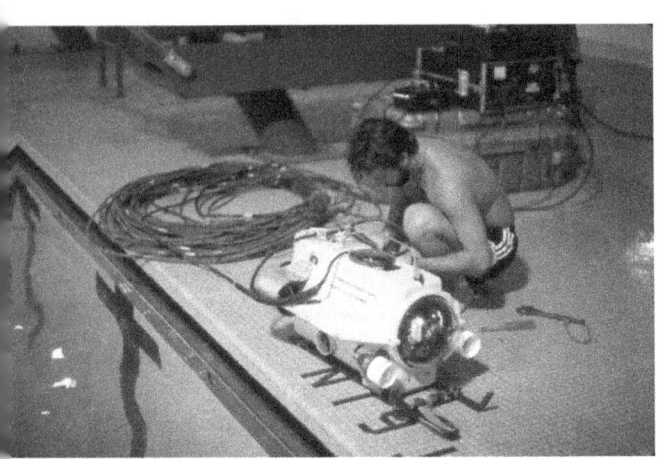

Figure 8.2 Vince Capone readies a remotely-operated-vehicle (ROV) for a training seminar on underwater archaeology held on September 12, 1987. (Credit: M.P. Meaney)

Figure 8.3 Vince Capone at a monitor screen piloting a remotely-operated-vehicle (ROV) during the September 13, 1987 underwater archaeology practicum at the Wiawaka sunken bateaux site at Lake George. (Credit: Joseph W. Zarzynski)

Lake George Bateaux Research Team formed the group—Bateaux Below—and it became a not-for-profit corporation whose primary mission was to archaeologically survey these colonial shipwrecks and to work to preserve and protect the sunken fleet of 1758.

Within a few months of our initial fieldwork at the Wiawaka bateaux following the September 1987 training program, we began to investigate other known bateaux sunk in the lake. Our fieldwork was often hampered by less than ideal underwater visibility due to storm water runoff, sediment disturbance from scuba divers, and other factors. All of this made underwater photography and the simple task of stretching a tape measure over bateau hull structure rather problematic at times.

By September 1987, twenty-seven years after the Wiawaka bateaux were located by recreational divers in 1960, these colonial warships had some of their sinking rocks, that once rested on top of their bottom boards, shifted around. Souvenir-seeking scuba divers moved the rocks off the shipwrecks to search for artifacts. Furthermore, frames that once were articulated to the bottom boards and strakes of the vessels' hull forms were now mostly dislodged. Though the Wiawaka bateaux had lost some of their contextual value, there was still much that could be learned about these significant eighteenth-century warships.

The New York State Museum (State Education Department) determined in 1987 that we did not require a formal archaeological study permit since our fieldwork was a minimally invasive study and not a formal archaeological excavation.[1] Nonetheless, I sent periodic reports about our fieldwork's progress to Lord's office at the state museum in Albany.

On October 22–23, 1988, thirteen months into our lake study, we conducted our first side-scan sonar survey in the waterway. I was fortunate enough to acquire the loan of a Klein side-scan sonar, donated by Klein Associates, a New Hampshire-based remote sensing manufacturing company.[2] Capone, a member of the Lake George Bateaux Research Team and employed as a remote sensing specialist with New Jersey-based Kaselaan & D'Angelo Associates, was our research team's sonar technician and ROV operator. David Van Aken, who worked for a local scuba business, was able to secure the loan of a pontoon boat for the 1988 side-scan sonar operation. Without the help of those businesses and individuals, our initial remote sensing project would probably not have occurred.

Side-scan sonar is a truly remarkable piece of remote sensing equipment sometimes employed by underwater archaeologists to look for shipwrecks and other large submerged heritage resources. Generally, this gear consisted of a towfish, a towing cable, and a recording unit. Nowadays, side-scan sonar is

Figure 8.4 Four archaeological divers with the Lake George Bateaux Research Team (later known as Bateaux Below) plan a scuba dive in 1988, at the same site where the 1758 sunken bateaux were rediscovered in 1960.
(Credit: Bateaux Below Collection)

Figure 8.5 This photograph is of a Klein 595 side-scan sonar with its recorder (right), cable (center), and towfish (bottom front). Klein Associates, Inc. was founded in January 1968. This Klein model (circa late 1980s) was being taken to sea off New England for testing and a training exercise. A Klein 595 side-scan sonar was employed during shipwreck inventory fieldwork at Lake George in 1990.
(Credit: Garry Kozak)

Figure 8.6 A state-of-the-art autonomous underwater vehicle (AUV), integrated with side-scan sonar and other equipment, being deployed from a research ship during an oceanic survey.
(Credit: Garry Kozak)

sometimes deployed using an **autonomous underwater vehicle (AUV)** rather than the sonar towfish and cable being towed from a **craft-of-opportunity**. The traditional side-scan sonar's towfish has two transducers, one mounted on each side of the towfish, where pulses of acoustic energy are transmitted in fan-shaped beams moving out along the seabed, lake bottom, or riverbed. At Lake George, side-scan sonar imaged the lake bottom creating sonograph records that somewhat resembled black-and-white aerial photographs. A quality side-scan sonar unit could acoustically map a swath about the length of a football field as the towfish was pulled through the water column behind a motorboat. Making numerous passes similar to mowing a lawn, a side-scan sonar could survey a sizeable area of the lake bottom in just a few hours.[3]

The type of side-scan sonar equipment we always employed at Lake George was a Klein unit. Martin Klein, founder of Klein Associates, Inc., started his business a half-century ago in January 1968.[4] At that time, and arguably still today, Klein side-scan sonar is considered to be the Rolls Royce of side-scan sonar technology. Our 1988 side-scan sonar survey of sections of the south end of the waterway mapped the Wiawaka bateaux site, and we also located several non-eighteenth century shipwrecks in that vicinity. However, our 1988 remote sensing survey found no previously unknown colonial bateaux.[5] Nonetheless, our 1988 side-scan sonar operation marked the inaugural application of this high-tech equipment at Lake George for underwater archaeology projects.

The Wiawaka bateaux site was not part of the original assemblage of sunken bateaux rediscovered near the southeast part of the lake in July 1960. Rather, the Wiawaka bateaux were found later in the early 1960s. As described earlier, Terry Crandall and the Adirondack Museum spent time over 1963 and 1964 investigating the Wiawaka shipwrecks during the institution's "Operation Bateaux."

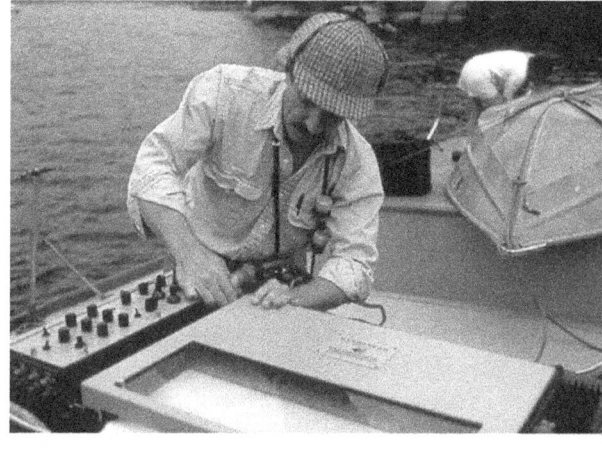

Figure 8.7 Martin Klein, the founder of Klein Associates, Inc., in Salem, New Hampshire, prepares the side-scan sonar recorder of one of his company's units for a 1988 remote sensing project at Lake Champlain, a waterway located just north of Lake George. Klein side-scan sonar was employed numerous times at Lake George during Bateaux Below shipwreck projects. (Credit: M.P. Meaney)

Figure 8.8 The shallow end of Bateau C at the Wiawaka bateaux site. A tape measure, for collecting hull measurements, runs down the centerline of the sunken watercraft. (Credit: Dr. Russell P. Bellico)

Our 1987–1991 fieldwork at the Wiawaka bateaux site was more intensive than that of the Adirondack Museum. We determined that the Wiawaka bateaux rested on an underwater slope in twenty to forty feet of water. Using the traditional equipment of underwater archaeologists—tape measures, slates, pencils, compasses, and underwater photography and videography—we mapped the Wiawaka bateaux.[6] Each of the seven Wiawaka bateaux was measured, photographed, videotaped, and drawn in a plan view (bird's-eye perspective). Unlike the Operation Bateaux project, we did not undertake any excavation. Nor were any artifacts or bateau pieces recovered.

Other remote sensing surveying was also conducted at the Wiawaka bateaux. Following the initial side-scan sonar fieldwork on October 22 and 23, 1988, on June 26, 1990, the sunken Wiawaka bateaux were again sonar documented using a Klein 595 side-scan sonar unit. Further, a remotely-operated-vehicle (ROV), a Benthos Mini-Rover Mk II on loan from Kaselaan & D'Angelo Associates in New Jersey, was deployed in the lake on August 18, 1990; our team first used the ROV at the Wiawaka bateaux on September 13, 1987. The 1990 ROV survey work, operated by Capone, acquired robotic videography of several of the Wiawaka bateaux.[7]

The seven sunken bateaux we studied lying off the Wiawaka Holiday House were designated, from south to north respectively, as Bateaux A, B, C, D, E, F, and G. Bateau A was the southern-most sunken warship in this shipwreck cluster, and Bateau G was the northern-most. The sunken bateaux rest on their flat pine planks

Figure 8.9 During Bateaux Below's archaeological mapping of the Wiawaka bateaux site, this photo was taken of Bateau C. Note the sunken vessel's bottom boards, some battens (cleats) lying across the sunken boat, and, in the foreground, some disarticulated frames. (Credit: Dr. Russell P. Bellico)

(bottom boards) upon a slight lake bottom slope. They are each partially covered with a layer of brown silt. Excluding Bateau D, which lies somewhat parallel to the nearby shoreline, six of the seven bateaux are pointed toward shore, most likely done that way when deliberately sunk in 1758 for ease of recovery the following year by British and provincial troops. From 1987 to 1991, the years mapping the Wiawaka bateaux site, some of the colonial shipwrecks still had several of their oak frames attached to the bottom boards with some of these articulated frames protruding from the lake bottom silt. Two disarticulated bateau stems were found, both buried at the site to protect them from theft. Unfortunately, we located no bateau sternposts. When we began our fieldwork in September 1987, the seven bateaux showed fairly good structural integrity of their lower hulls. Thirty percent or more of the vessels were still present—mainly bottom boards, battens, some frames, and fragments of the garboard strakes.

When the 1628 *Vasa* warship was raised from the harbor in Stockholm, Sweden, in 1961, it was recovered nearly intact. It had not collapsed and fallen apart on the sea floor even though many of its iron bolts and nails had wasted and rusted away. The hull was being held together by the thousands of treenails (trunnels), "approximately forty per square metre," that had been used to build the Swedish royal warship.[8] The Lake George bateaux were all fastened with iron nails that rust and degrade over time. It is thus rather remarkable that the lower hull structure of some of these sunken bateaux retained structural integrity.

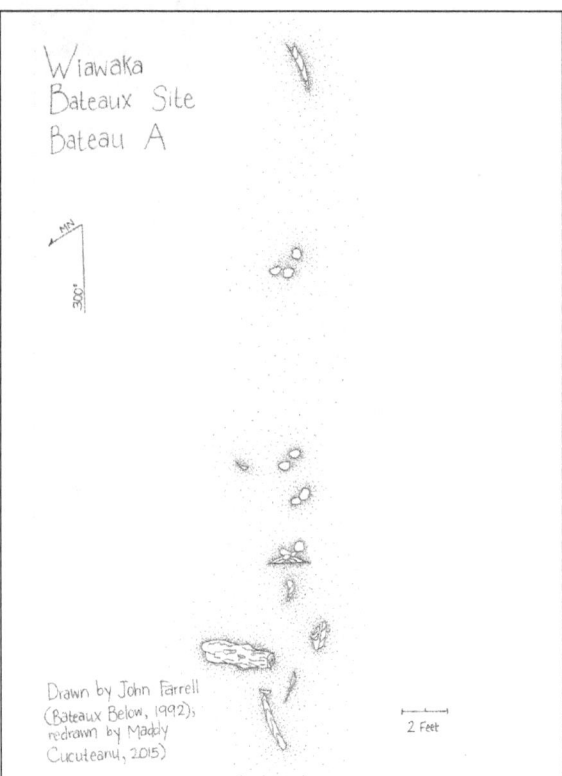

Figure 8.10 Drawing of Wiawaka Bateau A, part of the results of Bateaux Below's noninvasive archaeological mapping of this assemblage of 1758 British bateau shipwrecks. Much of this bateau is buried. (Credit: John Farrell/Bateaux Below and Maddy Cucuteanu)

Figure 8.11 Drawing of Wiawaka Bateau B, part of the results of Bateaux Below's noninvasive archaeological mapping of this assemblage of 1758 British bateau shipwrecks. In 1988, scuba divers vandalized this sunken bateau. (Credit: John Farrell/Bateaux Below and Maddy Cucuteanu)

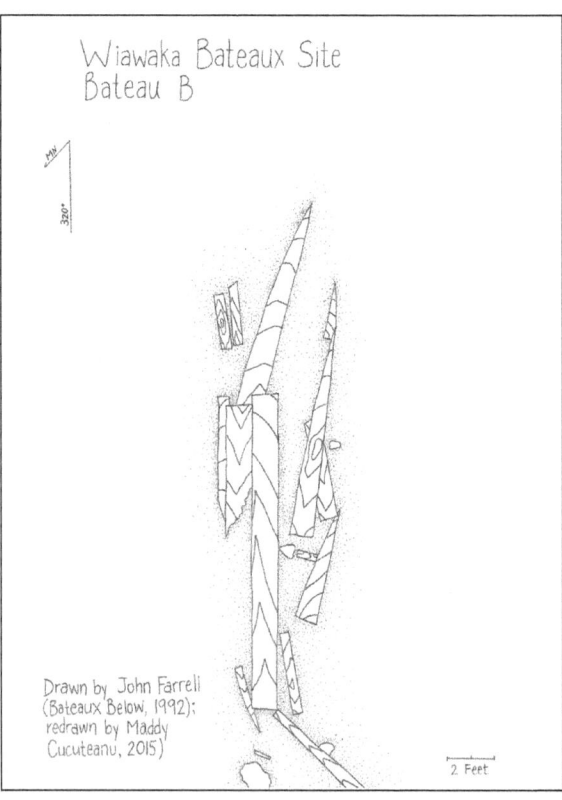

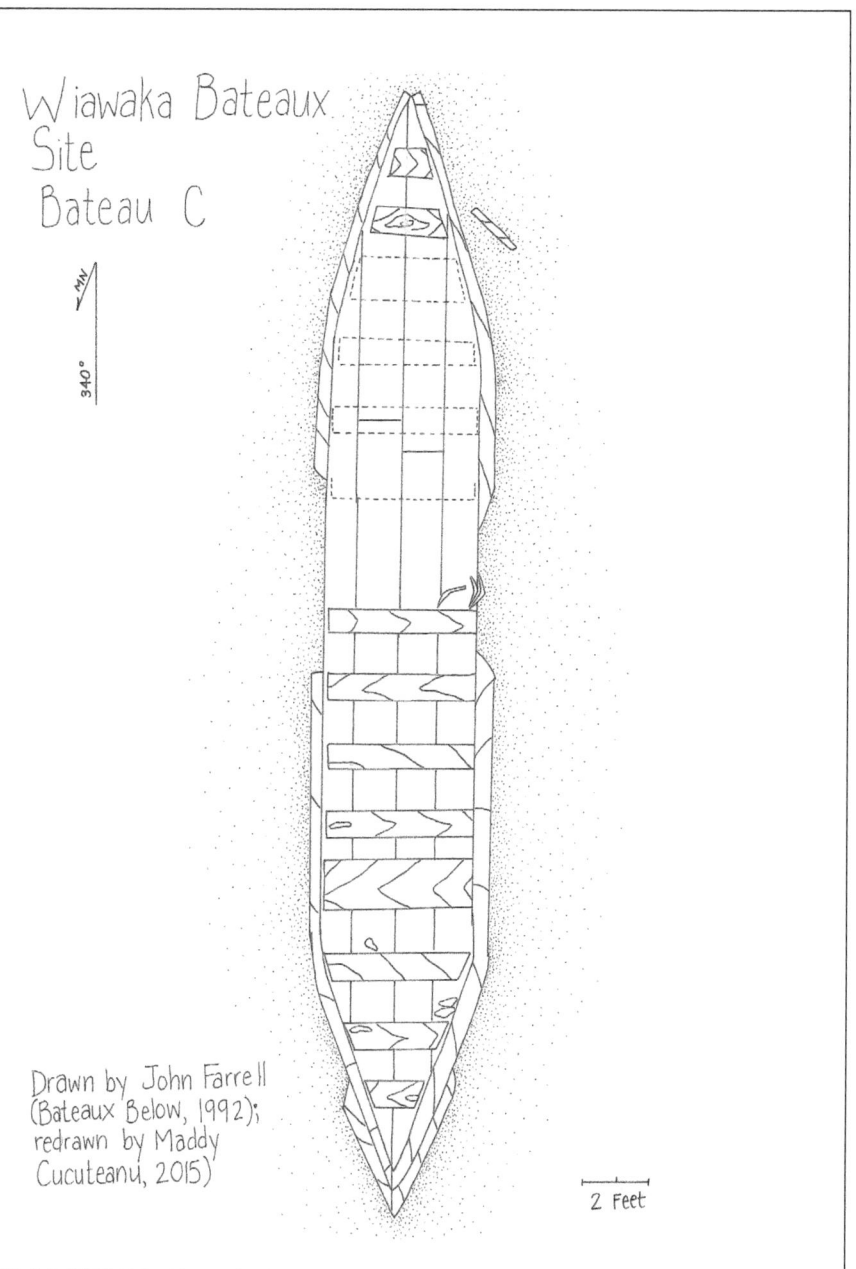

Figure 8.12 Drawing of Wiawaka Bateau C, part of the results of Bateaux Below's noninvasive archaeological mapping of this assemblage of 1758 British bateau shipwrecks. (Credit: John Farrell/Bateaux Below and Maddy Cucuteanu)

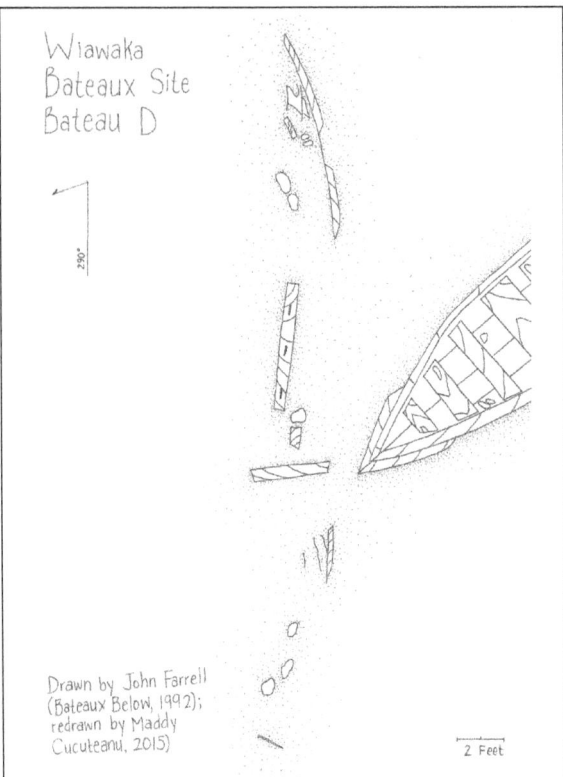

Figure 8.13 Drawing of Wiawaka Bateau D, part of the results of Bateaux Below's noninvasive archaeological mapping of this assemblage of 1758 British bateau shipwrecks. Note the nearby end of Bateau C off to the right. (Credit: John Farrell/Bateaux Below and Maddy Cucuteanu)

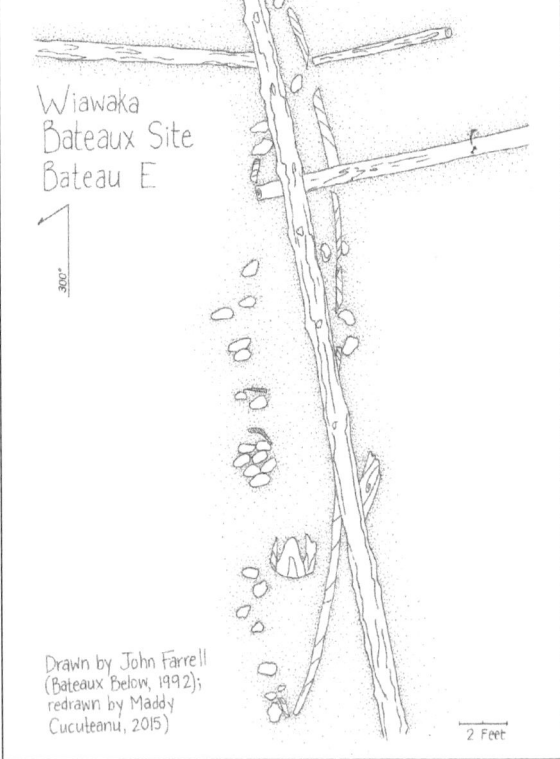

Figure 8.14 Drawing of Wiawaka Bateau E, part of the results of Bateaux Below's noninvasive archaeological mapping of this assemblage of 1758 British bateau shipwrecks. Several tree trunks lie near this colonial bateau. (Credit: John Farrell/Bateaux Below and Maddy Cucuteanu)

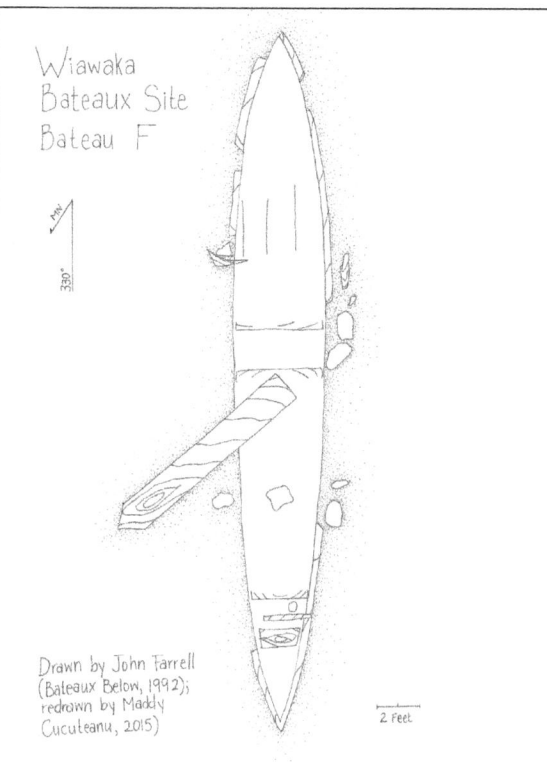

Figure 8.15 Drawing of Wiawaka Bateau F, part of the results of Bateaux Below's noninvasive archaeological mapping of this assemblage of 1758 British bateau shipwrecks. (Credit: John Farrell/Bateaux Below and Maddy Cucuteanu)

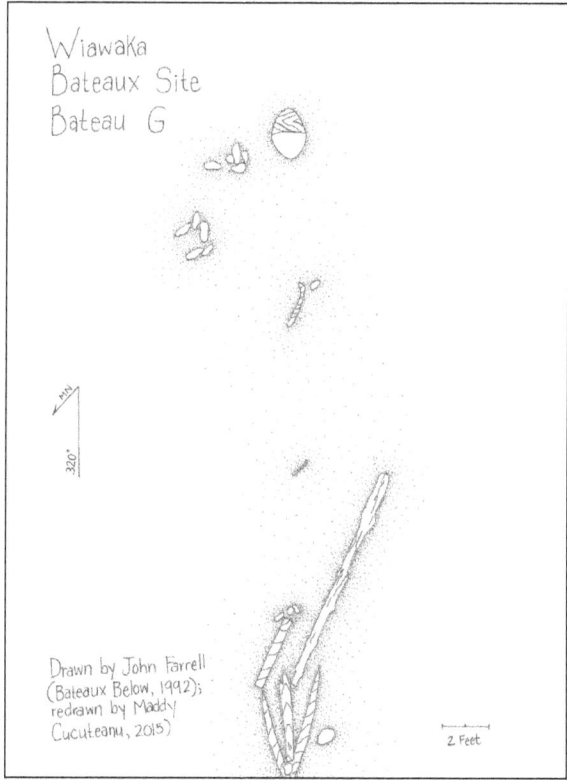

Figure 8.16 Drawing of Wiawaka Bateau G, part of the results of Bateaux Below's noninvasive archaeological mapping of this assemblage of 1758 British bateau shipwrecks. This sunken bateau is partially exposed at both ends but covered with sediment over the vessel's midsection. (Credit: John Farrell/Bateaux Below and Maddy Cucuteanu)

Figure 8.17 Educator Ted Caldwell's students built this twenty-three-foot replica bateau. After its use as a public school "floating classroom" in 1997, the wooden boat was sunk at a Lake George shipwreck preserve to enhance scuba diver visitation at the site. (Credit: Ted Caldwell)

One day in 1988, we discovered that Bateau B had been recently vandalized and that the site was now totally "wrecked." The vandalism of Bateau B made that sunken boat the least structurally sound of the seven sunken vessels of this assemblage. The other six bateaux had their pine bottom boards relatively intact, some transverse pine planks (battens), a few oak frames (some of those frames could be other hardwood), and they all still had remnants of their garboard strakes attached to the pine bottom boards.

During our team's hundreds of scuba dives undertaken at the site, we noticed that some of the Wiawaka bateaux had circular holes, approximately 1-1/4 inches in diameter, that were drilled into their bottom boards. British and provincial troops undoubtedly drilled these holes, probably to aid in sinking the watercraft in 1758. There were also some disarticulated bateau frames laying around the shipwrecks, most likely the result of sport diver intrusion and possibly from anchor damage over the past few decades. Some bateaux had rocks inside them, and other rocks were also scattered about, the latter due to disturbance from scuba divers. The rocks observed underwater at the site were probably employed to facilitate the deliberate sinking of the bateaux in the late summer and early autumn of 1758, and not so much to trim the vessels for better stability in the water. Logs and dock debris also resided around the Wiawaka shipwreck assemblage, making it difficult at times to discern what were wooden fragments from shipwrecks and what were pieces of errant logs and old timbers from a nearby dock at the Wiawaka Holiday House. From 1987 to 2016, the latter date when I made my last reconnaissance dive at the site, no colonial-era artifacts were observed by our research team on any of the seven Wiawaka bateaux. Most likely, any portable artifacts were collected during "Operation Bateaux" or were retrieved by artifact-hunting scuba divers, some possibly using underwater metal detectors.

There were also three non-bateau shipwrecks in the immediate Wiawaka bateaux area. Lying just west of the site in deeper water was a twentieth-century wooden canoe, sometimes mistaken by visiting sport divers as an eighteenth-century bateau. Resting in shallow water closer to shore and adjacent to the Wiawaka bateaux were the remains of a small disarticulated and lightly constructed wooden vessel, possibly remnants of a guide boat or a type of lightly built vernacular rowboat. Last, in 1997, with permission from state and local authorities, Bateaux Below archaeological divers and other volunteers sank a twenty-three-foot replica colonial bateau. The replica boat was sunk, with state government permission, to the immediate south of Bateau A. Ted Caldwell, an Adirondack-region public school educator, graciously provided the reproduction bateau. The wooden boat was fabricated by students from a partnership of three public schools in the Adirondacks known as the Tri-District Consortium (Bolton, Minerva, and Newcomb). After this watercraft outlived its usefulness as a "floating classroom," it became a very suitable candidate to be sunk to test our hypothesis on how colonial troops sank bateaux in 1758. Likewise, the bateau reproduction also has provided the opportunity for scuba divers visiting the site to examine what an intact bateau shipwreck would look like.

The archaeological mapping of the Wiawaka bateaux site from 1987 to 1991 determined that the seven 1758 sunken vessels lie approximately 120 feet off a meandering shoreline of the eastern side of Lake George near the Wiawaka Holiday House estate. The seven extant shipwrecks are located within a rectangle approximately 445 feet long by 105 feet wide. Our archaeological fieldwork revealed the following for each of these seven sunken 1758 bateaux, this information gathered during our 1987–1991 fieldwork:

Bateau A. Length: 35 feet, 6 inches (note that none of the seven colonial bateaux had an articulated stem or sternpost. Thus, the length measurements of these seven bateaux is from one end of the bottom boards to the other); shallow-end depth: 27 feet of water (note that water depth varies depending on seasonal rains and also because a small dam at the north end of Lake George manages the lake's water level); centerline orientation of the bateau: 310 degrees MN (Magnetic North). This shipwreck is the southern-most sunken vessel in the

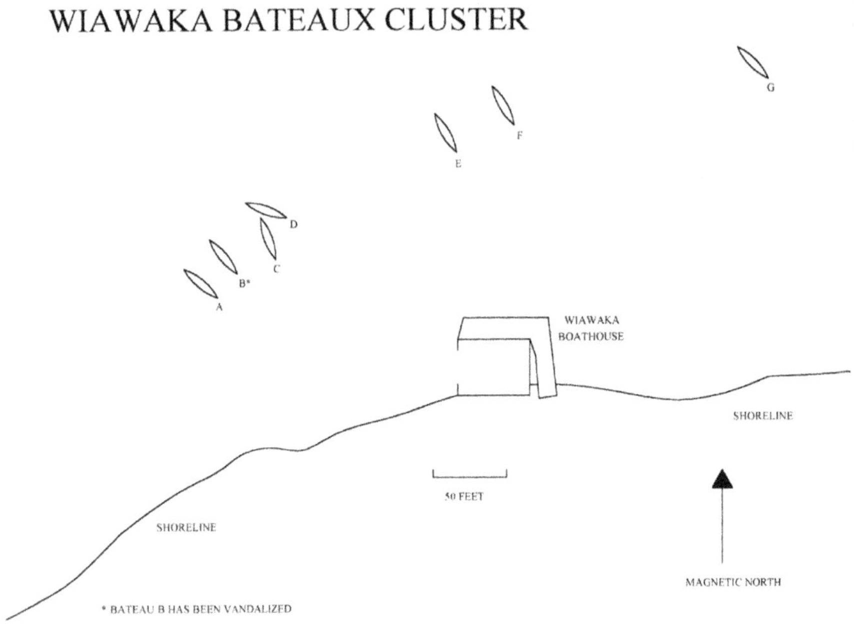

WIAWAKA BATEAUX CLUSTER

Figure 8.18 Map of the seven 1758 Wiawaka bateaux (plan view) created by Bateaux Below; cartography by John Farrell, CAD by Bob Benway. (Credit: Bob Benway/Bateaux Below)

Wiawaka bateaux cluster. It was heavily covered with sedimentation, with only a small portion of the submerged watercraft's pine bottom boards, battens, and hardwood frames visible. The upper strakes (side boards) were gone. There were some rocks, which were used as sinking rocks (possibly some for trim) visible on or adjacent to the shipwreck. Parts of the garboard strakes (lowest side boards) might be buried in the soft sediment that covers most of the bateau shipwreck.

Bateau B. Length: 28 feet, 4 inches; shallow-end depth: 26 feet of water; centerline orientation of bateau: 320 degrees MN. Sadly, within a year of our initial fieldwork, begun in mid-September 1987, we discovered that this bateau had been vandalized, probably in early 1988. We promptly reported this damage to state government agencies. Prior to that site disturbance, the bateau's bottom boards were relatively intact.

Bateau C. Length: 31 feet, 7 inches; shallow-end depth: 25 feet of water; centerline orientation of bateau: 340 degrees MN. This bateau was lightly covered with sedimentation. Partial garboard strakes were still attached to the bottom boards. Some scattered fragments of strakes (side planking) were lying around the submerged vessel. Some rocks were inside the bateau.

Bateau D. Length: 25 feet; shallow-end depth: 35 feet of water; centerline orientation of bateau: 290 degrees MN. Bateau D's centerline orientation was somewhat different from the rest in this bateaux assemblage, partially due to this shipwreck being disturbed during sampling fieldwork during Crandall's "Operation Bateaux" fieldwork. Dr. Robert Bruce Inverarity, director of the Adirondack Museum, instructed Crandall to sample (collect) bateau pieces and to excavate some of the colonial bateau shipwrecks he found in the lake. Crandall later wrote that Inverarity ordered him to excavate one of the Wiawaka bateaux "to remove selective timbers" for study and analysis. As part of this "sampling," done in 1963, Crandall and another diver on his scuba team removed "a variety of planks from one of the bateau"—Bateau D.[9] Crandall wrote that he then "wet wrapped many [bateau] structural pieces in wet newspapers and saran wrap and transported them" to the Adirondack Museum.[10]

Bateau E. Length: 36 feet; shallow-end depth: 25 feet of water; centerline orientation of bateau: 330 degrees MN. Much of Bateau E was covered with sedimentation. A large tree trunk with branches lay over the sunken vessel, probably a tree uprooted from the shoreline that fell into the lake and tumbled over the bateau shipwreck. There were two bateau frames visible, with rocks scattered about the Bateau E area. The south side of the bateau had a partial garboard strake. Other strakes were disarticulated and scattered around the shipwreck.

Bateau F. Length: 27 feet, 2 inches; shallow-end depth: 27 feet of water; centerline orientation of bateau: 330 degrees MN. Bateau F was lightly covered with sedimentation. One bateau frame was visible as well as a partial garboard strake, the latter located at the deep end of the shipwreck. One bottom plank was pulled away from the bateau. Scattered partial side planks (strakes) lay about the bateau site. Some rocks were lying inside the vessel as well as some scattered adjacent to the sunken bateau.

Bateau G. Length: 32 feet, 7 inches; shallow-end depth, 27 feet of water; centerline orientation of bateau: 315 degrees MN. Bateau G was heavily covered with sedimentation, probably the most soil overburden of any of the bateaux in this cluster. However, each end of the boat had significantly less sedimentation then the middle section of the watercraft. The garboard strakes might be somewhat intact. Rocks were still aboard the bateau and fragmentary strakes were scattered about. We observed some disarticulated frames to the south of the sunken bateau.[11]

The centerlines of six of the seven vessels are oriented perpendicular to shore with the seventh (Bateau D) vessel's centerline orientation somewhat parallel to shore. Thus it appears that when the British and provincial troops sank these vessels in 1758 for recovery in 1759 they oriented each boat's centerline toward the shoreline for easy recovery. According to Crandall, Bateau D, the vessel not pointed toward shore, moved slightly during his fieldwork over 1963–1964. Bateaux Below archaeological divers observed that the slope upon which Bateau D lies is a dynamic environment. So, it is probable the sunken vessel slid a bit down the lake bottom slope, altering its original centerline orientation.[12]

When not conducting fieldwork at the Wiawaka bateaux, the Lake George Bateaux Research Team and later Bateaux Below investigated other submerged bateaux in Lake George. In 1988, Terry Crandall was invited to become part of our research team. He turned out to be a very valuable member of our organization. On July 27, 1988, Crandall showed his new colleagues a cluster of nine bateaux on the east side of the lake, a considerable distance from the Wiawaka bateaux cluster. He dived the site that day with us and was quite upset to discover that these once rather pristine bateaux that he had observed a quarter-century ago (1963–1964) had been vandalized, greatly compromising some of their structural integrity. The damage to these bateaux was a rude awakening not only for Crandall but also for the other members of the Lake George Bateaux Research Team.[13] That same year, Lake George Bateaux Research Team divers with assistance from Les (Wit) Richmond, dived on the 1758 bateaux cluster that had been rediscovered in July 1960 by teenage divers Bolt and LaVoy. Unfortunately, by 1988, many of those sunken bateau warships had also been "trashed." This location is probably the site where the three bateaux were raised in the early 1960s during the recovery project conducted by the Adirondack Museum.

As noted earlier, on September 25, 1988, during a reconnaissance dive at the Wiawaka bateaux, we discovered that Bateau B of the Wiawaka site had been severely damaged by scuba diver intrusion. Our research team had not been to the Wiawaka bateaux since May 8 of that year because we had been making reconnaissance dives elsewhere in the South Basin searching for other sunken bateaux. So, by the autumn of 1988, the Lake George Bateaux Research Team undertook a new two-part strategy in our colonial bateau shipwrecks study: (1) we initiated a more intensive effort to locate vessels of the sunken bateaux of 1758 using scuba reconnaissance and remote sensing (side-scan sonar), and (2) we began to accelerate our mapping of the Wiawaka bateaux cluster fearing other vandalism might destroy the spatial and structural integrity of that historic site.

Figure 8.19 Martin Klein (left), Vince Capone (second from left), Garry Kozak (second from right), and the author (right) examine lake charts aboard a survey vessel during Klein side-scan sonar survey fieldwork in 1988 at Lake Champlain. This project helped form a long-term working relationship between Klein Associates, Inc., and the Lake George group that became known as Bateaux Below. (Credit: M.P. Meaney)

Therefore, in the autumn of 1988, I talked to Martin Klein and asked him to loan our team one of their side-scan sonar units. He wholeheartedly agreed. Thus, began our effort at side-scan sonar surveying the lake's South Basin, the area of the waterway that had the highest probability of us finding a nondisturbed colonial bateau shipwreck. Capone, our group's remote sensing specialist, was our side-scan sonar operator for that remote sensing project. Capone, whom I first met in 1987, had several years of experience using a Mini-Rover Mk II ROV. Over the past two summers, he had also helped me out in side-scan sonar projects at Lake Champlain, where I introduced him to Klein Associates' Garry Kozak, one of the world's foremost side-scan sonar specialists. Kozak provided Capone with valuable training that was put to good use during our autumn 1988 side-scan sonar surveying at Lake George. Capone later used that initiation into side-scan sonar technology to establish his own remote sensing company, today known as Black Laser Learning. The company specializes in not only side-scan sonar survey work for clients, but also provides training workshops in the operation and interpretation of side-scan sonar as well as using other marine remote sensing equipment.

Between 1987 and 2011, Bateaux Below and its forerunner organization, the Lake George Bateaux Research Team, investigated eight bateau vessel clusters in the South Basin of Lake George; five of those cluster sites had been reconnoitered by Terry Crandall for Adirondack Museum in the summers of 1963 and 1964.

During nearly a quarter-century of study of sunken colonial bateaux of the so-called "Ghost Fleet," we made three notable underwater discoveries in Lake George, all associated with the French and Indian War. On June 26, 1990, I directed the research team that discovered the 1758 *Land Tortoise* radeau warship, lying two miles north of the head of the lake in about 107 feet of water. The find was made using a Klein 595 side-scan sonar. Aboard the survey vessel that day were Vince Capone, Bob Benway, John Farrell, David Van Aken, and myself. Van Aken provided the loan of his father's family watercraft that served as our craft-of-opportunity. I secured the loan of the sonar gear from Klein Associates, courtesy of two of the company's employees, Garry Kozak and Bill Key.

The 1758 *Land Tortoise* radeau is a one-of-a-kind floating gun battery. It is a fifty-two-foot, eighteenth-century warship that was pierced for seven cannons. During its construction, the wooden juggernaut was sometimes called "Ord's Ark," named for the artillery officer, Captain Thomas Ord, who was quite involved in the building of the warship, and for its resemblance to Noah's ship in the Bible.[14] The unique seven-sided watercraft was somewhat shaped like the corner bastion of a Vauban-style eighteenth-century frontier fortification. The wooden shipwreck is the only radeau-class warship to have ever been discovered and studied by archaeologists. Maritime and military historian Dr. Russell P. Bellico appropriately dubbed the sunken battleship, "North America's oldest intact warship." Following its 1990 discovery and initial exploratory scuba investigation, Bateaux Below archaeological divers, archaeologists, and non-diving support personnel studied the radeau from 1991 to 1994. That all-volunteer effort was under the direction of Dr. D.K. (Kathy) Abbass, archaeologist and **Principal Investigator (P.I.)**. I served as project manager. Following our fieldwork, in 1995, the 1758 *Land Tortoise* was listed on the National Register of Historic Places, and in 1998 it was recognized as a **National Historic Landmark (NHL)**, only the sixth shipwreck in American waters with that federal designation.

Another exceptional sunken watercraft associated with Lake George's sunken bateaux of 1758 was discovered on June 18, 1995. During one of our Bateaux Below submerged cultural resources inventory reconnaissance dives, Bob Benway and I discovered a fifteen-foot yellow research submarine sunk in deep water in Lake George. The submarine, named *Baby Whale*, was stolen one night in 1960 from its dock on the east side of the lake, and was mysteriously sunk. The underwater vehicle was at the waterway for researchers to photograph the sunken bateaux of 1758.[15] For further information on *Baby Whale*, see chapter 12.

On October 1, 2000, Bateaux Below divers located the submerged remains of a colonial wharf (i.e., dock, pier, quay) primarily associated with the 1759 British campaign to oust the French from Fort Carillon and Fort St. Frédéric, two military strongholds along the shores of Lake Champlain. Undoubtedly, many British vessels, including bateaux, used this sturdy waterfront structure. The wharf might be one of the best-preserved docks from the French and Indian War and American Revolution; troops at Lake George used it in both military conflicts. Originally rectangular-shaped like a pier, our archaeological investigation suggests the waterfront structure underwent alteration and was probably modified from its original rectangular configuration into a T-shape. That newer design was necessary because some eighteenth-century warships on the lake, like sloops, row galleys, a radeau, and even schooners, were larger than bateaux and had deeper drafts. The waterfront structure's T-shape thus allowed more formidable vessels to dock at the 1758-built military wharf.[16]

Figure 8.20 Painting depicting the 1758-built British wharf located at the south end of Lake George. The waterfront structure was used to berth vessels of all classes, including bateaux and the sloop *Earl of Halifax*, pictured in this artwork. (Credit: Mark L. Peckham)

Chapter Nine

The "Mortar Bateau"

One of the enigmas of Lake George's sunken bateaux of 1758 is a colonial shipwreck that has been dubbed the "Mortar Bateau." The somewhat strange sunken boat is also sometimes called the "mortar bomb bateau" or the "**bomb ketch**." The unusual watercraft is named after its military cargo, a few dozen hefty iron mortar bombs or shells, and not because a mortar, a type of artillery piece, was fired from the wooden warship.

A colonial mortar was a muzzle-loaded heavy weapon with a short barrel that fired a projectile, typically an explosive bomb, over a shorter range than a cannon. A mortar bomb was circular in shape. Gunpowder was inserted into a hole in the ordnance and then a fuse plugged the orifice. The mortar bomb's fuse was lit just before the mortar was touched off and fired. The round ball, filled with gunpowder, was designed to explode over its target, thus maximizing damage and casualties. A mortar had a higher arcing trajectory than a cannon or howitzer. The so-called "mortar bateau" probably was a bateau-class vessel altered to transport its weighty load of iron ordnance.

The "mortar bomb" shipwreck lies in the middle of the waterway in the South Basin. It apparently was found sometime around the Bolt-LaVoy dive team's rediscovery of the lake's colonial bateau shipwrecks in the summer of 1960. On July 31, 1960, an *Albany Times-Union* article entitled "Bottom of Lake George: Divers Find Craft With 40 Mortars" reported that two Saratoga Springs, New York, scuba divers, Walter Stroup (attorney, age thirty-one) and Fred Tarrant (an executive with Tarrant Manufacturing Company, age thirty-two), discovered the unique submerged vessel. Stroup described the sunken boat as being about twenty-eight feet long and seven feet wide. Stroup was quoted in the article as saying, "We don't know what kind of craft it was. It appears to have been two-decked and the top deck looks as if it collapsed." The divers said there were about forty mortars bombs aboard the sunken vessel, each artifact about 150 pounds in weight and thirteen inches in diameter. The newspaper reported that the two Saratoga Springs scuba divers also "found a skeleton on the deck but left it untouched."[1]

The *Lake George Mirror* newspaper published a news story about the shipwreck discovery, dated August 5, 1960, entitled "Saratogians Discover 28-Foot Boat and 40 Mortars in the Lake."[2] The *Lake George Mirror* news story was basically an account quite similar to the *Albany Times-Union* article from July 31, 1960.

Both stories mentioned the discovery of a skeleton aboard the shipwreck. However, that skeleton reference probably was inaccurate. Follow-up eyewitness stories did not report any skeleton, human or animal, observed on the shipwreck. Likewise, local oral history and lore do not support the media's skeleton claim.

However, in a letter and affidavit sent by Dr. Lewis L. Smith (veterinarian) of Stillwater, New York, to Dr. Robert Bruce Inverarity (Adirondack Museum), Smith professed that his group of scuba divers (Bruce M. Smith, John Wheeldon, and himself) found a colonial bateau while diving in the south end of the lake on June 26, 1960. Smith said the sunken watercraft appeared to be filled with "rocks." However, based on Smith's description of the location and what one of his dive buddies described he saw, it could be that the sunken bateau they observed filled with rocks was possibly the so-called "Mortar Bateau."[3] There is another probable bateau shipwreck near the head of the lake that is completely covered with rocks. It is also possible that this is what the Smith team saw in late June 1960.

Another highly experienced scuba diver, Charles Diehl of Ridgewood, New Jersey, declared that his dive buddies and he were the ones that originally discovered the sunken Lake George "mortar bomb bateau." Diehl stated that they found the shipwreck in 1959, a year earlier than the other claimants.[4] Charles Diehl had a residence near the shores of Lake George.[5] He recalled the vessel being about twenty-five feet long. The account crediting Charles Diehl and his colleagues as first finding this sunken warship was published in 1998, nearly four decades after their reported discovery of the eighteenth-century shipwreck.[6] So, there certainly is some debate as to who actually first found this French and Indian War shipwreck. Regardless of what group initially discovered the "mortar bomb bateau," some information about this puzzling colonial shipwreck can be offered.

Gene Parker, a Schenectady-area scuba diver and an accomplished underwater photographer, inspected this shipwreck on several occasions in the early 1960s. Parker's expertise as a scuba diver would soon be supported, too, as in 1963 he revised a textbook on scuba instruction entitled *Dive: The Complete Book of Skin Diving*.[7] Parker's visits to the "mortar bateau" were undertaken after the shipwreck was reported to have been found. Gene Parker was contracted by the Adirondack Museum in 1962 to examine and remove artifacts from the "mortar bateau." On September 14, 1962, Gene Parker and two other divers, Robert Drose and Ronald

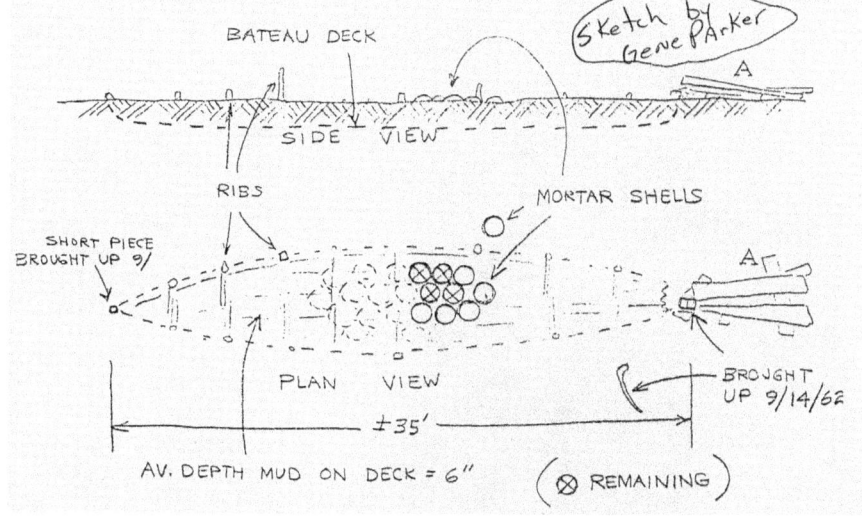

Figure 9.1 Gene Parker, a Schenectady-area diver, drew this sketch on September 14, 1962, shortly after his team dived the Lake George "mortar bateau" shipwreck. The scuba divers were working at the time for the Adirondack Museum. (Credit: Adirondack Experience)

Higgins, employed a dive plane that towed a scuba diver behind a motorboat, the *Scuba Queen*, to relocate the "mortar bomb bateau." Parker's team worked under the auspices of the Adirondack Museum, the institution that had a permit issued by the State Education Department to excavate and remove artifacts from sunken bateau vessels in Lake George. According to Parker, his divers removed several "mortar bombs," what Parker called "mortar shells." The ordnance was then stored temporarily in a Warren County Sheriff's department shed before being transported to the Adirondack Museum. Parker likewise snapped photographs of the sunken boat and the dive team's exploratory and artifact recovery operation.[8]

Parker later prepared a one-sheet description of the sunken mortar bomb-laden shipwreck supplemented by two drawings and a map. Gene Parker's sketches, one a profile of the shipwreck and another illustration in a plan view, show the remains of a sunken boat pointed at both bow and stern with several wooden planks affixed together, possibly a type of decking on the wooden boat. His profile drawing does not depict any strakes (side planks) sticking up above the lake bottom sediment, but does portray several articulated frames standing proud, protruding from the lake bottom's soft sediment. Parker estimated the shipwreck was over thirty-five feet long. He wondered if the so-called separate decking, which was not part of the vessel's bottom boards and found at the south end of the sunken vessel, might "be [the] portion of another bateau?" His plan view sketch also shows

Figure 9.2 Adirondack Museum's Terry Crandall aboard a pontoon boat with two thirteen-inch mortar bombs recovered in 1963 from the so-called "mortar bateau" shipwreck at Lake George. (Credit: Terry Crandall)

a cluster of several mortar bombs configured in a pile in the amidships (center) section of the sunken military watercraft.[9]

Terry Crandall dived the "mortar bomb" bateau on several occasions while employed by the Adirondack Museum in 1963–1964. Crandall wrote to Inverarity on September 15, 1963, stating that he was "greatly intrigued" by the "mortar bomb bateau."[10] Crandall said he recovered a few mortar bombs from the shipwreck site for the museum.[11]

The Richfield Springs, New York, diver also sketched the shipwreck following an October 12, 1963 dive.[12] Crandall came to the conclusion that this sunken vessel was not a "stock" bateau. Rather, it was constructed or modified specifically to haul heavy loads, since the vessel's frames were "more dense, heavier, and more closely spaced."[13] Further, Terry Crandall suggested that this boat might have been "purposely sunk," as he discovered "two very large rocks" inside the sunken watercraft and evidence of other rocks outside the shipwreck that might have been removed by other scuba divers. Crandall wondered if French General Montcalm scuttled the military vessel in August 1757 with its cumbersome cargo of mortar shells, rather than abandon the ordnance at Fort William Henry or attempt to take the mortar shells back to the Champlain Valley as spoils of war.[14] There is also the possibility that the rocks observed by Crandall were added to the cargo of ordnance to balance the vessel's stability to counteract Lake George's sometimes turbulent waters. Thus, it remains an enigma under what circumstance the unusual military vessel sank.

On June 30, 1965, James A. Magee, at the time the curator of the Fort William Henry Museum, composed a brief report offering a description of the sunken "mortar bateau." Magee was from nearby Thurman, New York, and a graduate of the Syracuse University School of Forestry. Over his career he also belonged to the New York State Archaeological Association—Auringer Seelye Chapter and the John Thurman Historical Society. Thus, Magee was well versed in the nuances related to timber types and the principles of archaeology.[15] Magee's narrative is the most detailed account available about the puzzling watercraft and its combat-related payload. Magee's document was written after interviewing several scuba divers—Charles Diehl, Robert LaVoy, Bernie Campoli, Terry Crandall, and Nick Pallissino—all who claimed to have examined this shipwreck.

Magee wrote in his monograph that the vessel was double-ended, and its lines were like that of a bateau, but with some construction features like that of another type of colonial vessel, a whaleboat. The vessel's "knees," meaning frames, were heavier than those on the typical bateau being three to four inches in cross-section; bateau frames were about two inches. The vessel's bottom was reinforced with oak "cross-beams" that measured three to four inches in cross-section. On top of these crossbeams rested decking that lay four or five inches above the boat's bottom boards. Furthermore, only part of the sunken vessel had this "double deck" feature. This decking was such that only one-third of the boat at the bow and one-third of the vessel at the stern were "decked or double floored." Thus, about twelve feet of the center was open, without decking.

Magee commented that when the unusual shipwreck was originally discovered there were about forty mortar bombs (that he called "round cast iron bombshells") aboard. These were described as being approximately thirteen inches in diameter and weighing about 175 pounds each. Furthermore, the iron mortar bombs were of two different kinds,

> one type having a small neck and a fuse opening of approx. one and one half (1-1/2) inches and carrying loops (2), one on each side of the neck. The other type had the same size fuse opening but with a wider rim at the top of the neck and no carrying loops. Some of the necks of the fuse openings had been knocked off, indicating that the bombs had been deactivated before the vessel was sunk.[16]

Magee related that the sunken vessel might have been from the 1758 Abercromby campaign and had sunk "after leaving the point of embarkation at the south end of Lake George."[17] Magee thought that the sinking by Abercromby's soldiers might even have been deliberate. The Fort William Henry curator suggested the British sank "the heavy bombs in the lake to destroy them and keep them from being salvaged by the French, rather than transport them all the way to Albany and bring them back the following season." It should be noted that in the autumn of 1758, Abercromby's British army had no fortification to protect their warships and ordnance. So, besides sinking their fleet for recovery, they may have scuttled this watercraft to keep the ordnance out of the hands of French salvage teams sent down to the south end of Lake George over the winter of 1758–1759. Regarding this vessel, Magee also believed "the true story will probably never be uncovered."[18]

Attached to Magee's short report was a handwritten note, the content of which differed somewhat from his typed report. His note indicated the sunken vessel was right side up on the lake bottom, pointed at each end, and about forty feet long, six feet wide, and three feet high. The sunken watercraft had "31 or 32 13-inch mortar bombs, some with stopper or plugs intact." Further, Magee stated that some of the mortar bombs were scattered outside the submerged vessel.[19] So, even Magee was somewhat unclear and conflicted about the scanty information he had collected about this cryptic craft.

Obviously, these details were based on eyewitness reports in which the divers' inspections were at times limited by poor visibility due to sediment disturbance, a problem at many shipwreck sites on a lake bottom comprised of fine silt and sand.

I first dived to find and examine the "mortar bateau" on May 16, 1987, searching for the site with diver Jack Sullivan, who first explored the shipwreck back in the early 1960s as part of the Adirondack Museum's "Operation Bateaux." Sullivan occasionally worked as a support diver for Terry Crandall's 1963–1964 fieldwork. Sullivan and I had no luck that day relocating the "mortar bateau," as his shore references—buildings, a flagpole, and trees from the early 1960s—were now gone nearly twenty-five years later. Additionally, there was no **Global Positioning System (GPS)** at that time that could have pinpointed the shipwreck's precise location.

In 1987, Dr. Russell P. Bellico and I considered this shipwreck as the site for the practicum of the three-day archaeological training workshop targeted for recreational divers, scheduled for September 11–13, 1987. Without that shipwreck, I asked Jack Sullivan to take Dr. Bellico to the Wiawaka bateaux that I had first dived in 1982. After Bellico's scuba visitation and his initial underwater photography of the Wiawaka bateaux, we were very satisfied with that choice for the workshop's September 13, 1987, practicum.

Nearly a year after the 1987 archaeology workshop, on May 22, 1988, our recently formed underwater archaeology group, the Atlantic Alliance Lake George Bateaux Research Team (quickly renamed the Lake George Bateaux Research Team), made another attempt to locate the "mortar bateau." We had an experienced scuba team—four divers, two non-divers, and two boats. One of the non-divers that day was Terry Crandall, the archaeological diver who was a major participant in the Adirondack Museum's "Operation Bateaux." I invited Crandall, recently retired from a public school administrative job at Richfield Springs, New York, to come to Lake George from his home on Canadarago Lake in central New York. Crandall gave us useful advice on where to dive for bateau shipwrecks. This was the beginning of my association with Crandall, an affiliation that would greatly benefit our organization's studies. Unfortunately, as on our May 16, 1987, exploratory dive, we did not locate the "mortar bateau" shipwreck, again due to the absence of the 1960s' shoreline visual landmarks. Buildings and other structures used in the 1960s as shore visuals to relocate the "mortar bateau" had been torn down. The Atlantic Alliance Lake George Bateaux Research Team (aka Lake George Bateaux Research Team), and later Bateaux Below, would spend a total of thirteen days from 1987 to 1998, using scuba diver-conducted circle searches, a typical underwater search method for finding shipwrecks, attempting to locate this sunken transport watercraft.[20]

Our fascination with finding the "mortar bomb" shipwreck was unexpectedly interrupted when we discovered another significant French and Indian War shipwreck in the lake, the fifty-two-foot 1758 *Land Tortoise* radeau. This incredible find was made on June 26, 1990, during a Klein 595 side-scan sonar survey project. Following the discovery of this one-of-a-kind British and provincial floating gun battery, Bateaux Below spent nearly four years studying the sunken British and provincial warship, an underwater mapping project complicated by its depth of 103 to 107 feet (depth varied due to seasonal lake level changes).

So, without any luck with scuba diver searches to relocate the "mortar bomb" shipwreck, we utilized side-scan sonar as a remote sensing tool; our first attempt at using this technology was in 1988. We had been employing a Klein side-scan sonar during our shipwreck inventory fieldwork. Every couple of years or so we were able to get the loan of a Klein side-scan sonar unit or find sufficient funds to rent the equipment with a trained and experienced operator. During one of those remote sensing searches conducted on October 18, 1998, we employed a Klein 2000 side-scan sonar unit. Vince Capone was our sonar operator. With the more advanced technology of this newer generation side-scan sonar, we detected a subtle sonar target that we believed could be the "mortar bomb bateau" shipwreck, an anomaly that had a low profile above the lake bottom and was mostly covered with sedimentation. Further, it was in the general location of our overall search area, a spot determined from interviews with Terry Crandall and Jack Sullivan, who dived the site in the early 1960s. It should be pointed out, we did have **LORAN (long range navigation)**, a type of nautical navigation positioning system, but it was notoriously inaccurate. Also, we did not have Differential Global Positioning System (DGPS) gear. GPS technology at that time was still in its infancy for civilian usage and DGPS units, which used a correction from a shore-based station to enhance positioning since the U.S. military distorted GPS data, were expensive. Finally, on November 8, 1998, the third day of scuba searching to locate the side-scan sonar-generated target, Bateaux Below divers finally spotted the "mortar bomb" vessel. Over the years of this search, our scuba forays were plagued by "brown water" diving due to low visibility caused by diver disturbance of the silty lake bottom. How much easier it is today since GPS units are now low cost, and also the U.S. military's selective availability has been turned off by an executive order executed during the Clinton presidency.

On November 15, 1998, we brought Mark L. Peckham, a civil servant with the New York State Office of Parks, Recreation and Historic Preservation agency, to dive with us to inspect the eighteenth-century shipwreck. Peckham had been our case officer from his state agency on Bateaux Below's sponsorship of the 1992 nomination of the seven 1758 Wiawaka bateaux site to the National Register of Historic Places, listed on the National Register in June 1992. Peckham examined the "mortar bateau," and since he was a superb architectural and maritime artist, he sketched part of the sunken boat, too.

The "mortar bomb" shipwreck's construction is difficult to decipher in part because its structural integrity appears to have been altered from intrusive scuba diver visitations during the 1960s. Further, the colonial vessel may have gone down under duress, and the sinking process during the 1700s might have "wrecked" the vessel. The sunken watercraft lies on a soft sediment lake bottom that can easily result in low visibility conditions from scuba divers swimming around the site, thus contributing to the difficulty in deducing the vessel's structural form.

Bateaux Below members made several noninvasive dives at the site after locating the vessel in 1998 to ascertain the shipwreck's class and its condition. We discovered that the sunken vessel appears bateau-like and its "centerline orientation" is perpendicular to the south end of the lake at a 28/208 degrees centerline orientation. However, Bob Benway, one of Bateaux Below's most experienced divers, commented that due to undetermined damage to the sunken vessel, the submerged watercraft's centerline appears to be somewhat "twisted." In 1998, no end posts (stem or sternpost) were standing proud above the lake bottom, thus making it difficult to accurately measure the length of the "mortar bateau." The most visible part of the partially buried sunken boat was at the south end of the shipwreck, exposed timbers fashioned into a type of short "deck." Was this to hold part of the cargo or for passengers or the bateau crew? Was it a helmsman's station to aid in employing an oar or paddle at the stern for steerage? Or was this "deck" part of a second bateau that served as flotation for a pontoon-type vessel employing two bateaux to support a platform to carry heavy ordnance?

Terry Crandall suggested the sunken vessel could be a pontoon-like boat with two bateaux for flotation and a platform in between, "like a catamaran."[21] Further, Crandall said there were pine planks scattered off the sides as well as a horizontal stage over part of a bateau.[22] Thus, from observation and without the luxury of having archaeologically excavated this shipwreck, there was no real consensus as to what this watercraft would have looked like back in the eighteenth century when it was transporting these heavy mortar bomb shells.

Bob Benway and I took measurements of the mortar bomb shipwreck over two consecutive scuba visits (November 8 and 15, 1998), but we had two different length measurements for the strange-looking craft. This was because of the subjective nature of trying to ascertain the two ends of the vessel, a shipwreck disarticulated and somewhat like a large wooden jigsaw puzzle lying on a soft sediment lake bottom that easily gets disturbed from diver visitation. One length measurement was thirty-nine feet, four inches long, and the other was nearly six feet shorter, or thirty-three feet, seven inches in length. Crandall reported in 1963 that the vessel was broken amidships,[23] so the sunken vessel's centerline orientation and length might have been compromised. The boat's width amidships was measured at four feet, seven inches, that being inside the vessel, across the bottom boards. Moreover, it was five feet, seven inches in width from the outside edge of one garboard strake to the other side's outer edge garboard strake. I observed eight articulated frames, five on one side of the sunken boat and three on the other. Three other frames were observed protruding from the soft sediment of the lake bottom, but these appeared to be off the sunken vessel. The latter frames may be disarticulated, that is, broken away from the hull structure. In 1998, Bateaux Below divers observed no mortar bombs during our inspections, but Peckham reported that during his dive with Bateaux Below on November 15, 1998, he saw an artifact, a bottle that could be of eighteenth-century vintage.[24]

Once news of the discovery of the "mortar bateau" got out to the public in 1960 from several newspaper stories reporting on the subject, recreational divers attempted to locate it. Many of the mortar bombs were thus removed from the shipwreck site. Some ended up in museums, while others found homes in personal collections.

The September 30, 1960, issue of *The Saratogian* newspaper reported that Fred Tarrant had been contacted by Mendel L. Peterson, the curator of the Department of the Armed Services History at the Smithsonian Institution. Peterson asked Stroup and Tarrant to donate one of the iron mortar bombs to the Washington, DC national museum.[25] Fred Tarrant and Walter Stroup reportedly donated two mortar bombs to the Smithsonian Institution.[26] Further, a 1962 issue of *The Bulletin of the Fort Ticonderoga Museum* cites that Fred K. Tarrant and Walter Stroup also donated a thirteen-inch "Mortar Shell" to the Fort Ticonderoga Museum.[27]

A photograph taken by Dr. Russell P. Bellico of a Lake George colonial bateau shipwreck, one of the three raised in the early 1960s and later exhibited at the Adirondack Museum from 1968 to 1993, shows three thirteen-inch mortar bombs in the museum's bateau display. Those three artifacts might be the ones that had been collected by Crandall and his dive team during "Operation Bateaux."

Charles Diehl and his dive partners removed mortar bombs from this shipwreck, too. His son, David Diehl, wrote an article in the *Lake George Mirror* newspaper in 1998 that reported on his father's scuba diving in Lake George. The story, based on an interview conducted by the son with his father, reported on Charles Diehl's scuba team recovering nine mortar bombs from the "mortar bomb" shipwreck site. David Diehl wrote that his father donated four mortar bombs to Fort William Henry Museum, two to Fort Ticonderoga Museum, one to the Smithsonian Institution, one to the Town of Bolton Historical Society Museum (aka Historical Society of the Town of Bolton), and one "found its way to The Boston Tea Party Ship Museum in Boston, Massachusetts."[28]

Bateaux Below's Bob Benway, besides being an excellent scuba diver, is a talented CAD technician. Benway measured, weighed, and created CAD illustrations of three publicly exhibited colonial mortar bombs, all believed to have come from the "mortar bomb bateau." Each artifact was about thirteen inches in diameter, but their weights differed slightly.

In 1993, the Lake George Historical Association, a Lake George, New York museum, received the loan of a "13-inch" mortar bomb from Fort William Henry Museum. At the time, the historical society was preparing a Lake George shipwreck exhibit at their museum. Benway later, in November 1993, measured this colonial mortar bomb. The military shell was 12.50 inches in diameter. The iron mortar bomb weighed 169 pounds. Its fuse lip was either broken and this part was mostly

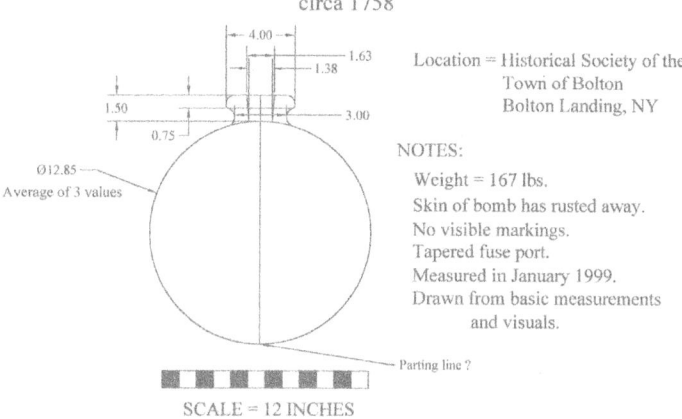

Figure 9.3 A CAD illustration of one of the thirteen-inch diameter "mortar bombs" recovered in the early 1960s from an enigmatic bateau-type shipwreck in Lake George. (Credit: Bob Benway/ Bateaux Below)

missing, or the artillery bomb was constructed without this protuberance that functionally served to receive the fuse. Also, the iron shell had no visible markings, such as the British broad arrow, a symbol that denoted British government ownership.[29]

With assistance from Ted Caldwell, one of the principals of the Historical Society of the Town of Bolton (Bolton Landing, New York), Benway scrutinized and then measured a second mortar bomb in January 1999. Charles Diehl donated the ordnance to the Bolton historical society. Unlike the mortar bomb at the Lake George Historical Association, this military artifact did have an extended fuse port. This piece of ordnance measured 12.85 inches in diameter and weighed 167 pounds. The mortar bomb also had no visible markings.[30]

In August 2001, Benway surveyed a third mortar bomb relic, reported to also have come from the "mortar bomb bateau." As with the examinations of the other two mortar bombs, this recordation was conducted under the auspices of Bateaux Below. The mortar bomb was being displayed in the Cooper's Cave Ale Company in Glens Falls, New York. The artifact had an extended fuse port, like the one in the Historical Society of the Town of Bolton. It weighed 176 pounds and was 12.90 inches in diameter. Similar to the other two artillery mortar bombs, it had no visible markings.[31]

In the mid-1980s, Kevin J. Crisman examined three mortar bomb shells in the collection at Adirondack Museum. These artifacts came from the "mortar bomb bateau," having been retrieved from Lake George in the early 1960s. Crisman's recording of these mortar bombs was in conjunction with his examination and study of one of the Lake George bateaux raised from the waterway in the early 1960s and on exhibit at the Adirondack Museum.

These three shells were 12.50 inches in diameter, and all had a circular raised opening, the part with the fuse hole. Two of the mortar bombs that Crisman studied at the Adirondack Museum showed evidence, too, of lifting handles. Remarkably, one of these Lake George "mortar bomb bateau" shells was partially filled with a small amount of black powder.[32]

To conclude, the "mortar bomb bateau" is truly a Lake George historical and archaeological conundrum. Based on newspaper reports, eyewitness accounts, and nonintrusive inspections by underwater archaeologists, the sunken vessel appears to have been a large and sturdy bateau-type watercraft. However, it might have been altered to transport the reported forty mortar bombs seen by divers at the shipwreck site in 1960.

If that estimate of the number of mortar bombs is accurate, then the estimated weight of that cargo would then be approximately 6,787 pounds. That amount was determined from the average weight of a mortar bomb recorded from the three mortar bombs (Lake George Historical Association, Historical Society of the Town of Bolton, and Cooper's Cave Ale Company) by Bateaux Below (average of three samples was 169.67 pounds \x\ forty mortar bombs). That total weight, about 3-1/3 tons, is certainly considerable. Quite possibly the excessive load of this cargo in the military vessel contributed to its sinking. Thus, the boat's sinking might have been a marine mishap and not necessarily deliberately done to scuttle the watercraft. It is unfortunate that a comprehensive professional archaeological study of the sunken watercraft was not undertaken in the early 1960s, prior to major disturbances of the submerged cultural site. Such an endeavor would probably have garnered much more information about this boat—its builders' nationality, its type, its vessel lines, its function, how a large bateau could have been modified to transport heavy mortar bombs, why it sank in the lake, and when.

Chapter Ten

What Lies Beneath

An Inventory

Two of the main tenets of terrestrial and underwater archaeology are survey and inventory of cultural resources.[1] This was a major component of the efforts of Adirondack Museum's "Operation Bateaux" (1960–1965) and also by Bateaux Below and its predecessor group, the Lake George Bateaux Research Team, from 1987 to 2011.

Over the early 1960s, Dr. Robert Bruce Inverarity's divers undertook a bateau shipwreck survey of select areas of Lake George, primarily in the south end of the waterway. Terry Crandall, who conducted fieldwork in the summers of 1963 and 1964, was sent by his employer to various locations around the lake to follow up on reports of sunken bateaux that had been collected by the Adirondack Museum. Crandall was also instructed to scuba reconnoiter locales with a high probability of finding colonial shipwrecks based on historical literature. In the first two appendices of this book you will find two articles by Crandall that provide insight into his *modus operandi*. Based on the results of "Operation Bateaux," as well as the inventory survey executed by Bateaux Below, we have some details to share as to how many colonial bateau shipwrecks have been found in Lake George. Collectively, I call these shipwrecks "Lake George's Sunken Bateaux of 1758." However, some of these bateaux might have sunk in the waterway before 1758 and others later on, during the American Revolution (1775–1783).

To promote resource protection, I am designating most of these shipwreck sites on a numbering system rather than by an exact geographic location; the Wiawaka bateaux are part of an existing state park for scuba divers, and their location is thus well known. The inventory is a combination of parts of "Operation Bateaux" as well as fieldwork completed by the Lake George Bateaux Research Team and Bateaux Below from 1987 to 2011.

Inventory of Lake George's Sunken Bateaux of 1758

Bateau(x) Site I Estimated ten to fifteen sunken bateaux located in the summer of 1960 by Fred Bolt and Robert LaVoy; this number range was also put at twelve to fifteen, or at fourteen. It is believed that three of these shipwrecks were raised from the lake in the early 1960s, the recovery executed under a formal permit issued by the New York State Education Department to the Adirondack Museum and its affiliate, the Adirondack Historical Association. Terry Crandall's 1963–1964 inventory of this site showed six sunken bateaux, with one located under modern-day dock structure. His low number of bateaux might be because some of the bateaux observed in 1960 could by 1963–1964 have been covered by sediment from visiting scuba divers. Bateaux Below's noninvasive inspection of this site did observe several bateaux, but they were heavily damaged, with many disarticulated pieces lying on the lake bottom or partially buried. Originally this site had an estimated ten to fifteen sunken bateaux, three of which were removed by Adirondack Museum in early 1960s. **Seven to twelve bateaux at Site I**.

Bateau(x) Site II ("Mortar Bomb Bateau") A single shipwreck, probably a robust bateau that was reinforced with partial "decking" to carry a cargo of an estimated forty thirteen-inch mortar bombs. Archaeological divers with the Adirondack Museum removed several mortar bombs, and sport divers probably recovered the others. The site was partially "excavated" during "Operation Bateaux"; Gene Parker reported he removed "mortar shells" in 1962, and Terry Crandall recovered a few mortar bombs during his 1963–1964 fieldwork, both recoveries executed under the auspices of the Adirondack Museum's state permit. **One bateau at Site II.**

*Bateau(x) Site III A single shipwreck on the west side of the lake reportedly discovered in August 1960 by scuba divers Darold Cerrone, Stan Zeccolo, and Daniel Donnelly. Crandall relocated this sunken bateau during his 1963–1964 fieldwork. Bateaux Below's underwater survey fieldwork failed to find the shipwreck. It is hypothesized that this sunken bateau is now buried under a growing stream delta. **One bateau at Site III.**

*Bateau(x) Site IV (Wiawaka Bateaux Site) Located on the east side of the lake in the South Basin. Sport divers first relocated the site in the early 1960s. Crandall did a preliminary site map in 1963–1964. In 1964, Crandall reported eight bateaux in this assemblage. Bateaux Below's fieldwork revealed there are now just seven bateaux; parts of one bateau shipwreck might have been recovered in

1965 during a combined training session and fieldwork conducted by the New York State Police dive team. Thus, eight bateaux mapped over 1963–1964, and one bateau believed to have been removed in 1965. **Seven bateaux at Site IV.**

*Bateau(x) Site V Located on the east side of the lake in the South Basin. Crandall did a preliminary site map of this cluster of colonial shipwrecks during "Operation Bateaux" and observed five sunken bateaux. Reconnaissance fieldwork by Bateaux Below in the late 1980s revealed only four bateaux at this site; oral history suggests one bateau shipwreck from this assemblage was removed from the waterway in a nonsanctioned recovery (salvage date unknown). The four surviving bateaux's lengths were measured in 1989 at thirty-one feet, four inches; thirty-one feet, seven inches; thirty-two feet, one inch; and thirty-two feet, five inches. Additionally, in 1993 Bateaux Below divers under the direction of Dr. D.K. (Kathy) Abbass conducted several days of noninvasive fieldwork on this shipwreck assemblage. Bateaux Below divers discovered that one of the four extant bateaux rested on a lumber frame with affiliated concrete blocks. The crude frame was nearly rigged for another salvage attempt of a bateau shipwreck. Thus, five bateaux originally located; one bateau reportedly removed during a nonsanctioned recovery, probably in the 1960s. **Four bateaux at Site V.**

*Bateau(x) Site VI Located on the east side of the lake in the South Basin. Crandall recorded nine sunken bateaux at site VI. Reconnaissance fieldwork by Bateaux Below archaeologists and archaeological divers in the late 1980s observed several shipwrecks heavily disturbed, probably vandalized post-1964. On July 27, 1988, Dr. Russell P. Bellico, Bob Benway, Mark Matucci, and I took Crandall to revisit the site that he last saw twenty-five years earlier. Crandall believes he might have been the first scuba diver to visit this site. In 1988, Crandall was shocked at the catastrophic damage he witnessed to some of these sunken bateaux. One bateau was a pile of disarticulated bateau bottom boards and frames and other hull structural pieces. **Nine bateaux at Site VI.**

*Bateau(x) Site VII (Diamond Island "Bateau") A single bateau-like hull timber was observed by Terry Crandall during "Operation Bateaux." Inverarity sent Crandall to dive this area based on information Inverarity received from Harold Veeder at the Fort William Henry Corporation. Years later, five scuba inspections were conducted by Bateaux Below members searching for evidence of this reported "bateau" (**gunboat**) shipwreck, but no hull structure was observed at the target site. A mid-twentieth-century wooden shipwreck lies relatively intact in the search area near Diamond Island, but it is highly unlikely that Crandall

Figure 10.1 July 27, 1988: the author diving at Site VI, a cluster of nine sunken bateaux. Sadly, since this site was first recorded in the early 1960s it has been heavily vandalized by souvenir-seeking scuba divers. Note the pile of disarticulated hull structure pieces torn up and in disarray on the lake bottom. (Credit: Dr. Russell P. Bellico)

Figure 10.2 A Klein side-scan sonar image of Bateau(x) Site VIII showing two to four sunken bateaux. This sonograph, collected early in Bateaux Below's shipwreck inventory fieldwork, shows the subtle image of bateau-class shipwrecks. The sunken warships are mostly buried in a soft sediment lake bottom, thus showing little structural relief. (Credit: Bateaux Below Collection)

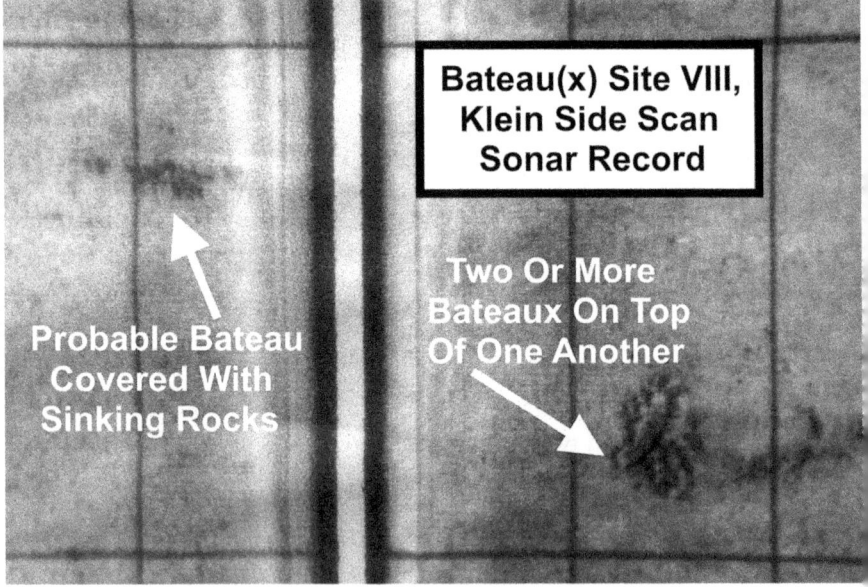

would have misidentified it as an eighteenth-century bateau, if in fact, this wooden cabin cruiser was even there in 1963–1964. The modern wooden cabin cruiser probably was sunk at this site after Crandall's 1963–1964 inventory scuba dives. Furthermore, the reputed "bateau" shipwreck might not be associated with Lake George's sunken bateaux. Rather, this missing shipwreck could be affiliated with the British occupation of the island in 1777 during the Burgoyne campaign of the American Revolution. Another possibility is that the sunken "bateau" fragments first observed in 1954 and again later during "Operation Bateaux" were from a French watercraft that carried an eighteen-pounder French cannon (originally misidentified as a twenty-four-pounder) raised in 1954.[2] In 2014, I directed a team that did an inventory of the historic and replica artillery in the collection of the Fort William Henry Museum; the inventory was undertaken by a group of volunteer archaeologists, archaeology students, and amateur archaeologists and was completed for the French and Indian War Society, a not-for-profit corporation.[3] It is conceivable that after the French victory over the British at Fort William Henry in August 1757 a French bateau transporting a French eighteen-pounder iron cannon went down off Diamond Island. In 1966, a local newspaper article articulated the same thought, probably a theory professed by James A. Magee, who at that time was the Fort William Henry Museum curator. Magee was interviewed for a newspaper story. The 1966 news article reported "Because of the weight of the cannon and the lack of large water craft on Lake George in 1757, it is surmised that the cannon and its carrying batteaux [sic], or raft, sank on the trip to French Territory."[4] One bateau or other type of warship was reported to once be at Site VII; the shipwreck "appears" to be "gone." If so, possibly it was removed board by board by souvenir-collecting scuba divers, as the waters around Diamond Island and nearby reefs are among the most frequently dived in Lake George. **Zero bateaux at Site VII.**

*Bateau(x) Site VIII The wooden remains of at least two, possibly three, bateaux lying on top of one another in a cross-like formation. The cluster is in mid-lake off the head of the waterway. One sunken vessel was measured at about thirty feet long, and the other was twenty-four feet, three inches. There might be another bateau buried under this cross-like formation of bateau-class shipwrecks. The longer visible bateau rests partially over one end of the second visible bateau. Thus, the length of the shorter bateau could be more. Nearby was a mystery "vessel," possibly another buried bateau. A little over a hundred feet away is a pile of rocks, configured like a typical stone ballast pile, possibly rocks used to help sink a bateau. The rock pile, roughly in the oval shape of a bateau, was about the length of a typical colonial bateau. A couple of pieces of wood lay nearby, too, but we were unable to determine if these were bateau planks or simply miscellaneous wooden debris. We always wondered if the structural remains of another bateau lay buried under these rocks because of its shape, length, and proximity to the other two or three bateaux. Two bateaux at this site show heavy structural damage. A modern-era anchor lies embedded at the site, too. Bateaux Below's Russell P. Bellico first informed me of this site. He was told of the assemblage in the 1980s by a local scuba shop proprietor. **Two to four bateaux at Site VIII.**

*Bateau(x) Site IX Two sunken bateaux lie off Fort William Henry Museum. This is believed to be the bateaux site observed by scuba diver Carl Dunn in the early 1950s. Bateaux Below divers first visited this site on April 27, 1996. The physical remains of one bateau shipwreck were measured at twenty-eight feet, six inches long, and the second shipwreck, about twenty feet away and closer to shore, was thirty-five feet, six inches long. Both shipwrecks had sinking rocks, football-sized cobble, and angular-shaped rubble on and around the two shipwrecks. **Two bateaux at Site IX.**

*Bateau(x) Site X This is a site of about five colonial bateaux off the west side of the lake in the waterway's South Basin. This shipwreck assemblage has unfortunately been heavily vandalized. After a lecture entitled "Documenting Lake George's Shipwrecks" that I presented on May 7, 1991, at the Schenectady Public Library in Schenectady, New York, a recreational scuba diver in the audience talked to me about this site. He said that years earlier he recovered a small caliber cannonball from this location. He did not indicate if he kept the artifact or donated it to a museum or historical society. **Five bateaux at Site X.**

*Bateau(x) Site XI At this site in the lake's Narrows, Crandall found a single "frame member" during his 1963–1964 fieldwork. He said the hull structure piece was like a bateau frame, but longer. This frame could be from a bateau-type vessel that had a protective bulwark atop the bateau hull, thus creating a type of floating gun battery. This site was later relocated by Bateaux Below divers. **One large bateau-like sunken vessel or a small floating battery at Site XI.**

*Bateau(x) Site XII ("Wit's Bateaux") This site, nicknamed "Wit's Bateaux" by the Bateaux Below team, was located by Bob Benway, John Farrell, and myself during shipwreck inventory reconnaissance on September 4 and 10, 1995. We were conducting scuba fieldwork to ground truth side-scan sonar targets from Klein side-scan sonar surveying conducted earlier in the year. On September 4, 1995, we located the first of two sunken bateaux. We noticed bateau frames protruding from a rocky pile area, probably bateau sinking rocks. Parts of the vessel were also embedded and covered with lake bottom sediment. This site was in the South Basin, and the first bateau we located had a centerline orientation perpendicular to shore. We revisited the bateau shipwreck on September 10, 1995, and discovered a second sunken bateau nearby but closer to shore. To our surprise, the second eighteenth-century boat's centerline orientation was parallel to the nearby shoreline. Most of the sunken bateaux we examined over the years tended to be oriented with the shipwrecks' centerline orientation toward shore, probably done by British soldiers when they deliberately sunk scores of bateaux in the late summer and early autumn of 1758. **Two bateaux at Site XII.**

Counting the bateaux for an inventory has been rather problematic. This inventory is based on both Terry Crandall's work over 1963–1964 and that of the Lake George Bateaux Research Team and Bateaux Below from 1987 to 2011. There certainly could be, and probably are, more sunken colonial bateaux in the waterway, especially near the north end of the waterway. Nonetheless, Bateaux Below's shipwreck inventory totals approximately forty to forty-seven sunken bateaux found in Lake George. However, not many decades ago, there were more bateau shipwrecks in the lake. Three bateaux were raised by Adirondack Museum in the early 1960s. One bateau was reportedly raised, probably post-1960, during a nonsanctioned recovery. State Police divers are believed to have retrieved one bateau in 1965. One possible bateau-like vessel, first found in 1954, has apparently disappeared or been covered over by sediment. Another colonial bateau is today probably covered by growing stream delta overburden. So, prior to these seven missing bateaux, there were about forty-seven to fifty-four known bateau warships embedded in the bottom sediments of Lake George. What is remarkable is that, based on these numbers, General Amherst's British forces were able to raise approximately two hundred or more bateaux from the lake in 1759. Presumably, many or all of these military bateaux were then allowed to dry, were repaired if necessary, and were then incorporated into Amherst's successful 1759 campaign against the French military in the Champlain Valley.

Also, stories have been emanating from back in the 1960s that a colonial bateau was discovered in the early 1960s near Sabbath Day Point. Additionally, oral history from the 1960s indicates a possibility of sunken bateaux in the Dunham's Bay area as well as around the north end of the lake. These are not included in the inventory numbers above. I hope that one day that ever elusive, relatively intact, and totally undisturbed colonial bateau shipwreck—so desperately sought during "Operation Bateaux" and by the Lake George Bateaux Research Team and Bateaux Below teams—will be found for archaeological study.

Chapter Eleven

Missing Bateau Shipwrecks

As described in the last chapter, one aspect about Lake George's sunken bateaux of 1758 remains rather mystifying. Approximately forty to forty-seven bateau shipwrecks are on Bateaux Below's submerged cultural resources inventory list. However, several sunken bateaux located nearly six decades ago are missing. I gave some information about these in chapter 10, but in this chapter we will consider these "disappeared" bateaux in greater detail.

Adirondack Museum diver Terry Crandall mapped eight bateau-class shipwrecks lying off the Wiawaka Holiday House, a mile north of the southeast corner of Lake George. However, in the late 1980s, Bateaux Below archaeological divers found only seven bateau shipwrecks in this assemblage. There is also a more modern wooden canoe lying in deeper water, just west of the Wiawaka bateaux cluster. Recreational divers have sometimes misidentified this twentieth-century canoe as an eighteenth-century bateau, thus adding to the confusion of sorting out the total number of sunken bateaux off the Wiawaka Holiday House estate.

Also missing from Lake George is a bateau shipwreck first located in 1960. It was observed again in 1963–1964 lying on the lake bottom near the mouth of a stream on the west side of the lake. The remnants of another bateau-like shipwreck, searched for by Crandall near Diamond Island, has also apparently disappeared. Additionally, there was a bateau shipwreck, one of five bateaux on the east side of the lake, that is now gone.

I now think I might know what happened to some of these lost or missing eighteenth-century watercraft. Let's start with the Wiawaka bateaux. On June 27, 1965, the *New York Times* published a story about a New York State Police scuba project, described in the newspaper as a "training program." State Police divers at Lake George reportedly raised an unknown number of 1758 sunken bateau shipwrecks from the historic waterway. A photograph in that *New York Times* article showed scuba divers recovering and handing bateau planks and frames to support staff aboard a State Police pontoon vessel.[1] During scuba dives in 1999 at "The Sunken Fleet of 1758" shipwreck preserve (aka Wiawaka bateaux), Bateaux Below divers were able

THE SUNKEN FLEET OF 1758: DETAIL AT SOUTHERN END

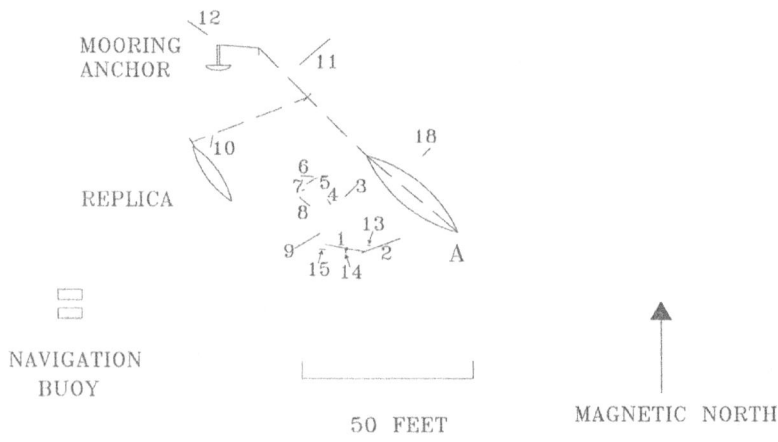

Figure 11.1 This map, generated by the Bateaux Below staff, shows an assemblage of disarticulated bateau frames and other hull structure lying to the south of Bateau A at "The Sunken Fleet of 1758" shipwreck preserve, sometimes called the Wiawaka bateaux. This is likely the location where an eighth 1758 sunken bateau at the Wiawaka site once rested. Parts of the colonial warship were recovered in a 1965 project undertaken by the New York State Police for the Adirondack Museum. (Credit: Bob Benway/Bateaux Below)

to determine the exact location of the missing eighth bateau shipwreck, presumably removed during this 1965 State Police training exercise. Numerous disarticulated bateau hull pieces, observed lying embedded in the lake bottom to the south of Bateau A, likely mark the spot of the so-called missing eighth bateau.[2]

On October 7, 1995, during shipwreck inventory fieldwork, Bateaux Below's Bob Benway and I made a reconnaissance dive to search for a sunken bateau reported to be lying off a stream, called English Brook, that flows into the west side of the lake. We spent nearly an hour swimming search **transects**, but we discovered no evidence of a sunken bateau. According to 1960s newspaper accounts, this colonial bateau was part of what the media called the "Ghost Fleet." The English Brook-area bateau was discovered in mid-August 1960. The August 15, 1960, issue of *The Troy Record* reported in an article entitled "Find Another 'Ghost Fleet' Boat," that three Albany, New York, divers—Darold Cerrone, Stanford Zeccolo, and Daniel Donnelly—located the sunken boat on the west side of the lake lying in twenty-five feet of water. The newspaper account indicated that the divers reported the sunken eighteenth-century watercraft to be in excellent condition.[3]

This was the third bateau-related discovery of the summer of 1960. The first was a find of approximately "14 craft" made on July 15, 1960, by two teenage sport divers; sometimes this number of sunken bateaux was listed at ten to fifteen. The second discovery was "a large double deck mortar carrier" reportedly found a week later by two Saratoga Springs, New York divers Walter Stroup and Fred Tarrant. As previously noted, another news story suggests that Charles Diehl and some of his dive buddies might have first located the shipwrecks in 1959.[4] Further, Lewis L. Smith claimed that on June 26, 1960, he and his scuba buddies found a vessel that might have been the "mortar bomb bateau." The "motor bomb" watercraft was possibly an oversized bateau, or perhaps two bateaux affixed in outrigger fashion to support its weighty cargo of about forty iron mortar bombs.[5]

The English Brook bateau shipwreck could also have been French since that area was just a few hundred yards from Artillery Cove, where French General Montcalm landed his forces in August 1757. Following Bateaux Below's October 7, 1995, scuba search to relocate the sunken bateau near English Brook, we made other dives at the area, but we did not find any remains of a submerged bateau craft.

Later, I reviewed aerial photography and compared the photos with maps from the 1960s. I then discussed this with a scientist at the Darrin Fresh Water Institute in Bolton Landing, New York. We concluded it is most likely that the sunken colonial bateau lying off English Brook is now covered with alluvial sedimentation from the ever-growing delta at the mouth of the stream, rapidly formed over the past several decades.

The remnants of a third bateau shipwreck, documented by Terry Crandall (Adirondack Museum) in 1963–1964 near Diamond Island, have seemingly vanished from its reported location on a sand and silt lake bottom.[6] If so, this was likely due to extensive sport diver visitation in this area and souvenir-collecting neoprene explorers. For decades, Diamond Island has been one of the most popular scuba destinations on the lake. The island is easily accessible by small boat from the south end of the lake, has several state-administered docks for day use by visitors, has picnic tables for visitors to have meals, and the waters around the state-administered island are known for very good visibility, generally twenty-five feet or greater.

The Diamond Island sunken "bateau" might not have been part of Lake George's sunken bateaux but instead associated with British-directed forces stationed on Diamond Island during General John Burgoyne's 1777 British campaign to seize Albany, New York. If this reputed bateau is from the Revolutionary War era, this would certainly be a noteworthy submerged cultural resource to

Figure 11.2 Robert Lennan stands next to two grapnel anchors that his dive buddy Jim Carney and he discovered in 1954 at the site of a Lake George colonial shipwreck, possibly a bateau. (Credit: Fort William Henry Museum)

investigate to be able to compare bateau dimensions and construction techniques from two different colonial conflicts—the French and Indian War (1755–1763) and the American Revolution (1775–1783).

However, as briefly mentioned earlier, another possibility exists as to the origin of the so-called Diamond Island "bateau" that deserves further consideration. In 1954, two recreational divers found a large French iron cannon sunk off the island. The reputed Diamond Island "bateau" was probably associated with this artillery piece.

Two sport divers, Robert Lennan and Jim Carney, first observed the shipwreck in 1954 during scuba exploration. They recovered a cannon and two anchors from the sunken vessel. The iron artillery piece was depicted as being French, and the two anchors were described as "five-pronged anchors." The cannon was said to have been "resting on the planks of a French and Indian War gunboat."[7] The term—gunboat—is a popular term for any light watercraft mounted with artillery. Thus an armed bateau could be characterized as a gunboat.

It should also be mentioned that nearly a quarter-century earlier, on June 26, 1930, the *Binghamton Press* reported that "Near the head of the lake [Lake George] is a sloop, sunk during the Revolutionary War, and a brass cannon, near Diamond Island, a relic of the Battle fought between Captain Aubrey and Colonel Brown, during the Revolution."[8] This short news account might be a reference to the Diamond Island shipwreck where divers Lennan and Carney retrieved the French siege cannon. However, the 1930 report might be about another shipwreck, an armed sloop, lost in 1777 by Colonel John Brown, an American patriot officer, during a retreat following an artillery duel between his flotilla of warships and enemy soldiers stationed on Diamond Island. Brown's sloop was reportedly lost a mile or more to the east of Diamond Island.[9]

Lennan described their unexpected underwater discovery as occurring during a recreational scuba dive while "out for our health."[10] Lennan was a schoolteacher from the suburbs of New York City. He also worked as a waiter that summer at a Lake George lodge. Lennan's scuba buddy that day was Jim Carney, his boss at the lakeside hotel. The two divers first spotted a single iron anchor and then a second. About fifteen feet from the second anchor they noticed an old sunken boat embedded in the lake bottom with wooden planks and protruding ribs (frames). Lennan later commented that as they approached the shipwreck, "we found the cannon. It looked tremendous in the dimness."[11]

The two anchors and French cannon discovered by Lennan and Carney were raised on September 3, 1954. A floating derrick named the *Beaver*, owned by the Lake George Steamboat Company, was employed to raise the heavy artillery piece

Figure 11.3 Robert Lennan poses next to a massive French siege cannon as it is being delivered to Fort William Henry Museum in 1954. Lennan and a dive buddy discovered the artillery piece lying inside a Lake George shipwreck, possibly a bateau. (Credit: Fort William Henry Museum)

from the lake bottom. The divers sold the cannon and the two anchors to Harold Veeder, president of the Fort William Henry Corporation.[12]

The cannon was tentatively identified as a French smoothbore eighteen-pounder, meaning it fired an eighteen-pound cannonball. The two grapnel anchors recovered were rather tall in height, nearly coming up to Lennan's shoulders. This style of anchor was generally employed to grab onto an object underwater, suggesting there possibly was a salvage attempt to either raise the sunken vessel or retrieve its valuable cargo, the massive iron siege gun. It is unlikely a cannon of this size and weight would have been employed to "arm" a standard-sized bateau for combat purposes on a waterway.

Today, the enormous cannon sits on exhibit on the parade ground of replica Fort William Henry (aka Fort William Henry Museum). The two anchors are also displayed in the museum's historical exhibitions, a popular tourist attraction at the south end of the lake that is generally open to the public from May into early November of each year.

In 2014, I directed a group of dedicated volunteers in an inventory of artillery pieces, both historic and replica, in the collection at Fort William Henry Museum. The 1954-recovered French cannon was one of the armament pieces that we examined. The Fort William Henry Museum staff originally gave the artillery artifact the inventory catalogue designation—LM-48. Earlier in its museum career, the cannon rested on a garrison carriage, but today it is mounted on a field carriage. The artillery piece measures 9 feet, 1/2 inch long (from the forward end of the muzzle to the aft end of the tube, less the cascabel). It measures 9 feet, 9-1/2 inches in its extreme (overall) length. At the breech (rear) end of this ordnance you can still make out several letters—LA MARINE. Though the cannon has had no professional conservation—only coats of black paint, a popular method of "conserving" and displaying artillery artifacts in the 1950s and 1960s—the military artifact is in remarkable condition. It is certainly well worth a visit to Fort William Henry Museum to peruse this exceptional eighteenth-century artillery relic.

Fortunately, this unique cannon survived a September 17, 1967, arson fire at replica Fort William Henry that destroyed much of the west side of the museum. The large French gun appears to have been undamaged during the fierce inferno.[13]

The shipwreck site found in 1954 by Lennan and Carney was later dived by Lewis L. Smith and his dive partners. Harold Veeder, one of the principals of Fort William Henry Corporation, probably provided Dr. Robert Bruce Inverarity with the exact location where the French cannon and two anchors were found and recovered in 1954. In 1960, Inverarity asked Lewis L. Smith to dive the area, and Smith relocated the shipwreck.

Smith described seeing frames and about thirty-five feet of a "keel" of what he called a "Gunboat."[14] I believe the historic Diamond Island "bateau" shipwreck was probably removed by non-preservation scuba enthusiasts during the 1960s, 1970s, and early 1980s when scuba diving was becoming quite popular at Lake George.

Archaeological sleuthing has likewise revealed that a fourth missing bateau, one of a cluster of five bateau-class shipwrecks in the South Basin, was removed from the waterway during an illegal salvage conducted in the 1960s or 1970s.[15] Sadly, another sunken bateau in that assemblage lies dilapidated on a crude lifting frame fashioned from cinder blocks and lumber. That bateau's structural integrity has been severely compromised from this second unauthorized recovery venture.

Approximately forty to forty-seven known bateau shipwrecks appear on Bateaux Below's Lake George submerged cultural resources inventory list. However, the seven sunken Wiawaka bateau vessels are the only bateau-class shipwrecks listed on the National Register of Historic Places (N.R. listing, 1992). Additionally, the Wiawaka bateaux are part of a state-administered shipwreck park for visiting scuba divers. This shipwreck preserve site for scuba divers is called "The Sunken Fleet of 1758" and is part of a unique state park administered by the New York State Department of Environmental Conservation. The three shipwreck preserve sites—"The Sunken Fleet of 1758," "The *Forward* Underwater Classroom," and "*Land Tortoise*: A 1758 Floating Gun Battery"—are collectively known as Lake George's "Submerged Heritage Preserves." It holds the distinction as being the first state park in the Empire State for scuba diver visitation.

Fortunately, national, state, and local historic preservation laws protect Lake George's historic shipwrecks. However, local and state authorities need to conduct a more aggressive campaign to inform both scuba divers and the general public about these finite heritage resources. Better shore side signage is needed. An ongoing public outreach campaign in which marine patrols, dive shops, marinas, and tourism outlets disseminate brochures to boaters and divers, as well as other innovative educational programs, would aid in safeguarding these vulnerable submerged cultural resources. Granted, there is a much greater historic preservation ethic practiced by scuba divers today who visit the "Queen of American Lakes." We can only hope that the surviving colonial shipwrecks will not be vandalized or have boat anchors dropped on them. They require protection so that future generations can enjoy and gain greater knowledge about the lake's historic past. Archaeology alone cannot protect these non-renewable cultural resources.

Chapter Twelve

Lake George's *Baby Whale* Submarine

The year 1960 was certainly significant in the history of Lake George's sunken bateaux. Two teenage sport divers rediscovered several bateau shipwrecks at the head of the lake. Later that summer, a fifteen-foot yellow research submarine, constructed by three local men to photograph Lake George's sunken bateaux of 1758, disappeared one summer night from its dock on the east side of the lake. The missing small research submarine caused a news sensation. Scuba divers were brought in to search for the stolen sub as airplanes flew over the lake looking for a submerged yellow object. The media spent days covering this fascinating news story.

This submarine, called *Baby Whale*, disappeared from its berth over the evening of August 4, 1960. Local residents James Parrott, Gerald Root, and Art Jones fabricated the underwater exploratory craft. In many respects, the yellow submarine was "a product of its time."

On January 23, 1960, the Italian-built bathyscaphe, later purchased by the U.S. Navy, made a deep plunge into the Marianas Trench of the Pacific Ocean. The bathyscaphe, a free diving, self-propelled submersible-type undersea vessel, reached a record depth of 35,813 feet. It carried a crew of two, Jacques Piccard, the son of the vessel's designer, Swiss oceanographer Auguste Piccard, and James Walsh, a U.S. Navy officer.[1] That scientific dive into the

Figure 12.1 Photograph of the fifteen-foot *Baby Whale* research submarine during its construction. The underwater vehicle was built in 1960 to help photograph the sunken bateaux of 1758. (Credit: Bateaux Below Collection)

Figure 12.2 The *Baby Whale* submarine in 1960 as it is being attached to its concrete keel before being put on Lake George. (Credit: Bateaux Below Collection)

deepest part of our oceans captivated Americans and probably inspired Parrott, Root, and Jones to design and fashion a homemade submarine to explore the underwater world of Lake George.

Following the *Baby Whale*'s disappearance, stolen from its dock in August 1960, there was a surge of activity to recover the missing submarine. That initial search effort failed to locate the underwater vehicle. The yellow submarine soon became part of the lore of the lake, a "Holy Grail of shipwrecks" awaiting curious explorers.

On June 18, 1995, Bateaux Below's Bob Benway and I were fortunate enough to be the first to discover the sunken *Baby Whale* submarine during a shipwreck reconnaissance dive in deep water in Lake George's South Basin. Bateaux Below's shipwreck inventory that year was supported by a grant from the Rural New York Historic Preservation Grant Program administered by the Preservation League of New York State with support of the J.M. Kaplan Fund. Our submarine discovery was announced in early August 1995 to mark the thirty-fifth anniversary of the submarine's disappearance.[2]

The research submarine reportedly weighed 3,700 pounds and was constructed of aluminum, iron, and concrete. The sub had a single glass viewport, twelve inches in diameter, located on its starboard side. The portal was for photography and undoubtedly to aid in navigating the underwater vehicle. The submarine also had a conning tour, exterior ballast tanks, and handrails.

The sub was not quite finished when it was stolen. Newspapers reported that the subsurface vessel had been tested in the lake, being towed behind a motorboat to determine if the underwater vehicle was stable for surface navigation. Surfacing gear, a propeller, and a battery-powered motor were yet to be installed in the sub. The *Baby Whale* was designed for use in twenty-five to thirty feet of water, the depth of many of the waterway's sunken colonial bateaux. According to an article in the August 4, 1960, issue of the *Glens Falls Times*, the submarine would be used to photograph "the fleet of old bateaux" recently relocated in the lake, as well as to acquire photographs of the "twin-deck sloop" (i.e., "mortar bomb bateau") discovered that summer in Lake George. The submarine had not yet been rigged with its "glass ball turret for photography."[3]

Following news coverage of our 1995 discovery of the yellow submarine, Bateaux Below researchers received information from a man who claimed to have been involved with the submarine's 1960 disappearance. The person recalled that the sub's disappearance thirty-five years earlier was a prank. The informant told Benway that one night a couple of people tried to transport the unique vessel from one part of the waterway to another. The pair tied a line to the submarine that was berthed at a dock on the lake and used a powerboat to tow the vessel on the surface, intending to transport it to another pier across the lake. The "tom foolery" nearly turned deadly when the person riding inside the submarine attempted to use a hammer to free something from the interior of the sub. The iron mallet unexpectedly struck the only glass port on the underwater vehicle, and the sub began to slowly sink. Both young pranksters escaped as the *Baby Whale* descended into the dark depths of Lake George.[4]

Figure 12.3
Following scuba diving by Bateaux Below personnel to photograph, videotape, and map the *Baby Whale* submarine, this interpretive image of the 1960 sunken submarine was created. (Credit: Linda Schmidt/ Bateaux Below)

After the submarine's 1995 discovery, several scuba visits were made to the underwater craft where archaeological divers videotaped, photographed, measured, and drew the odd-looking shipwreck. The Bateaux Below research team consisted of Benway (archaeological diver), Vince Capone (remote sensing specialist), John Farrell (archaeological diver), Scott Padeni (archaeological diver), Linda Schmidt (illustrator), and myself (project director).

Bateaux Below's John Farrell, an accomplished ship modeler and diorama artist, later fashioned a scale model of the *Baby Whale* submarine based on Bateaux Below's recordation of the underwater vehicle. During an interview for the 2010 documentary "Wooden Bones: The Sunken Fleet of 1758," he gave a brief description of the unusual craft:

> [T]he Lake George sub known as *Baby Whale* or aka "Yellow Submarine" ... seemed to be ... fabricated from oil tanks 275 gallon oil tanks welded together and that was the main body of the sub and then ... the flotation on either side was provided by what appear to be water tanks, ... two on each side on the upper part of the vessel. The ballast were ... two water tanks supposedly filled with concrete giving ... it an approximate mass of 2,000 pounds as ballast for the bottom of the submarine. And ... shrouding in the ... bow and stern of the submarine was provided by ... 55 gallon drums which had been cut in half and the conning tower was a half of an upright 55 gallon drum.[5]

The 1960 *Baby Whale* research submarine is noteworthy because it represented one of the first attempts to apply modern underwater technology to document Lake George's sunken bateaux of 1758. The fifteen-foot-long subsurface vehicle was constructed shortly after the U.S. Navy's success with the *Trieste*'s dives to over 35,800 feet in the Marianas Trench. Therefore, you could argue, the Lake George submarine is an icon of that era of early underwater scientific exploration.

Shortly after the unexpected discovery of the *Baby Whale*, the State of New York ruled that because none of the submarine's three owners had kept looking for the sunken submarine that the underwater research vehicle was "abandoned." It was thus determined that the aluminum and iron submarine shipwreck was the property of the State of New York. The Submerged Lands & Natural Resources Manager, Bureau of Land Management, New York State Office of General Services granted permission to Bateaux Below to place a sign next to the submarine shipwreck to help protect and preserve the submerged cultural resource.[6] The sign, installed on July 28, 1995, read:

Figure 12.4 Photograph of the sunken Lake George *Baby Whale* submarine after it was found in 1995 by Bateaux Below divers. (Credit: Bob Benway/Bateaux Below)

Property of the
State of New York
Submarine "Shipwreck"
Do Not Touch or Disturb
Sign Funded by Bateaux Below, Inc.

Today, because the shipwreck is over fifty years old, because it is significant in the history of early underwater technology being employed in the documentation of Lake George shipwrecks (Criterion B, National Register of Historic Places Criteria for Evaluation), and because future underwater archaeology at the submarine site might one day yield more information about the history of the Lake George watercraft (Criterion D, National Register of Historic Places Criteria for Evaluation), the *Baby Whale* shipwreck should be nominated by the State of New York for listing on the National Register of Historic Places.

The story of Lake George's 1960 *Baby Whale* research submarine was wonderfully told in the 2010 documentary "Wooden Bones: The Sunken Fleet of 1758" (Pepe Productions & Bateaux Below, Inc.).

Chapter Thirteen
Wiawaka Bateaux and the National Register of Historic Places

From a personal perspective, one of the most gratifying projects that I had the pleasure to be involved with during our quarter-of-a-century fieldwork study of Lake George's sunken bateaux of 1758 was collaborating with other Bateaux Below members to research, write, and help get the seven shipwrecks of the Wiawaka bateaux cluster listed in 1992 onto the National Register of Historic Places. Bateaux Below members initiated the undertaking after being encouraged to do so by James P. Delgado, the Maritime Historian of the National Park Service and the Head of the National Maritime Initiative in the early 1990s. Delgado had also recently served as the lead author for *National Register Bulletin 20*. That informative publication provided a rationale for and the step-by-step methodology to nominate historic floating ships and shipwrecks to this important registry. Years later, Delgado would go on to become a prolific author, specializing in books on a vast variety of topics in underwater archaeology and maritime history. When drafting the National Register nomination for the Wiawaka bateaux, we were also fortunate to have the guidance and support of one of our state's most dedicated public servants, Mark L. Peckham. He was the New York State Office of Parks, Recreation and Historic Preservation's case manager for the Wiawaka bateaux shipwreck site nomination, and a scuba diver as well. During the National Register nomination process, Peckham was a Program Assistant at the Field Services Bureau of the New York State Office of Parks, Recreation and Historic Preservation. He later served as director of the Bureau of Historic Sites and Parks, New York State Division for Historic Preservation.

The primary writers for the Bateaux Below nomination draft were Dr. Russell P. Bellico and myself. Others who contributed to the nomination writing or draft review process were Bob Benway, Vince Capone, Terry Crandall, John Farrell, R. Duncan Mathewson III, Jack Sullivan, and David Van Aken.[1] I am very grateful for their helpful input into the nomination draft.

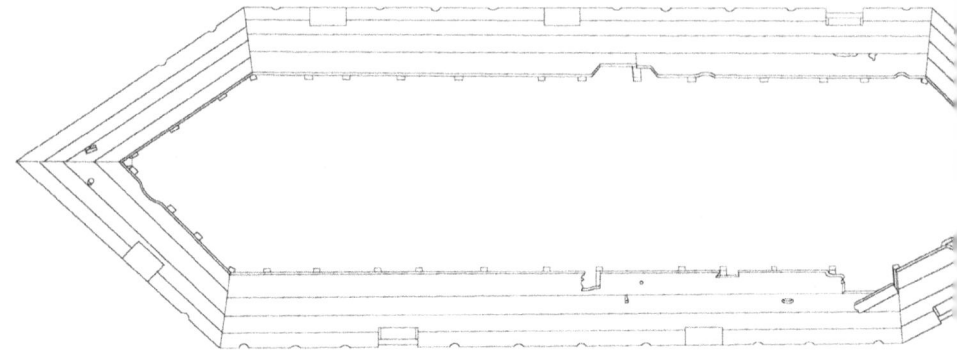

Figure 13.1 Drawing of the 1758 *Land Tortoise* radeau shipwreck. Discovered in 1990 during a Klein side-scan sonar survey at Lake George directed by the author, this fifty-two-foot British warship was studied by Bateaux Below over 1990–1993. Dr. D.K. (Kathy) Abbass, a Rhode Island archaeologist, oversaw the mapping endeavor, and the author served as project manager. In 1995, the one-of-a-kind radeau shipwreck was listed on the National Register of Historic Places, and in 1998 was designated a National Historic Landmark. (Credit: Bateaux Below Collection)

Figure 13.2 Bill Appling, one of Bateaux Below's volunteer scuba divers, holds two signs later installed at Lake George shipwreck sites listed on the National Register of Historic Places. (Credit: Bateaux Below Collection)

The Wiawaka bateaux site nomination and subsequent listing were quite noteworthy for the Empire State. The June 14, 1992, National Register listing of the Wiawaka bateaux site was the first shipwreck nomination in New York state in a dozen years. It was also the first National Register nomination proposal of a shipwreck from New York since the passage of the Abandoned Shipwreck Act of 1987. Bateaux Below sponsored the nomination.[2] Furthermore, this National Register nomination was a precedent for Bateaux Below to nominate and get several other significant Lake George shipwrecks listed on the National Register of Historic Places: the 1758 *Land Tortoise* radeau shipwreck (N.R. listing, 1995; National Historic Landmark listing, 1998), *Cadet* ex *Olive* shipwreck (N.R. listing, 2002), and the *Forward* shipwreck (N.R. listing, 2008).

Although the Bateaux Below team was able to get several different types of Lake George shipwrecks onto the National Register of Historic Places, one of my greatest personal disappointments was that we could get only one assemblage of sunken bateaux, the seven Wiawaka bateaux, designated to the National Register. Other bateau shipwrecks should also have been nominated and listed.

Shipwrecks in New York state waters—and for that matter, around the country—are an "underlisted" National Register category. Brick-and-mortar properties, primarily standing structures, such as historic buildings, appear to be top priority for the National Register of Historic Places designations. Simply put, greater emphasis needs to be directed to prepare more nominations of significant historic shipwrecks for listing onto the National Register of Historic Places. A lot of sweat equity goes into the National Register nomination process, but the result is well worth the time and effort.

Chapter Fourteen
Submerged Heritage Preserves

One of the most innovative submerged cultural resources public education programs at Lake George that promotes recreational and heritage tourism is the waterway's shipwreck preserve project. Kenneth J. Vrana, at the time an underwater archaeologist at Michigan State University, wrote in 1997, "Shipwreck preserves can be viewed as a type of protected area created primarily to enhance preservation of sunken watercraft in archaeological context."[1] A shipwreck preserve is much more, too. It is an underwater park for visiting scuba enthusiasts where divers can literally "dive into history."

In chapter 6, I addressed the Abandoned Shipwreck Act that would give additional protection for historic shipwrecks. Following the passage of the law, eleven public meetings were held around the country in September and October 1988 for the public to comment on the legislation and provide input into what should go into the act's forthcoming guidelines. Over 120 people presented their viewpoints at these forums, and approximately 130 people sent letters.[2] I was among those citizens who attended and testified at one of these hearings. Among the many points in the Abandoned Shipwreck Act's guidelines, the document encouraged states to create "underwater parks or preserves" and to facilitate "sport diver access to State-owned shipwreck sites."[3]

One of the early Lake George advocates for an "underwater museum" or shipwreck preserve at Lake George was Harrison K. Bird Jr. of Huletts Landing, New York. In 1964, Bird presented a visionary plan to create an "underwater museum" at the lake. At the time, historian Harrison K. Bird Jr. was the author of the books *Navies in the Mountains: The Battles on the Waters of Lake Champlain and Lake George, 1609–1814* and *March to Saratoga: General Burgoyne and the American Campaign, 1777*.

Most likely, Bird's idea was derived from the media publicity of the early 1960s about Lake George's so called "Ghost Fleet." Bird's 1964 proposal would have begun with a "Five Year Plan" to search for and locate all shipwrecks in the waterway, an endeavor that today is known as a "submerged cultural resources

Figure 14.1 In 1964, Lake George historian Harrison K. Bird Jr. believed that one day an "underwater museum" of shipwrecks at the waterway could be created by the state agencies so tourists could visit these sites using scuba or emerging technologies—submersibles and submarines. This hypothetical drawing shows the early twentieth-century gasoline-powered *Forward* shipwreck at Lake George with a scuba diver and submarine inspecting the watercraft. (Credit: Linda Schmidt/Bateaux Below)

inventory." However, that strategy would have been quite costly, though not as expensive as "salvaging" submerged artifacts and shipwrecks and then spending lots of money to conserve these submerged cultural resources for land-based exhibit. Harrison K. Bird Jr. suggested it "would be nice" if the state agencies worked cooperatively to facilitate tourist visitation to Lake George's numerous sunken vessels, thus promoting their historic preservation. With the emergence of submersibles during the 1960s, Bird thought that guided excursions for tourists to sunken vessels might one day become feasible.[4] Unfortunately, Bird's vision for an underwater museum of shipwrecks for public visitation under the direction of the State of New York was not adopted.

Over two decades after Bird's suggestion, Dr. Russell P. Bellico, a lake historian and avid scuba diver, organized a grassroots initiative to create a shipwreck park for scuba divers at Lake George. I was fortunate to be able to collaborate with Bellico in the mid- to late-1980s trying to get the 1910-built *Sayonara*, recently retired as an excursion and personal launch, donated to be sunk to establish a shipwreck park. The *Sayonara* had outlived its usefulness as a floating vessel and sat in a private boathouse near the lake's Narrows. We hoped that the aging hulk could be donated to our initiative, cleaned and sanitized of pollutants, and—with local and state government permission—sunk in a remote area of Lake George to establish a shipwreck-protected area. That vision of the small group that Bellico called the "Save the *Sayonara* Committee" was regrettably not realized. Sadly, the *Sayonara* yacht's owners had the historic vessel partially dismantled, removing its propulsion hardware and some of its upper works.[5] Then, in 1988, local firefighters in a controlled burn torched the remaining hull structure of the watercraft and also the boathouse where the vessel rested.[6] At the time, that ended our effort to establish a shipwreck preserve for visiting scuba divers at the "Queen of American Lakes."

Finally, after further hard work by Bateaux Below members, archaeologist Dr. D.K. (Kathy) Abbass, and some local and state governmental agencies, the first shipwreck preserve system in New York opened at Lake George on September 25, 1993. The Lake George shipwreck preserves system certainly benefitted from the Abandoned Shipwreck Act and also because Vermont, a state bordering New York, had in 1985 established an underwater dive park system, known as the "Vermont Underwater Historic Preserve Program."[7] Lake George's "Submerged Heritage Preserves" are administered by the State of New York's Department of Environmental Conservation, and the program initially consisted of two shipwreck sites.[8] As the first shipwreck preserve system in the Empire State, this essentially served as a pilot project for other waterways in the state. Although Lake George's shipwreck preserves program was directed by the New York State Department of Environmental Conservation, there were several other original "cooperating organizations and agencies"—New York State Office of Parks, Recreation and Historic Preservation, New York State Office of General Services, Lake George Park Commission, New York State Museum, New York State Divers Association, Warren County, and the Lake George Historical Association.[9] From 1993 to 2011, Bateaux Below, the principal non-government organization in this coalition, provided volunteer underwater archaeological services as well as scuba divers and boat support personnel to conduct the preserve system's seasonal set-up, to undertake seasonal monitoring of the shipwreck preserves, and to help close the shipwreck

THE SUNKEN FLEET OF 1758

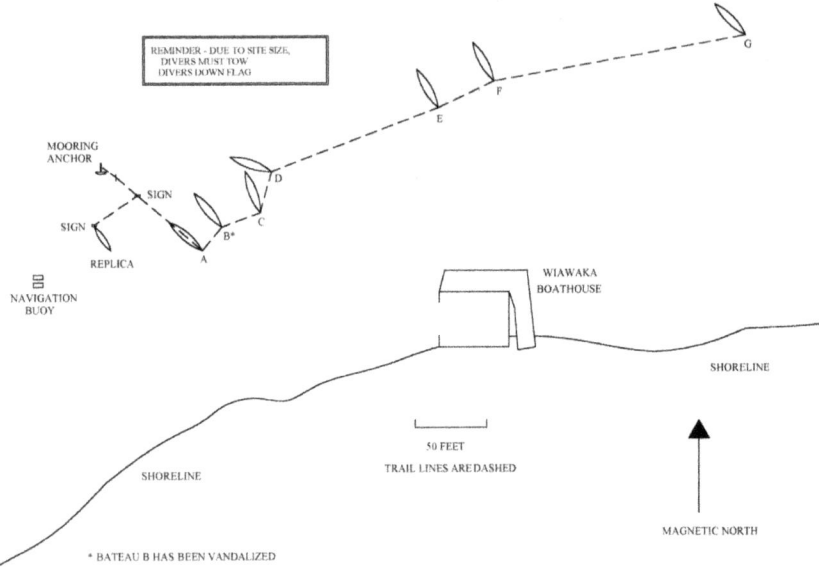

Figure 14.2 "The Sunken Fleet of 1758" shipwreck preserve opened in 1993. Four years later a replica bateau was sunk in Lake George to enhance diver visitation to the site. Original cartography by John Farrell; CAD by Bob Benway. (Credit: Bob Benway/Bateaux Below)

preserve sites at the end of each diving season. Such broad-based community and government support generally means the program has sustainability and will meet with much success.

Lake George's "Submerged Heritage Preserves" started in September 1993 with two shipwreck sites and had plans to expand that number. One of the first two preserves was "The *Forward*," a forty-five-foot-long, 1906-built, early gasoline-powered motor launch that rests in thirty-five to forty-five feet of water. The shipwreck preserve lies about 1,500 feet east of Diamond Island. The other shipwreck preserve was called "The Sunken Fleet of 1758."[i] This is the cluster of seven French and Indian War shipwrecks commonly known as the Wiawaka bateaux. These colonial-era bateaux measure from twenty-five to thirty-six feet in length and lie in about twenty to forty feet of water. "The Sunken Fleet of 1758"

---

i   As you have gathered, the Sunken Fleet of 1758 is a reference to British forces sinking over 260 warships at Lake George to protect the ships over the winter of 1758–1759, with a plan to raise the vessels in the late spring and early summer of 1759. What is somewhat confusing is that "The Sunken Fleet of 1758" is also the name of one of the three shipwreck preserves in Lake George, also known as the Wiawaka bateaux or Wiawaka bateaux cluster.

shipwreck preserve is located less than a mile north of Million Dollar Beach on the east side of Lake George.

The sunken vessels in Lake George's "Submerged Heritage Preserves" were first studied by archaeologists with Bateaux Below before they opened. Months were initially spent delving into the history of these shipwrecks, and then a few years were invested archaeologically mapping each shipwreck. Furthermore, numerous meetings were held with government officials as well as scores of letters sent over several years as part of a major lobbying effort to establish the state-administered shipwreck preserve system. Once the shipwreck park plan was adopted, the physical hardware then had to be acquired and installed. This included underwater signs, trail lines to guide divers around the site, a mooring system for each preserve, and a navigational aid buoy for each shipwreck preserve. Further, shipwreck preserve brochures had to be written and designed. Then funds had to be secured within the state government to print the shipwreck preserve brochures. This was not an easy task in a state known to move quite slowly in decision making (due in part to its mammoth government bureaucracy). As mentioned, in 1985, the tiny state of Vermont opened a shipwreck preserve program in Lake Champlain called the "Vermont Underwater Historic Preserve Program."[10] It was rather quickly established not only because of the efforts of the Champlain Maritime Society and the Basin Harbor Maritime Museum (later renamed the Lake Champlain Maritime Museum), two instrumental maritime heritage not-for-profit corporations, but also because of Vermont's smaller government administration. Vermont's less cumbersome state government was able to more easily cut through the red tape that often slows larger governments.

Each Lake George shipwreck preserve site was marked by a set of two buoys, one spherical mooring buoy for tying up a dive boat, and a second buoy, a barrel-shaped navigational aid with a light, to denote that there are surface buoys in the area, thus promoting boat navigation safety. Access to these two

Figure 14.3 Paul Cornell, at the time the president of the New York State Divers Association and also a volunteer with Bateaux Below, holds an informational sign installed at one of Lake George's Submerged Heritage Preserves. (Credit: Joseph W. Zarzynski)

State of New York

Submerged Heritage Preserve

The Sunken Fleet of 1758

French scouts on Rogers Rock observe the movement of General Abercromby's fleet to attack Carillon (Fort Ticonderoga) in July 1758. (Drawing courtesy of Gary Zaboly)

Figure 14.4 The cover of the tri-fold brochure for the 1993-established Submerged Heritage Preserve known as "The Sunken Fleet of 1758," the seven Wiawaka bateau shipwrecks. (Credit: New York State Department of Environmental Conservation and Bateaux Below)

preserve sites has been on a first-come, first-served basis. After a dive vessel ties up to the mooring buoy, scuba divers gear up and descend the mooring line (cable) to the lake bottom. There, informational signs greet scuba divers, who tour the preserve by following trail lines with similar signage.

When the shipwreck park program first opened in 1993, each preserve had its own informational brochure: "State of New York Submerged Heritage Preserve— The Sunken Fleet of 1758" and "State of New York Submerged Heritage Preserve— The *Forward*."[11] These brochures provided scuba divers with a brief history of the shipwreck(s), a drawing (in plan view) showing the shipwreck site, diver guidelines for safety and emergency information, a suggested reading list of books for more background about the sunken vessel(s), and a map that showed the location of each shipwreck preserve on the lake. After the initial 1993 season, in which the two preserves opened in late September, these two shipwreck preserves then opened over Memorial Day weekend (late May) and generally closed for the season in early October.

Bateaux Below had a Memorandum of Understanding (MOU) with the State of New York specifically spelling out what hardware and services the state would provide and what scuba monitoring services Bateaux Below would undertake. Basically, every seven to fourteen days, divers with Bateaux Below would visit each of the shipwreck preserves to check the hardware and inspect the shipwrecks. This "tender loving care" was necessary, too, as it ensured that the shipwreck preserves were safe for visiting scuba enthusiasts and that the submerged cultural resources, the historic sunken vessels, had not been vandalized or damaged during public visitation. About two to four times a month, I would send a short report to officials of the state agencies responsible for the custodial care of these historic shipwrecks. The state dispensed no pay to Bateaux Below

LAKE GEORGE
"Submerged Heritage Preserves"

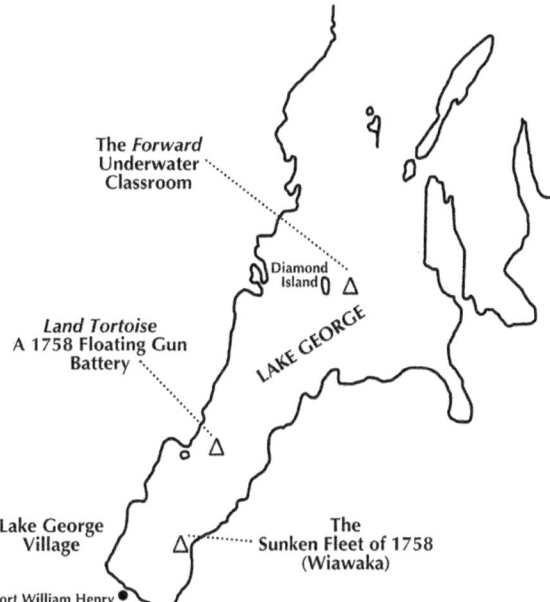

Figure 14.5 Map showing the south end of Lake George with the locations of the waterway's three shipwreck preserves for visiting scuba divers. (Credit: Peter Pepe)

members for their years of services, but the Town of Lake George did graciously provide dock space to berth a Bateaux Below boat. The town's generosity certainly helped Bateaux Below members execute their volunteer duties at the shipwreck preserves.

On July 26, 1994, less than a year after "The Sunken Fleet of 1758" and "The *Forward*" shipwreck preserves opened to the scuba diving public, two Long Island scuba divers were arrested for removing artifacts (bottles and leather goods) from "The Sunken Fleet of 1758" preserve. According to a local newspaper account, the two men were also scuba diving without using the red-and-white dive flag, required during scuba diving in the state, and they reportedly also possessed a spear gun, which was against local regulations.[12] This incident certainly tested the concept of shipwreck preserves for scuba divers on Lake George. Luckily, none of the bateau shipwrecks were damaged at that time.

A few weeks later, in August 1994, a third site, "*Land Tortoise*—A 1758 Floating Gun Battery," joined the lake's shipwreck preserve system.[13] This shipwreck is one of the most historic and significant sunken warships in the country.

When the shipwreck was found in June 1990, that discovery, along with the passage of the Abandoned Shipwreck Act of 1987 and the act's guidelines, persuaded the State of New York to begin working toward establishing a shipwreck preserve system in the Empire State. The ASA federal legislation combined with the efforts of Bateaux Below, the Lake George Historical Association, and the New York State Divers Association certainly pushed and finally influenced the State of New York to create Lake George's "Submerged Heritage Preserves." Kathy Abbass, who occasionally worked with Bateaux Below, was also instrumental in guiding the creation of the shipwreck preserve system to fruition. The New York State Department of Environmental Conservation had a "footprint" on Lake George, with logistical facilities on Green Island in the Town of Bolton and at Fort George Battlefield Park at the head of Lake George. Thus, that department was selected to be the state government agency to formally administer the shipwreck preserves on Lake George. Though the rank-and-file employees of this state agency were very dedicated in helping to manage the shipwreck preserves, the upper administration of the agency was sometimes not as enthusiastic in their administrative duties for the underwater park. In retrospect, it might have been more appropriate if back in 1993, when the shipwreck preserve system was established, that the New York State Office of Parks, Recreation and Historic Preservation was assigned the task of state governmental management of the lake's "Submerged Heritage Preserves." That state government entity's very name incorporates all three facets of what a shipwreck preserve for scuba divers is supposed to be—it's a park, it supports recreational tourism, and it promotes historic preservation of submerged cultural resources.

By the late 1990s, the Department of Environmental Conservation went to a single brochure format, with all three of the Lake George shipwreck preserves being incorporated into one publication. After a few years, the Department of Environmental Conservation was unable to generate sufficient funds to reprint several thousand copies of the shipwreck preserve brochures for dissemination to the public. The New York State Office of General Services, one of the state government partners in this recreational and heritage tourism experiment, thus stepped in and funded several printings of the brochures. As the Internet grew in popularity, the Department of Environmental Conservation finally put the "Submerged Heritage Preserves" brochure onto their agency's website (www.dec.ny.gov/lands/315.html), thus making the information easily available to both diving and non-diving sectors.

In 1997, "The Sunken Fleet of 1758" shipwreck preserve was enhanced when Bateaux Below, with state government permission, sank a twenty-three-foot, three-fourths-scale replica bateau at the preserve site. Ted

Figure 14.6 Bateaux Below's Bob Benway (right) and Bill Appling (left) examine the twenty-three-foot Caldwell replica bateau. After being donated by Ted Caldwell, the vessel was initially sunk near this dock in four feet of water so that its planks could swell and, when dried, reduce leaking. After a few weeks underwater, the boat was raised, and on September 7, 1997, it was sunk at "The Sunken Fleet of 1758" shipwreck preserve. The sunken replica provides scuba divers an opportunity to view an intact bateau in an underwater environment. (Credit: Joseph W. Zarzynski)

Caldwell of Bolton Landing, New York, kindly donated the replica bateau, which had been constructed several years earlier by Caldwell's students from the Bolton, Minerva, and Newcomb school systems. On September 7, 1997, Bateaux Below divers and other volunteers sank the replica bateau to provide visiting sport divers to the shipwreck preserve an opportunity to see what an intact bateau would look like.[14]

The replica vessel also gave Bateaux Below researchers an opportunity to test deliberate boat-sinking techniques practiced at Lake George in 1758. This likewise allowed "for the study of the long-term deterioration process of a wooden shipwreck in cold water."[15] The replica bateau sinking in 1997 was covered as a news story by both a local newspaper and television station, informing many non-diving regional community members about the merits of **experimental archaeology**.

Over 1997 and 1998, "The *Forward*" shipwreck preserve was remodeled and as a result became known as "The *Forward* Underwater Classroom." Supported by a $2,420 grant from the Fund for Lake George, Inc., Bateaux Below completed a transformation of the shipwreck preserve site. With formal permission granted by the State of New York, a wooden cabin cruiser was acquired. It was then inspected by a marine surveyor and was cleaned and sanitized of pollutants before it was deliberately sunk in Lake George. Bateaux Below divers then installed a triangular-shaped underwater trail system with informational stations. Subsequently, visiting scuba divers could learn about the site's underwater geology, fish life, types of vegetation, and how colors are lost at depth underwater. In August 1998, Bateaux Below published a 120-page report of the 1997–1998 remodeling of the shipwreck preserve entitled *Lake George's Forward: Historic Vessel, Shipwreck Preserve, and "Underwater Classroom."*[16]

One of the complementary aspects of historic preservation of Lake George's "Submerged Heritage Preserves" is that all three shipwreck sites in the preserves have been listed on the National Register of Historic Places. This will be covered in more detail later in the book, but to summarize, in 1992, the Wiawaka bateaux cluster, later also known as "The Sunken Fleet of 1758" shipwreck preserve, was listed on the National Register. In 1995, the 1758 *Land Tortoise* radeau was listed on the National Register, and in 1998 was designated a National Historic Landmark. The shipwreck preserve is known as *"Land Tortoise*: A 1758 Floating Gun Battery." Finally, in 2008, the *Forward* shipwreck site was listed on the National Register of Historic Places. As mentioned, today the *Forward* site is known as "The *Forward* Underwater Classroom" shipwreck preserve.[17]

Lake George's three shipwreck preserves enjoyed early popularity, but after several years, diver visitation began to decline. Part of this was due to a lack of publicity about the program by the state. Many scuba-diving destinations around the country, especially in Florida, are heavily promoted and advertised for their recreational tourism. Over the years, the Department of Environmental Conservation was not able to find funds to regularly reprint the shipwreck brochures to make them readily available to regional dive shops, chambers of commerce, and other tourist-related venues in the greater Lake George/Adirondacks region. Nor was there a central Internet website that promoted scuba diving around the many waterways of the Empire State. After eighteen seasons (1993–2011) of volunteer work with the archaeology, seasonal preserve set-up, preserve monitoring, and annual preserve closing, in 2011, Bateaux Below relinquished its volunteer monitoring duties of Lake George's "Submerged Heritage Preserves." Simply stated, Father Time had caught up with Bateaux Below as members became older, one member resigned, another key volunteer turned to scientific diving, studying aquatic invasive species at Lake George, and two members suffered health problems that limited their abilities to conduct scuba fieldwork. The organization thus simply retired from its formal fieldwork duties. In midsummer

2011, three non-government organizations—a scuba shop, a dive club, and a dive charter—collectively picked up the monitoring responsibilities for the Department of Environmental Conservation. My hope is that this coalition of volunteers and others can work effectively with the state agencies on the cultural resources management aspect of this noteworthy program—Lake George's "Submerged Heritage Preserves." I am certainly appreciative of this collective effort.

The three shipwreck preserves have also become focal points of interest for heritage tourism for non-divers. At the time of this writing, two excursion boat companies at the south end of the lake—the Lake George Steamboat Company and Lake George Shoreline Cruises—run several tour vessels on the waterway that regularly motor past all three shipwreck preserves. Narrated information about the shipwreck preserves are sometimes included by the excursion boat pilots during these popular boat tours. These maritime tourism companies should be applauded for their public outreach efforts.

Sadly, the waterway's shipwreck preserves have had a few cases of diver vandalism. One of the most publicized occurred in July 1994, as described earlier. Several other incidents of scuba diver vandalism have occurred as well, especially at the 1758 *Land Tortoise* radeau shipwreck preserve, where visiting sport divers have tried to steal cannon port lids. Nonetheless, the positive aspects of the shipwreck preserve program, promoting such things as historic preservation, heritage tourism, and sport diver recreation, far outweigh the relatively few problems.[18]

Largely because of Bateaux Below's work on Lake George's shipwreck preserves and other related programs, in August 2009, Bateaux Below received a letter from the White House and First Lady Michelle Obama notifying us that the Volunteers of Bateaux Below, Inc. were recipients of a "Preserve America Steward" designation. Preserve America is "a federal initiative that encourages and supports community efforts to preserve and enjoy" the nation's "priceless cultural and natural heritage."[19] The Preserve America program is administered "in cooperation with the Advisory Council on Historic Preservation and in partnership with the U.S. Departments of Agriculture, Commerce, Defense, Education, Housing and Urban Development, Interior, and Transportation; U.S. General Services Administration; National Endowment for the Humanities; President's Committee on the Arts and the Humanities; Institute of Museum and Library Services; and the President's Council on Environmental Quality."[20]

Bateaux Below and its volunteers were one of only two recipients nationwide to receive the prestigious recognition during that designation period in 2009. The honor recognized the Volunteers of Bateaux Below, Inc. for exemplary efforts caring for the historic resources sunk in Lake George, especially as volunteers maintaining

PRESERVE AMERICA
Explore and Enjoy Our Heritage

BATEAUX BELOW, INC.
is designated as a
2009 PRESERVE AMERICA STEWARD
in recognition of its

PRESERVATION OF LAKE GEORGE'S
SUBMERGED HERITAGE PRESERVES

*With appreciation for the efforts
of its volunteers
in preserving cultural resources
for the benefit of present and future generations.*

Michelle Obama
MICHELLE OBAMA
First Lady of the United States

Figure 14.7 Bateaux Below's 2009 "Preserve America Steward" certificate awarded for the "Preservation of Lake George's Submerged Heritage Preserves." (Credit: Bateaux Below Collection)

a state-administered shipwreck park for scuba divers called "Submerged Heritage Preserves." The shipwreck park opened in September 1993 and was the first of its kind in the state. Bateaux Below members and other docents conducted the volunteer monitoring of the shipwreck park from 1993 into mid-2011, when the team finally retired from that duty.

The Preserve America Steward award recognized the efforts of Bateaux Below's eleven principal volunteers: Dr. Russell Bellico, Bob Benway, Dr. Samuel Bowser, Vince Capone, Paul Cornell, Terry Crandall, John Farrell, Elinor (Mossop) Gottschalk, Peter Pepe, Steven C. Resler, and Joseph W. Zarzynski.

Among Bateaux Below's other contributions that helped in receiving this federal designation were (1) getting several historic shipwrecks listed onto the National Register of Historic Places; (2) opening the first shipwreck preserve system in the Empire State; (3) working with a local documentary production company to produce a national award-winning documentary about Lake George's 1758 *Land Tortoise* radeau shipwreck; and (4) initiating other public outreach programs.

First Lady Michelle Obama was the Honorary Chair for the Preserve America program in 2009. In her letter, the First Lady thanked Bateaux Below for its efforts "to care for our Nation's important historic resources"—a recognition that all Bateaux Below volunteers certainly appreciated.[21]

Chapter Fifteen

Stabilizing a Bateau Shipwreck Site

One of the more unusual projects for site protection of the seven sunken bateaux of "The Sunken Fleet of 1758" shipwreck preserve was an endeavor conducted in 1999. The project was supported by grant funds from the Fund for Lake George, Inc. The effort was a cleanup of modern-era debris that threatened the structural integrity of the seven colonial bateau shipwrecks. We also accomplished a site stabilization assessment of the shipwreck preserve site, especially since Bateau B, one of the seven 1758 bateau shipwrecks in the Wiawaka bateaux, had been vandalized by one or more scuba divers in 1988.

With permission from the ad-hoc Committee for Submerged Cultural Resources, the multi-agencies state government entity with the responsibility to manage the welfare of the Empire State's shipwrecks, Bateaux Below devised a plan to stabilize the Wiawaka bateaux site. We identified logs, large branches, and modern-day (under fifty years old) dock debris that was located "up slope" from several of the historic bateau shipwrecks. Those debris pieces were mapped and then removed. This refuse could have easily become dislodged from the muddy embankment where the sunken bateaux are embedded and rolled down the underwater slope. This would probably damage one or more of the sunken warships.

In 1999, Bateaux Below divers made twenty-three team dives on this project. A representative from the New York State Office of Parks, Recreation and Historic Preservation also dived with our group. Since the Wiawaka Holiday House estate had been listed on the National Register of Historic Places in 1998,[1] the state agency was concerned that some of the submerged debris could be from one of the historic structures that once stood nearby on shore. The archaeological divers did locate a single submerged nineteenth-century wooden building structure fragment. The Office of Parks, Recreation and Historic Preservation officer informed Bateaux Below that the piece was deemed "historic" and should therefore not be removed or touched.

THE SUNKEN FLEET OF 1758: DEBRIS THAT WAS MOVED OR REMOVED

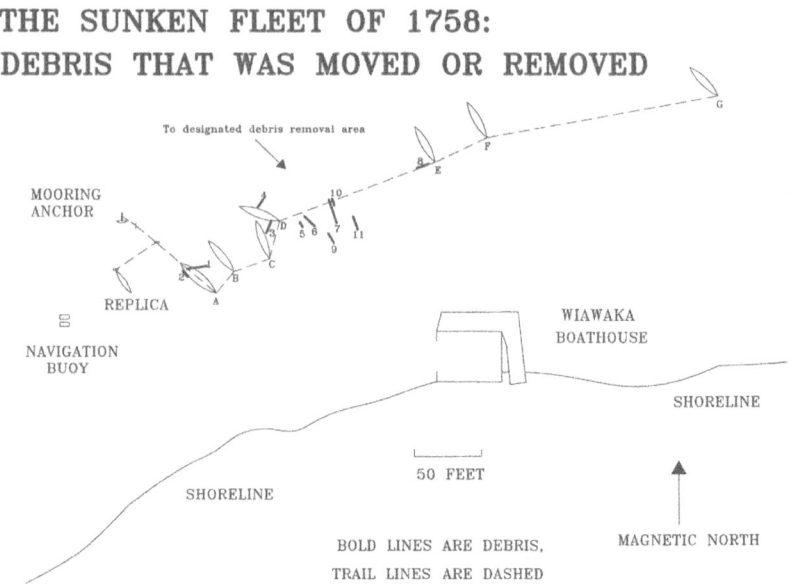

Figure 15.1 Map showing eleven pieces of debris that were either removed from Lake George or moved to another spot in the waterway because they threatened the structural integrity of the historic bateau shipwrecks. This work was completed during a 1999 site stabilization project at "The Sunken Fleet of 1758" shipwreck preserve. Cartography by John Farrell and Bob Benway; CAD by Bob Benway. (Credit: Bob Benway/Bateaux Below)

During the initial phase of the site stabilization project, debris pieces were first mapped into the preserve site plan. The ad-hoc Committee for Submerged Cultural Resources directed that the scuba team could move the natural debris—logs and branches—away from the sunken bateaux, but to keep those sunken tree logs and branches in the lake. However, manmade materials, such as the modern-era dock planks, that were not determined to be historic were to be removed from the waterway. During this fieldwork, Charles Vandrei, the Department of Environmental Conservation's Historic Preservation Officer, was on hand one day aboard a state boat to direct the Bateaux Below divers. Five pieces of large natural debris (logs and sturdy tree branches) were moved to a designated area in the lake northwest of the Wiawaka bateaux. Six pieces of abandoned dock fragments were removed from the waterway. The dock refuse lumber was later cut up for campers to use as firewood at state campsites around the lake. During the project, the larger lumber and timber fragments necessitated that the dive team employ a lift bag to move the heavy material.[2]

THE SUNKEN FLEET OF 1758: DEBRIS THAT WAS REMOVED FROM LAKE

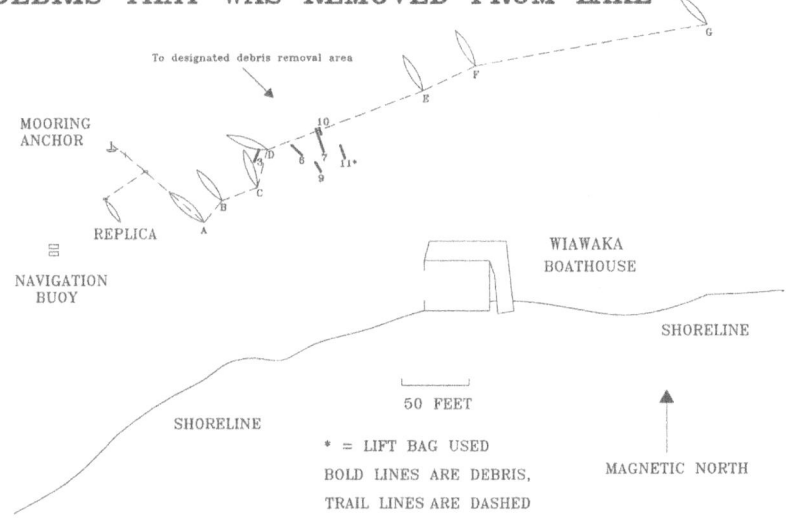

Figure 15.2 Map showing manmade debris (six modern-era dock planks: 3, 6, 7, 9, 10, and 11) removed from the lake as part of a 1999 site stabilization program at "The Sunken Fleet of 1758" shipwreck preserve. Cartography by John Farrell and Bob Benway; CAD by Bob Benway. (Credit: Bob Benway/Bateaux Below)

The next phase of the 1999 operation involved a site stabilization assessment of the seven 1758 bateaux and any disarticulated bateau pieces lying around the site. Bateaux Below divers did a reconnaissance of the bottomlands at the preserve and located and mapped eighteen disarticulated bateau pieces among the seven 1758 bateau shipwrecks. These eighteen bateau timbers included bottom planks, frames, battens, and strakes (side planks). The effort was primarily to determine if any of the eighteen disarticulated bateau pieces came from Bateau B, a shipwreck vandalized by souvenir-seeking scuba divers in 1988. Reconnaissance dives at the north end of the Wiawaka bateaux cluster site also noted several disarticulated bateau pieces lying visible on the lake bottom.[3]

The management of the seven bateaux known as the Wiawaka bateaux cluster (aka "The Sunken Fleet of 1758" shipwreck preserve) has been a challenge for cultural resources managers. Future strategies for the site's historic preservation welfare might include the following:

1. Conduct an assessment of Bateau B to ascertain its condition and determine if a site stabilization of the bateau is necessary, possibly a combination of partially reassembling the "wreck" and/or berming of the vandalized shipwreck.

2. Sketch, photograph, videotape, and then bury the disarticulated bateau pieces lying throughout the shipwreck preserve (eighteen bateau pieces noted during the 1999 mapping).

3. Make periodic dives to remove debris, not only to maintain the physical integrity of the historic shipwrecks in the cluster, but to also beautify the shipwreck park for the enjoyment of visiting sport divers.[4]

Site protection of the Wiawaka bateaux cluster using periodic debris clean-up and possible site stabilization strategies is an intricate process and one that would probably need to include a long-term investment of time and labor.

Chapter Sixteen

Students Build Underwater Archaeology Equipment and Replica Bateaux

Students Build Underwater Equipment for Bateaux Study, 1987–1988

Over the 1987–1988 school year, seventh-grade students at the Saratoga Springs Junior High School in Saratoga Springs, New York, had a rare opportunity to explore underwater archaeology and technology by constructing a nine-foot-by-twenty-seven-foot grid fashioned using PVC (polyvinyl chloride) piping. This undertaking was conducted during after-school enrichment sessions directed by Jeff Sova, a dynamic Industrial Arts (now known as Technology class) instructor. The Lake George Bateaux Research Team provided all the materials required to erect the archaeology grid. Underwater archaeologists often use grids like this to aid in mapping shipwrecks in a plan-view perspective.

I served as the advisor on this educational project. Prior to the student construction activity, the participating junior high school students were presented with background on the project and viewed underwater video shot by an ROV, a tethered robot, of underwater fieldwork at the Wiawaka bateaux site. The ROV-generated video was shot on September 13, 1987. The after-school project not only introduced students to the principles and facets of underwater archaeology but also acquainted them with emerging technology, robotic aids to complement scientific research. You might say this was an early example of a STEM (science, technology, engineering, and math) interdisciplinary learning experience, today a staple in American education.

At the time in 1988, I was quoted in a local newspaper: "Besides being of educational value to these students, their efforts shall have a practical side in that the grid will be used by divers to help measure some Lake George bateaux sunk there in the French and Indian War."[1]

147

The Caldwell Replica Bateau Sunk for Scientific Study and Scuba Tourism, 1997

Experimental archaeology, sometimes called replica archaeology, is often undertaken to gain a greater understanding of the lifeways of people from the past. One of the most publicized early examples of experimental archaeology with a watercraft was Thor Heyerdahl's 1947 balsa vessel *Kon-Tiki*. Heyerdahl's crew sailed the craft from Peru to Polynesia, testing the Norwegian explorer's theory that pre-Columbian people from South America could have sailed west across the Pacific Ocean to settle in Polynesia.[2]

At Lake George, the past two decades have seen several examples of experimental archaeology pertaining to the waterway's colonial bateaux. Energetic colonial re-enactor groups have constructed replica bateaux and hybrid vessels, the latter using structural designs combining bateau-, whaleboat-, and **dory**-class characteristics. These have been viewed by the public and been extremely valuable in informing people about eighteenth-century military life.

Ted Caldwell, a Bolton Landing, New York, educator, and his students accomplished one of the best regional projects of experimental archaeology when they designed, built, and tested replica colonial bateaux. I mentioned Caldwell earlier, but a more in-depth examination of his replica archaeology work with students is warranted. Caldwell, now retired, was an innovative instructor who worked for a partnership of three public schools in the Adirondacks known as the Tri-District Consortium (Bolton, Minerva, and Newcomb). Caldwell wanted his students to construct replicas of eighteenth-century military bateaux for a re-creation of Benjamin Franklin's 1776 bateau voyage on Lake George during the American Revolution. Though the replica voyage was not related to the sunken bateaux of 1758, the vessel design selected by Caldwell and his students had its roots in Lake George's 1758 bateaux. Beginning in 1993, Caldwell and his students, supported by a grant of several thousand dollars from the Lake Champlain Basin Program, constructed a few replica bateaux. To prep for the construction, the students went to Adirondack Museum in Blue Mountain Lake, New York, and received instruction from the facility's boat curator on one of Lake George's sunken bateaux that had been raised from the waterway in the early 1960s, conserved at the museum, and exhibited there for years. Caldwell said his bateaux were about twenty-three feet long with a forty-eight-inch beam, roughly two-thirds to three-fourths the size of the 1758 sunken bateaux in Lake George. Caldwell minimized the use of power tools to show the students "the labor intensity of eighteenth-century carpentry." Each of the Caldwell bateaux held eight students, with six students on the oars, one student steering at the stern, and another student

Figure 16.1 Two of the Caldwell replica bateaux being rowed by local school students on the waters of Lake George. (Credit: Ted Caldwell)

sitting at the bow providing navigation information. Caldwell said that each bateau weighed about 350 pounds.[3] The project was successful, as Caldwell and his students constructed several colonial bateau replicas.[4]

Following numerous trips on Lake George and other Adirondack waterways in the 1990s, after a few years, the Tri-District Consortium bateaux were retired. However, one of those modern-day nautical replicas would be incarnated as the focal point for a highly successful project. At the request of Bateaux Below, Caldwell donated one of the replica boats for another experimental archaeological endeavor. In mid-July 1997, Bateaux Below took the twenty-three-foot boat to the Bateaux Below dock, located behind the Old Courthouse Building in the Town of Lake George, where it was tied up to an open berth. Rocks, for sinking the bateau, were then collected. A total of 1,491 pounds of cobble-type rocks, each about the size of a football, were used to sink the bateau in three to four feet of water just off the dock. This allowed the replica bateau's wood to swell, closing the seams between the wooden floorboards and strakes. Several weeks later, the rocks were removed. An electric-powered pump, donated by Bateaux Below volunteer Bill Appling, was employed to remove the water inside the boat, and the vessel was refloated. Bateaux Below members later towed the replica watercraft across the

Figure 16.2 September 7, 1997: Bateaux Below divers and other volunteers sink a replica bateau at "The Sunken Fleet of 1758" shipwreck preserve. (Credit: Carolynn Raven Carpenter)

lake to the Wiawaka Holiday House, the property immediately adjacent to "The Sunken Fleet of 1758" shipwreck preserve.

With the approval of the appropriate State of New York agencies, on September 7, 1997, Caldwell's bateau was deliberately sunk at the shipwreck preserve. Two state government officials, Dale R. Kelly and Alan C. Bauder of the New York State Office of General Services, attended the replica bateau sinking, along with about thirty other invited guests. To sink the watercraft, the archaeological team used the 1,491 pounds of rocks plus another 194 pounds of cobblestone. These "sinking rocks" were similar in size and shape to those employed by the colonial soldiers at Lake George to submerge their lake mountain fleet in 1758. Two holes were also hand-drilled into the replica's pine bottom boards, holes about the same diameter as those found in some of the colonial bateaux sunk at this site. As the replica boat was gradually taking on water and slowly sinking, an additional 150 to 175 pounds of rocks were loaded into the vessel. Water then engulfed the bateau, and the watercraft went down, sinking in a swinging pendulum fashion before hitting the lake bottom in shallow water and sliding down a sediment slope into about forty to forty-five feet of water. The bateau came to rest just to the south of the southern-most colonial bateau shipwreck in the Wiawaka bateaux cluster. The experimental archaeology replica team, divers and non-divers, consisted of Bill

Appling, Bob Benway, Tim Cordell, Paul Cornell, Marie Ellsworth, John Farrell, Maria Macri, Scott Padeni, Mark L. Peckham, Carolynn Raven Carpenter, Susan Winchell-Sweeney, and myself. Several members of Speakman's Rangers, a French and Indian War re-enactors group, were also present, watching from a nearby boathouse dock. The boat sinking, which took a little over twenty minutes, was videotaped by one of Bateaux Below's underwater videographers.

Following the replica archaeology project, divers placed signage underwater informing visiting sport divers of the new "shipwreck." A trail line was also installed from the corridor line at the shipwreck preserve to the replica bateau to guide scuba enthusiasts to observe Caldwell's colonial replica boat. As part of the underwater state park, the watercraft has given sport divers an opportunity to see what an intact eighteenth-century sunken bateau would look like.

Several lessons were learned from this archaeological exercise:

1. Approximately 1,800 to 1,850 pounds of rocks were needed to sink the replica twenty-three-foot bateau. The archaeology team was surprised at the amount of weight required. Several of the sunken Wiawaka bateaux that date to 1758 show evidence of similar looking sinking rocks.

2. The replica bateau's centerline is approximately 325 degrees (MN), quite similar to that of six of the seven bateaux whose centerlines range from 310 to 340 degrees (MN). One of the 1758 bateaux was disturbed during excavation during "Operation Bateaux," and thus its centerline orientation differs. Terry Crandall reported that this bateau (Bateau D) slid a bit down the underwater slope, altering its original orientation on the lake bottom.[5]

3. The deliberate sinking of a bateau to orient its centerline axis toward shore for ease of recovery is an exercise in patience, skill, and labor. The research team came away with increased appreciation for the skills of the British and provincial soldiers who were tasked with this undertaking back in the late summer and autumn of 1758.[6]

Maple Avenue Middle School Replica Bateau "Wreck," 2007-2008

In 2007, I met with several Technology class teachers at Maple Avenue Middle School in Saratoga Springs, New York, to discuss the possibility of an enrichment project to construct a full-scale thirty-foot-long British military bateau "wreck." Upon completion, the replica bateau shipwreck would be deliberately sunk in the shallows of Lake George for pedestrian viewing. Jeff Sova, Preston Sweeney,

Figure 16.3 Two students at Maple Avenue Middle School (Saratoga Springs City School District, Saratoga Springs, New York) trace an eighteenth-century bateau stem in preparation for constructing a replica of a colonial bateau shipwreck during the 2007–2008 school year. (Credit: Joseph W. Zarzynski)

Figure 16.4 In June 2008, a replica bateau shipwreck sits along a walkway at Lake George prior to being sunk in four feet of water for pedestrian viewing. (Credit: Bob Benway/Bateaux Below)

and Karen Cavotta, the school's Technology teachers, with support from their department colleagues Bill Snyder and Bill Cooper, agreed to collaborate with Bateaux Below to complete the task. As described at the beginning of the chapter, I had worked with Jeff Sova on an earlier underwater archaeology- and technology-related project. Over the autumn, winter, and spring of the 2007–2008 school year, a core group of ten to fifteen students, under the direction of the Technology instructors and with Bateaux Below members acting as advisors, worked on constructing a full-scale replica shipwreck based on the 1758 Lake George bateau shipwreck exhibited at the Adirondack Museum.

Prior to construction activities, I presented an introductory lecture on the goals of the project and outlined the history of Lake George's sunken bateaux. Fort William Henry Museum loaned several colonial bateau pieces from their collection that were traced by the middle-school students to complete a template for construction of the replica wreck. Most of the actual bateau building was done by students as an after-school activity, with Sova and Sweeney as the principal instructors. Bob Benway, John Farrell, Steve Resler, and I assisted the school instructional staff in the execution of the project. Will Fortin, an eighth-grade student, worked with underwater archaeologists to draft the plans that became a blueprint for the replica watercraft. Fortin's drawings were largely based on the archaeological record, that is, the Lake George colonial bateau that was one of the three raised in the early 1960s and later exhibited at the Adirondack Museum.

Bateaux Below paid for the cost of the building materials. The educational and archaeological teams worked with Mayor Bob Blais (Village of Lake George), Alan C. Bauder (New York State Department of General Services), Charles Vandrei (New York State Department of Environmental Conservation), and other state and local agencies to acquire permission to sink the "shipwreck" in the lake. The location was a shallow water site, near shore along the Blais Walkway at the southwest corner of the lake. This locale would allow for pedestrian viewing of the replica shipwreck.

As the construction project inched closer to completion, the Technology teachers had some of their classes assist in the project so they, too, could experience the replica archaeology program. In mid-June 2008, with help from Northern Dean, a construction firm near Saratoga Springs, the replica bateau shipwreck was loaded onto a flatbed trailer and driven the twenty-five miles to Lake George. The replica "wreck" was then off-loaded, and a team of volunteer archaeological divers and non-divers used rocks to sink the replica in four feet of water.

Throughout the project, Pepe Productions, a Glens Falls, New York video production company, videotaped the students and instructors at work. The project was later featured in the 2010 DVD documentary, "Wooden Bones: The Sunken Fleet of 1758."

The replica bateau shipwreck was named *BAT*, after three of the project's principal supporters: Mayor **B**ob Blais (Village of Lake George Mayor), **A**lan C. Bauder (New York State Office of General Services), and **T**erry Crandall (Bateaux Below). The Office of General Services printed an informational brochure that described the replica shipwreck project, and Village of Lake George staff erected signage along the shoreline adjacent to where the replica shipwreck was sunk. The replica shipwreck was not for scuba diving but strictly for pedestrian viewing from a nearby lakeside walkway that overlooked the site.[7]

School projects such as Caldwell's replica bateaux and Maple Avenue Middle School's replica shipwreck illustrate the educational value of experimental archaeology endeavors and serve to promote local history.

Chapter Seventeen

"Raising the Fleet"

An Art/Science Initiative

Over 2008–2009, Dr. Samuel Bowser, then an Albany-area polar biologist, and Bateaux Below partnered with other organizations and individuals on a project to observe the 250th anniversary (1759–2009) of the British and provincial troops raising the submerged warships of the sunken fleet of 1758.

Bowser was a scientific diver who spent years traveling to Antarctica to collect and study single-cell organisms called foraminifera. The **National Science Foundation (NSF)** funded his groundbreaking work on how these creatures have adapted to extreme environments ("extreme" being relative to the frailties of human physiology). Bowser undertook annual training dives at Lake George to keep his **American Academy of Underwater Sciences (AAUS)** qualifications current, and the cold, deep water of the lake allowed him to remain proficient with the same type of scuba equipment he used in Antarctica. As part of his training, he frequently assisted Bateaux Below with its shipwreck monitoring duties at Lake George's Submerged Heritage Preserves. One day during a casual discussion aboard my dive vessel, Sam and I conceived a venture to combine natural sciences studies, cultural research, and art.

Our topside boat deliberation culminated in a 2009 Lake George tri-exhibition entitled "Raising the Fleet: An Art/Science Initiative." The project commemorated the 250th anniversary (1759–2009) of the British military raising part of their sunken fleet of 1758. Many of those recovered warships were repaired and used by British General Amherst's army in the 1759 military campaign that pacified the French forts in the Champlain Valley and ultimately propelled the British to victory in the French and Indian War.

The tri-exhibit was an art/science interpretation of the study of testate amoebae, single-celled organisms found in the sediment adjacent to eighteenth-century shipwrecks at Lake George. Because these amoebas reproduce asexually, they can be thought of as immortal—in essence, serving as "time

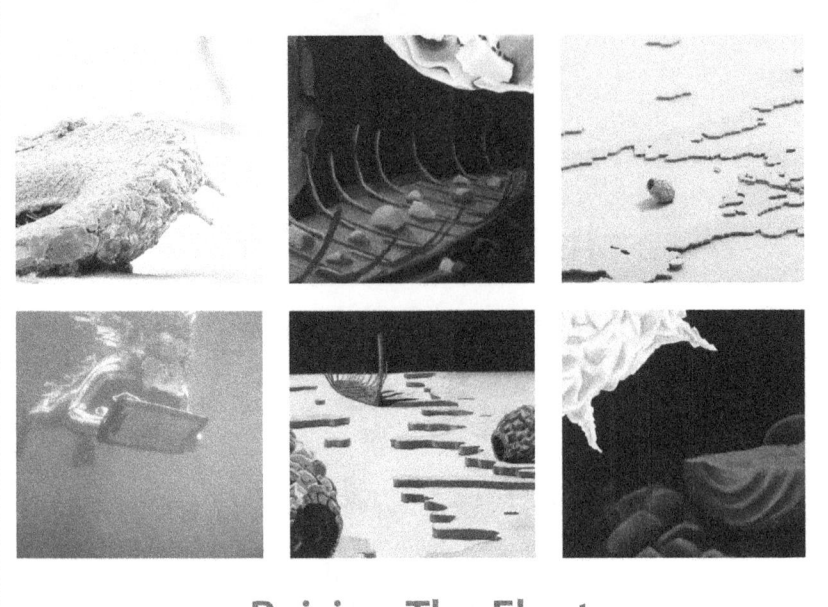

Raising The Fleet
An Art/Science collaboration exploring the underwater frontiers of Lake George.

Figure 17.1 This Lake George Arts Project's postcard promoted a summer 2009 art/science collaboration exhibit at their Lake George art gallery. The show was part of a tri-exhibition that commemorated the 250th anniversary (1759-2009) of the British military raising many of their vessels of the Sunken Fleet of 1758. (Credit: Laura Von Rosk and Dr. Samuel Bowser)

travelers" to tell the story of the 1759 military campaign. The project included (1) an exhibition of over three dozen art and science pieces held at the Lake George Arts Project gallery, (2) an underwater art/science exposition for scuba enthusiasts with easels erected around a replica bateau at "The Sunken Fleet of 1758" shipwreck preserve, and (3) an Internet display at the **Museum of Underwater Archaeology (MUA)**. The gallery program ran from August 25 to September 10, 2009, and featured work by science artist Elinor (Mossop) Gottschalk and ship modeler John Farrell. The gallery exhibition also included a mini-video documentary on the project prepared by Peter Pepe of Pepe Productions.

In 2009, Kurt Knoerl, director of the Museum of Underwater Archaeology, stated, "The 'Raising the Fleet' Internet exhibit had the most visitors over the shortest period since I started the Museum of Underwater Archaeology." Though the art/science exhibition has formally ended, the cyberspace exhibit is still available to view at www.themua.org/raisingthefleet.

Figure 17.2 Painting done by science artist Elinor (Mossop) Gottschalk for the 2009 "Raising the Fleet: An Art/Science Initiative" tri-exhibition. The artist's illustration shows a thirty- to thirty-five-foot sunken bateau shrunk down to the approximate size of minuscule amoeba tests (shells). The latter would normally be examined using a scanning electron microscope. Gottschalk painted the sunken bateau and amoeba tests on one landscape. (Credit: Elinor [Mossop] Gottschalk)

Figure 17.3 In 2009, Bateaux Below maritime archaeologist Joseph W. Zarzynski inspects the underwater art exhibit at "The Sunken Fleet of 1758" shipwreck preserve in Lake George. (Credit: Bob Benway/Bateaux Below)

Following the underwater display, divers with Bateaux Below recovered the art and easels. Nonetheless, the art that had been exhibited underwater continued to be a source of public introspection and scientific investigation. For example, some art reproductions that were exhibited in forty feet of water in Lake George were preserved for future study. Bowser later said that the submerged art will be examined using a scanning electron microscope to inventory the micro-organisms that settled onto it during the subsurface display. This information will provide an inventory of the micro-fauna and -flora that settled onto the preserve's shipwrecks without having to conduct an invasive investigation of the cultural resources.

The "Raising the Fleet: An Art/Science Initiative" tri-exhibit was also the subject of a poster presentation at the Society for Historical Archaeology's Annual Conference on Historical and Underwater Archaeology that convened at Amelia Island, Florida, in January 2010.[1]

"Knowing which organisms colonize newly submerged surfaces is an important part of understanding preservation processes underwater," declared Bowser. Local K–12 teachers will also use some of the underwater artwork in forthcoming art/science instruction.

According to Bowser, "Integrating art and science is not a fad—it's a proven way to draw interest to science, especially among youngsters who think science is 'too complicated' or 'not real' to them. These kids just need to see how art and science are really 'done' the same way—with equal parts of imagination and concentration."[2]

Chapter Eighteen

Documentary Filmmaking, Bateaux, and Archaeologists

One of the hallmarks of Bateaux Below's public outreach program was a collaboration on documentary video productions with documentarians Peter and Joe Pepe (Pepe Productions), animation specialist John Whitesel (Whitesel Graphics), and Vince Capone (Black Laser Learning). That documentary filmmaking partnership, begun in 2004, resulted in three award-winning documentaries: "The Lost Radeau: North America's Oldest Intact Warship" (2005, 57 minutes), "Wooden Bones: The Sunken Fleet of 1758" (2010, 58 minutes), and "Search for the *Jefferson Davis*: Trader, Slaver, Raider" (2011, 50 minutes). "The Lost Radeau" and "Wooden Bones" were about Lake George shipwrecks, and the latter, "Search for the *Jefferson Davis*," was Pepe Productions' collaboration with the Lighthouse Archaeological Maritime Program (LAMP) and the St. Augustine Lighthouse and Museum (today known as the St. Augustine Lighthouse and Maritime Museum) in their scientific investigation to locate a Confederate privateer shipwreck lost in 1861 off Florida's "First Coast" (i.e., near St. Augustine). These documentary projects, particularly the Lake George-related DVDs, were successful as tools to inform the public about the history and underwater archaeology of Lake George shipwrecks.

Documentaries are film or video productions that tell truthful stories about people, events, and places. Originally, they were called "documentary films" because they were shot on film stock, not videotape. Today, documentaries are more frequently shot in digital video format and the term "documentary" is commonly used when referring to this genre.[1] In 1926, John Grierson, a Scotsman, first coined the term "documentary." On February 8 of that year, Grierson's review of Canadian Robert J. Flaherty's film "Moana," a factual story about exotic Polynesia, was published in the *New York Sun* newspaper. Grierson, at the time writing under the pen name "The Moviegoer," wrote, "Of course *Moana*, being a visual account of events in the daily life of a Polynesian youth

159

Figure 18.1 In 2010, Pepe Productions and Bateaux Below released the documentary "Wooden Bones: The Sunken Fleet of 1758." Documentary filmmaking is an excellent way for archaeologists to disseminate information about their research projects. (Credit: Pepe Productions)

and his family, has documentary value."[2] Grierson's term soon became popular in describing most nonfiction films.[3]

However, film and documentary historians overwhelmingly profess that the first documentary came out a few years before Grierson first coined the term. In 1922, when motion pictures were about three decades old, the so-called first documentary production was released. Entitled "Nanook of the North: A Story of Life and Love in the Actual Arctic," the French-funded documentary film premiered on June 11, 1922. The seventy-nine-minute film, also directed by Flaherty, told the story of an Inuit hunter and his family living in the Arctic region. "Nanook" was an instant success, as it took theater viewers to a place they would otherwise probably not have the opportunity to visit.[4] Today, the documentary genre is extremely powerful and a trendy vehicle for telling stories about intriguing archaeology projects.

In mid-2004, Peter Pepe, Joe Pepe, and John Whitesel approached Bateaux Below's Bob Benway and myself to collaborate on a documentary project about Lake George's 1758 *Land Tortoise* radeau shipwreck. That partnership resulted in three documentaries, two related to shipwrecks associated with the sunken fleet of

1758. Black Laser Learning provided technical support for the first documentary, "The Lost Radeau: North America's Oldest Intact Warship,"[5] which came out in late 2005. It had taken eighteen months to complete the documentary, which tells the history of the 1758 *Land Tortoise* radeau, a one-of-a-kind floating gun battery shipwreck in Lake George, and Bateaux Below's underwater archaeological investigation of the historic warship. The documentary was released on DVD, and later was also broadcast on PBS television stations around New York state, thus increasing the public's knowledge of this unique and historic French and Indian War shipwreck.[6] "The Lost Radeau" also contained references to Lake George's eighteenth-century bateau watercraft.

In 2010, Pepe Productions and Bateaux Below again teamed up to release the fifty-eight-minute DVD documentary "Wooden Bones: The Sunken Fleet of 1758." This documentary examined Lake George's 1758 bateaux, the 1960 research submarine *Baby Whale* constructed to photograph the sunken bateaux, and the autumn 1758-built military wharf located at the head of the lake.[7] The production took nearly four years to complete, and the documentary was co-winner of the Maritime Heritage Award at NOAA's 2010 Gray's Reef Ocean Film Festival in Savannah, Georgia.[8]

In December 2012, Left Coast Press released *Documentary Filmmaking for Archaeologists*. Peter Pepe and I co-wrote the book, described as "a concise guide to filmmaking designed to help archaeologists navigate the unfamiliar world of documentary film."[9] The text includes a great deal of information about the making of "Wooden Bones: The Sunken Fleet of 1758."

Most people take great pleasure viewing quality films, good television programs, and informative documentaries. Well-made documentary videos such as those discussed above have helped spread the story of Lake George's colonial past, including the many shipwrecks of the sunken fleet of 1758. These video productions have likewise encouraged viewers to be advocates for historic preservation of these finite submerged cultural resources.[10] Video documentary productions are also one of the most effective ways for archaeologists to disseminate the results of their research.

Chapter Nineteen

Public Education Programs

A frequently overlooked aspect of submerged cultural resources management is informing and educating the populace about the results of archaeological projects. This campaign is often referred to as "public outreach." Unfortunately, this aspect of maritime archaeology is sometimes minimal, or even neglected by some archaeologists. This chapter reviews the numerous public education programs from the 1960s to the present that promoted historic preservation of the sunken bateaux of 1758.

National Fisherman Magazine's Series on Lake George's Colonial Bateaux, 1966-1967

Numerous newspaper articles published during the 1960s kept the public informed about Lake George's sunken colonial bateaux. In 1966–1967, *National Fisherman*, a widely read trade magazine published in Maine, printed a series of articles on Lake George's sunken bateaux that included informative details on their construction. John Gardner wrote the articles. He was a nationally recognized authority on small watercraft design and served as a consultant for Adirondack Museum on the reconstruction of the 1758 bateaux recovered from Lake George in the early 1960s.

State Education Department Publishes Booklet, *Diving into History: A Manual of Underwater Archaeology for Divers in New York State*, 1969

In 1969, the State of New York's State Education Department helped to educate the Empire State's populace about shipwrecks when it published the thirty-three-page booklet *Diving into History: A Manual of Underwater Archaeology for Divers in New York State*. The publication, written by Paul Scudiere, a senior historian in the Office of State History, State of New York, included information, too, about Lake George's sunken bateaux of 1758. The booklet enlightened readers about state historic preservation laws and principles and provided a primer on the principles and techniques of underwater archaeology. The publication was widely distributed around the Empire State.[1]

Three-Day Training Session, "Archaeological Research Assistant Workshop," 1987

By the early 1970s, the public's fascination in the 1758 bateaux had declined from the rabid interest in the "Ghost Fleet" during the early 1960s. Not until 1987 did a renaissance of attention to Lake George's colonial bateaux occur.

In September 1987, the Atlantic Alliance for Maritime Heritage Conservation, a Washington, DC not-for-profit educational corporation, sponsored a three-day workshop at Lake George to train sport divers in the principles of underwater archaeology. Dr. Russell P. Bellico, Vince Capone, Jack Sullivan, and I organized the program. Over twenty scuba divers participated in the educational workshop, which became the genesis for the Atlantic Alliance Lake George Bateaux Research Team.[2] Soon after the group's founding, the organization simplified its name to the Lake George Bateaux Research Team. That volunteer entity promptly began a public outreach campaign to educate local residents and visitors to Lake George about the waterway's eighteenth-century bateaux.

Bateaux Below Newsletter, 1988-1990

From 1988 to 1990, the Lake George Bateaux Research Team published a newsletter entitled *Bateaux Below*. Only a total of four issues were published, but the newsletter was disseminated to Lake George Bateaux Research Team members, state historic preservation officials, and other interested people. It presented its readers with news about recent developments in our team's study of the sunken bateaux of 1758. In the early 1990s, the principals of the organization decided to rename our underwater archaeology organization. We selected the moniker "Bateaux Below," named after the Lake George Bateaux Research Team's newsletter of that title.

Shipwreck Weekend at Lake George, 1990-1995

Another successful educational initiative about maritime archaeology and shipwreck preservation at Lake George was an annual weekend conference called "Shipwreck Weekend" (later renamed "Shipwreck Weekend at Lake George"). It was held annually each September in the Lake George area from 1990 to 1995 and was generally co-sponsored by the Lake George Historical Association, Bateaux Below, and New York Sea Grant/Oswego. Generous support came also from several other groups and businesses. The event attracted sport divers and maritime history aficionados who heard lectures and participated in workshops on topics related to shipwrecks, underwater archaeology, and shipwreck preservation. The Third Annual Shipwreck Weekend, held in September 1992, also featured three shipwreck scuba charters at Lake George. One of those dive charters was at the Wiawaka bateaux site and included a pre-dive lecture presented by Terry Crandall, the 1963–1964 archaeological diver during Adirondack Museum's "Operation Bateaux." Crandall's knowledgeable pre-dive talk certainly enhanced the divers' visitation to the colonial bateaux site.[3] Proceeds from the Shipwreck Weekend events were donated toward the purchasing of blue-and-yellow historic markers erected along the lake's shoreline. The historic markers had maritime or military history themes, and the signage enlightened the public about Lake George's underwater heritage.[4] Unfortunately, a few years after the conference was initiated, the program ended, due in part to growing operating expenses and a difficulty in getting quality speakers. This type of informational program about shipwrecks and maritime history was later emulated by other organizations. For years after Lake George's Shipwreck Weekends had ended, the New York Sea Grant/Oswego staff and its partners held a similarly designed scuba and shipwreck program at the State University of New York at Oswego in Oswego, New York. In many respects, their events were modeled after the annual Lake George "Shipwreck Weekend" festivities. The Oswego programs, likewise, were enjoyable annual events for scuba enthusiasts and maritime history buffs to learn more about historic shipwrecks, shipwreck diving, and underwater archaeology.

Figure 19.1 Kendrick McMahan, a New Jersey scuba diver and accomplished computer technician, was a guest speaker at one of the "Shipwreck Weekend at Lake George" conferences held in the 1990s. (Credit: Bateaux Below Collection)

THE LAKE GEORGE
NAUTICAL
NEWSLETTER

THE NEWSLETTER OF LAKE GEORGE REGIONAL NAUTICAL HISTORY AND ARCHAEOLOGY

35 Years Later—
Lake George's Lost Submarine Found By Bateaux Below, Inc.

During the night of August 4, 1960, a 15-foot long yellow research submarine, built to photograph Lake George's sunken colonial artifacts and warships, was taken from its dock and reportedly sunk by pranksters. After an extensive boat, air, and scuba search, the submarine was nearly forgotten.

However, Bateaux Below, Inc. (BBI), which in 1990 discovered the 1758 LAND TORTOISE radeau shipwreck in Lake George, long hoped of finding the lost submarine.

The "Baby Whale," the name the craft was reportedly going to be christened had she not been stolen from her dock, was found earlier this year during a shipwreck inventory survey by BBI. That survey was funded by BBI with partial assistance from a small grant by the Rural New York Historic Preservation Grant Program administered by the Preservation League of New York State with the support of the J.M. Kaplan Fund.

In early August 1995, BBI announced the discovery of the submarine to mark the 35th anniversary of its disappearance.

The submarine lies in deep dark water and according to BBI's Bob Benway "it is in excellent condition due to its deep and cold water environment."

BBI has notified State authorities of the find and has discussed with the State developing a management plan for the submarine's future. BBI has also placed

1960 photograph showing Lake George submarine and Jim Parrott, one of the submarine's original owners.

signage at the wreck, with State-approved wording, asking divers not to disturb the site. One of the options for the submarine is to make it part of the lake's shipwreck park for divers.

Members of BBI's submarine survey team included Bob Benway, Vincent J. Capone, John Farrell, Scott Padeni, Linda Schmidt, and Joseph W. Zarzynski.

The Lake George submarine was built 35 years ago by local residents—James Parrott, Gerald Root, and Art Jones. According to newspaper reports from the time, the submarine weighed 3,700 pounds and was made of aluminum, iron, and cement. It had a 12

(continued on page 8)

Figure 19.2 The cover of an issue of Bateaux Below's The *Lake George Nautical Newsletter.*
(Credit: Bateaux Below)

The Lake George Nautical Newsletter, 1992-1996

In 1992, the principals of Bateaux Below introduced *The Lake George Nautical Newsletter*, an eight-page quarterly periodical published from 1992 to 1996. After fifteen issues, the newsletter ceased publication.[5] Both of the newsletters, *Bateaux Below* and *The Lake George Nautical Newsletter*, filled a void. They provided eager subscribers, as well as local and state cultural resources managers that received complimentary copies of the newsletters, with information about one of the waterway's most significant cultural resources, the fleet of Lake George's French and Indian War shipwrecks.

Exhibit at the Schenectady Urban Cultural Park (Schenectady, New York), 1992

In 1992, to celebrate the 200th anniversary of the departure of a bateau on the Mohawk River from the Western Inland Lock Navigation Company, the Schenectady Museum (Schenectady, New York) opened a major exhibit.[i] The exhibition focused on the role of bateaux along the Mohawk River in New York state and included a pictorial display with descriptive captions about Lake George's Sunken Bateaux of 1758. The museum exhibition showcased the founding of the Western Inland Lock Navigation Company started in 1792 by Philip Schuyler of Albany, New York. The company's goal was to improve navigation along the Mohawk River and other waters west of Albany. Karen Engelke (Schenectady Urban Cultural Park), with assistance from Phil Lord, a senior scientist with the New York State Museum (New York State Department of Education), organized the 1992 exhibit activities at the Schenectady Museum. Bateaux Below members provided several photographs and research information about Lake George's sunken colonial military bateaux that were incorporated into the 1992 exhibit. The Lake George Historical Association also loaned for exhibit a colonial bateau frame from one of the lake's shipwrecks that was in the historical society's collection.[6]

As part of the Schenectady Museum's 1992 exhibit, on May 29, 1992, Bateaux Below's Bob Benway, Vince Capone, and myself assisted Philip Lord in a one-day Klein side-scan sonar survey of a section of Onondaga Lake near Syracuse, New York. The remote sensing team sonar scanned an area of the lake where a Durham boat,

---

i   It should be added that the New York State Museum also celebrated the bicentennial of the Western Inland Lock Navigation Company by building a river "batteau" replica in 1991 that was called *Discovery*.

a forty- to sixty-foot flat-bottomed vessel, was reported to have sunk. These vessels, similar in design to bateaux, but longer, were common watercraft on the Mohawk River and other waterways of New York during the era of Philip Schuyler's Western Inland Lock Navigation Company. Unfortunately, our remote sensing team did not locate any Durham boat-like sonar targets to further investigate.[7]

"Historic Vessels and Shipwrecks of Lake George" Exhibit at the Lake George Historical Association, 1993

On May 22, 1993, the Lake George Historical Association in conjunction with Bateaux Below opened a new long-term exhibit in the society's museum on Canada Street in the Town of Lake George. Called "Historic Vessels and Shipwrecks of Lake George," the display included dozens of photographs and archaeological drawings from the collections of the historical society and Bateaux Below. Dr. Russell P. Bellico and Bob Benway contributed most of the underwater photographs, and John Farrell donated several boat and military figure-scale models. A thirteen-inch diameter mortar bomb was loaned to the exhibit, courtesy of Fort William Henry Museum. The British ordnance is believed to have been recovered by scuba divers in the 1960s from the so-called sunken "mortar bomb bateau." To complement this museum exhibit, the Lake George Historical Association and Bateaux Below erected a blue-and-yellow metal historic marker entitled "SUNKEN FLEET"[8] behind the Old Courthouse Building in the Town of Lake George.

Shoreline Signage, 1993–2005

Lake George has miles of picturesque shoreline, all of it visible from boats and some of it accessible by pedestrians using public walkways. Therefore, signage erected along or near the shore is a traditional and extremely effective method to disseminate information to the public about the waterway's maritime and military history. For decades, the most popular signage along the waterway has been the New York State Historic Marker Program initiated in 1926. These durable metal signs with a blue background and high-visibility yellow lettering are found in several locations around the waterway. The signage provides brief text about historic buildings or sites, prominent people, and shipwrecks. Each marker is three feet wide by two feet tall, a half-inch thick through the body, and one inch thick along the border. Today, the signs are made of cast aluminum, and each metal marker weighs about fifty pounds. The base of the metal marker is cored

Figure 19.3 This blue-and-yellow metal historic marker informs visitors and residents about Lake George's maritime and military history. Behind this signage, along the shoreline, is the author's welded aluminum dive boat, frequently used on archaeology projects associated with Lake George's sunken bateaux of 1758. (Credit: Joseph W. Zarzynski)

to receive a 2-1/2-inch-wide by seven-feet-long metal pole.[9] When this historic marker program started, over ninety years ago, the signage was funded by the State of New York. However, that ended in 1939. In 1966, a new historic marker initiative using the same type of signage was begun with funding provided by local historical societies and civic groups.[10]

Each historic marker includes a title line followed by five lines of text and generally one or two credit lines. A logo, generally a silhouette of the map of New York, is included on the marker face.[11]

Bateaux Below, acting independently or in partnership with other interested parties, drafted the text and funded several of these historic markers. Three of these signs pertain to shipwrecks of the sunken fleet of 1758. The titles of these, plus the years of installation, are SUNKEN FLEET (1993), RADEAU WARSHIP (1995), and WIAWAKA BATEAUX (1996). Other state historic markers about the lake's submerged heritage resources produced by Bateaux Below and its partners and related to the waterway's maritime and military heritage are MILITARY DOCK (1992), SUBMERGED TRACK (2002), and CADET SHIPWRECK (2005).[12]

The two bateaux-related blue-and-yellow markers from 1993 and 1996 read in full:

SUNKEN FLEET
FALL 1758 BRITISH/AMERICANS
SANK RADEAU LAND TORTOISE
SLOOP HALIFAX, 260 BATEAUX
TO AVOID WINTER PLUNDER
BY FRENCH RAIDING PARTIES
LGHA AND
BATEAUX BELOW[13]

and

WIAWAKA BATEAUX
7 French and Indian War
BATEAUX SUNK HERE IN
1758. LISTED ON NATIONAL
REGISTER OF HISTORIC PLACES
IN 1992.
BATEAUX BELOW, INC.[14]

Walking Tours Established, 1995-1999

On May 13, 1995, I led a guided tour—"Colonial Walking Tour of Lake George"—around the south end of the lake. The tour helped celebrate the May 1995 "New York State Archaeology Month." That walking tour later became the genesis for a 1996 project entitled "Colonial Wars of Lake George Self-Guided Tour." The six-page, twenty-stop, 3.3-mile self-guided tour was researched and written by Dr. Russell P. Bellico, Bob Benway, Tim Cordell, John Farrell, Scott Padeni, and myself. The walking tour sheet was a free handout available to the public at several locations around the lake. The self-guided tour was funded by several principal sponsors: Lake Champlain Basin Program, Bateaux Below, Village of Lake George, Lake George Historical Association, State Senator

Ronald Stafford, Kiwanis Club of Lake George, Jack Mannix, Lake George Steamboat Company, Tall Pines Motel, Marine Village Resort, Shoreline Cruises, Inc., and Tom Mathias.[15] For several years, until our supply of the tour leaflet was exhausted, the tour was among the most popular through the Town and Village of Lake George.

On May 6, 1999, the New York State Department of Environmental Conservation opened new signage around Battlefield Park, a state-administered historic and recreation site located at the south end of the lake. The official opening of that signage circuit, administered by the Department of Environmental Conservation, coincided with the **North American Society for Oceanic History**'s 1999 annual conference held that year at the Sagamore Resort on Green Island in Bolton Landing, on the west side of Lake George. Dr. Russell P. Bellico, Scott Padeni, and I worked with the Department of Environmental Conservation's Charles Vandrei to research and write the text for the signage of the self-guided tour. The Battlefield Park's historical signs primarily interpreted the ground's eighteenth-century history for the tens of thousands of tourists who visit the state park each year. Several of the markers were directed specifically toward maritime history, including the lake's colonial bateaux heritage.[16]

Underwater Signage at 1758 Shipwreck Sites, 1996

On May 22, 1996, Bateaux Below divers erected underwater signage at "The Sunken Fleet of 1758" and "*Land Tortoise*—A 1758 Floating Gun Battery in Lake George" shipwreck preserves.[17] The signage was installed at the start of both shipwreck preserve trail lines that lead from the mooring anchorage to the shipwreck(s). The signs notify divers that these shipwrecks are listed on the National Register of Historic Places. The seven shipwrecks of the Wiawaka bateaux site were listed on the National Register in 1992.[18] The 1758 *Land Tortoise* radeau shipwreck's National Register of Historic Places listing was in 1995.[19] Unfortunately, several years ago, the National Register informational signage at the *Land Tortoise* shipwreck preserve was damaged from diver intrusion, and the sign was removed. It was not replaced.

As mentioned in chapter 12, on July 28, 1995, Bateaux Below scuba divers installed signage at the sunken 1960-built *Baby Whale* yellow submarine. The sign informs scuba divers that the sunken underwater vehicle is "Property of the State of New York" and that the submarine "shipwreck" should not be touched or disturbed.

New York State Archaeological Association Conference–Bateaux Program, 1997

Lake George was the site of the Eighty-First Annual New York State Archaeological Association (NYSAA) Conference, held May 2 through 4, 1997. The host for the conference was the NYSAA-Adirondack Chapter. The conference drew over two hundred people, mostly from the northeastern part of the United States. Over thirty archaeology papers were presented. John Broadwater, former Virginia State Underwater Archaeologist and then manager of NOAA's *Monitor* Marine Sanctuary, presented the keynote address for the conference. His lecture was entitled "Archaeology on the Revolutionary War Yorktown Fleet and the Civil War's *Monitor* Ironclad."

Two other highlights of the conference were tours presented by Bateaux Below staff. On May 2, 1997, some conferees were taken on guided walking tours entitled "Colonial Wars of Lake George." The tours ran along the south end of Lake George and included stops that informed participants about Lake George's sunken fleet of 1758.

On May 4, 1997, another cultural outing—"Video Virtual Reality Tour of a Sunken Colonial Bateau Site"—was presented to conference attendees. Nearly two hundred participants attended this outing, which convened aboard one of the Lake George Steamboat Company's excursion boats, courtesy of Bill Dow, the principal of the tour boats business. Non-divers got to view a bateau shipwreck, one of the Bateau(x) Site IX sunken warships, and archaeological divers from a video camera mounted on a camera frame set up overlooking an eighteenth-century bateau shipwreck. Divers recording measurements of a sunken bateau were viewed on a television monitor aboard a large excursion vessel. Bateaux Below docents aboard the excursion craft then explained to people what they were watching on the television monitor. Engineering technician Bob Benway designed and constructed the underwater camera housing and stationary camera frame. A two-thirds scale (twenty-three feet) replica bateau built by local students and loaned to Bateaux Below by Tim Caldwell was also exhibited at the Lake George Steamboat Company's wharf for conferees to peruse. Additionally, Tim Cordell, a Queensbury, New York artist, set up an exhibit inside the excursion ship, displaying his many maritime-themed paintings of Lake George. Cordell was present to answer questions about his artwork.[20]

Underwater Blueway Trail Exhibit at the Lake George Visitor Center, 2006

On June 29, 2006, the Lake George Visitor Center opened to the public.[21] The attractive building, a gateway for visitors to Lake George and the surrounding environs, included a wide variety of 2-D and 3-D exhibits, as well as some short video productions designed to inform people about local tourism opportunities. Included in the exhibition hall was a display about the emerging New York State Underwater Blueway Trail, a New York State Department of State initiative. Pepe Productions, a Glens Falls, New York multimedia company, was contracted to provide mini-video productions and 2-D poster designs about the Underwater Blueway Trail initiative. I assisted Pepe Productions on this project. The informational exhibit incorporated graphics created by Bateaux Below's Bob Benway and John Farrell, Pepe Productions, John Whitesel, and Mark L. Peckham. With creative video and museum-quality displays, including material about the sunken fleet of 1758, this exhibit quickly became a popular attraction.

Exhibit at Fort William Henry Museum, 2012

Fort William Henry Museum, which opened to visitors in May 1954, is a replica of the 1755–1757 British and provincial military structure at the south end of Lake George. The French and Indian War tourist attraction is located on a low plateau overlooking the head of the waterway. The historical facility is owned and managed by the Fort William Henry Corporation. In 2012, the French and Indian War Society, a 501(c) not-for-profit corporation that assists the museum in developing exhibits and programs, invited Bateaux Below to create a display on the history of underwater archaeology at Lake George. Though Bateaux Below ceased active archaeological fieldwork at Lake George in mid-2011, several principals of our group nonetheless enthusiastically planned this exhibition.

1992: "Wiawaka Bateaux Cluster" Listed on National Register of Historic Places

In 1992, Bateaux Below members completed the underwater archaeology mapping and the seven shipwrecks of the "Wiawaka Bateaux Cluster" were listed on the National Register of Historic Places, the first shipwrecks in Lake George with that noteworthy designation.

This blue-and-yellow historic marker was erected by Bateaux Below and its supporters on the grounds of the Wiawaka Holiday House at a location overlooking the seven 1758 Wiawaka Bateaux (credit: Joseph W. Zarzynski/Bateaux)

Figure 19.4 One of over twenty posters of Fort William Henry Museum's long-term exhibit "Underwater Archaeology of the Sunken Fleet of 1758" that opened in 2012. (Credit: Joseph W. Zarzynski and Fort William Henry Museum)

Public Education Programs 173

Bateaux Below's Dr. Russell P. Bellico, Terry Crandall, John Farrell, and myself collaborated with the staff at Fort William Henry Museum. The new exhibit was entitled "Underwater Archaeology of 'The Sunken Fleet of 1758.'" The exhibit premiered on August 9, 2012, its grand opening corresponding with the 255th anniversary of the August 9, 1757, surrender of the British garrison, Fort William Henry, to the French during the French and Indian War.

The exposition includes over twenty pictorial display posters, several scale models of Lake George vessels and shipwrecks associated with the sunken fleet of 1758, bateau- and other maritime-related artifacts from the Fort William Henry Museum collection, and a video component created by Pepe Productions. The short video includes excerpts from two Lake George shipwreck documentaries, "The Lost Radeau: North America's Oldest Intact Warship" and "Wooden Bones: The Sunken Fleet of 1758."

This Fort William Henry Museum exhibit examines the history, underwater exploration, and maritime archaeological investigation of the sunken fleet of 1758. As of this writing, this popular display, housed in the John Farrell Archaeology Exhibit room, is still running for public viewing. Fort William Henry Museum's James Hood, Hanna Rhodes, Melodie Viele, and Lauren Sheridan contributed to the exhibit's design.

Museum of Underwater Archaeology Exhibit, 2014

In July 2014, the Museum of Underwater Archaeology, an Internet-based showcase created by Dr. T. Kurt Knoerl, launched its seventh full exhibit, entitled "The Search for Underwater Sites from the French and Indian War." Knoerl described it as an exhibit that "reviews the underwater archaeology studies of Lake George's 'Sunken Fleet of 1758' conducted by Bateaux Below from 1987 to 2011, as well as earlier fieldwork undertaken by other research groups." You can view the Museum of Underwater Archaeology exhibit at www.themua.org/exhibit_1758. According to Knoerl, in 2014, "This is the second digital recreation of a physical museum exhibit."[22]

The MUA Internet exhibition was written by Dr. Knoerl and myself based on the display that opened at the Fort William Henry Museum in 2012. The MUA exhibition was dedicated to John Farrell (underwater archaeologist, Bateaux Below) and Al Bauder (cultural resources manager, New York State Office of General Services), both of whom had recently passed just prior to the exhibition. The two men were very involved in the study and historic preservation of Lake George's sunken fleet.

Lectures

Lectures and professional papers presented to the public and to archaeologists and maritime historians at conferences are two of the traditional means of "broadcasting" the results of archaeological studies. From 1987, the year the Atlantic Alliance Lake George Bateaux Research Team (later Bateaux Below) began lake studies, to the year 2018, Bateaux Below members have given over four hundred public lectures. Bellico and I gave most of these presentations, including lectures, professional papers, school instructional lessons, workshops, tours, and radio and television interviews. These lectures reached over fifteen thousand people from a wide range of educational and socioeconomic backgrounds. The programs were on topics related to the history, underwater archaeological investigation, and historic preservation and protection of Lake George's shipwrecks and other underwater heritage resources, including its sunken bateaux of 1758.

Classes

To commemorate and celebrate the 250th anniversary of the sunken fleet of 1758, a class for adult learners at the Schenectady County Community College (SCCC) explored that city's link to Lake George's sunken bateaux. The class, "Shipwreck Archaeology for Non-Divers," included eight lessons. One session, held on October 15, 2008, provided adult learners with insight into how to archaeologically map a

Figure 19.5 In 2008, the author (center) taught a class on the techniques of underwater archaeology to adult learners at the Schenectady County Community College in Schenectady, New York. The focal point of the instruction was a simulated mapping exercise using a 1:1 scale model of a 1758 bateau shipwreck. (Credit: M.P. Meaney)

colonial bateau shipwreck in a non-water environment. A two-thirds scale model of an eighteenth-century bateau shipwreck, fashioned out of sturdy insulation boards painted brown to resemble wood, was used for the simulated mapping exercise.

The location for the 2008 course was ideal, too. The old Schenectady harbor was located at the juncture where the Binnekill tributary meets the Mohawk River. This locale was once a major boatbuilding center during the colonial era and into the nineteenth century. The once bustling boatyards are today an urban environment. Unfortunately, remnants of the old harbor and its nearby bateau "factories" are not evident to the naked eye. However, this former colonial boat-building complex borders the SCCC campus.

After the American Revolution, the riverine boatyard became a terminus center for the Western Inland Lock Navigation Company founded in 1792. The Western Inland Lock Navigation Company initiated a commercial water route westward to Utica, Rome, and Oswego, New York. This necessitated a bigger watercraft than the twenty-five- to thirty-five-feet bateau. So, a longer flat-bottomed vessel, capable of carrying more cargo and supplies, emerged. Often known as a Durham boat, this watercraft ranged in length from forty to sixty feet. Durham boats ferried General George Washington's American soldiers across the Delaware River at Trenton, New Jersey, and thus helped in that important American victory over German mercenary soldiers in December 1776. The Durham boat design was borrowed from Pennsylvania, and in northern New York this vessel became more commonly known as the "Schenectady boat."

The SCCC class was timely since the autumn 2008 marked the 250th anniversary of Lake George's sunken fleet of 1758, when British and provincial troops sank 260 bateaux and other classes of warships to protect these vessels from the French and their Native American allies over the winter of 1758–1759. Many of those sunken warships were raised in 1759 by British General Jeffery Amherst's regular and provincial forces. The recovered vessels from the depths of Lake George were repaired and then employed in 1759 in the military offensive against the French forts in the Champlain Valley. This successful campaign was instrumental in the British winning the French and Indian War.

In the mid-1980s, nautical archaeologist Dr. Kevin J. Crisman completed line drawings of the Lake George bateau shipwreck exhibited at the Adirondack Museum, one of three bateau wrecks recovered in the early 1960s from the lake by scuba divers who worked for the Adirondack Museum. The bateau shipwreck model studied during the mapping class at SCCC in 2008 was loosely based on the archaeological record and Dr. Crisman's superb nautical line drawings of that legendary watercraft.

Lake George historian Russell Bellico wrote in his book *Sails and Steam in the Mountains: A Maritime and Military History of Lake George and Lake Champlain* that the British and provincials constructed bateaux in boatyards in Schenectady and Albany during the French and Indian War. In 1758, many of these boats were transported by water and then wagons to Lake George, where they were used on the waterway. Specifically, the bateaux built in Schenectady were moved east on the waters of the Mohawk River to the falls at Cohoes. The vessels were then pulled from the river and transported on wagons around the falls to Albany on the Hudson River. On that waterway, river bateaumen rowed them north to Fort Edward, a British and provincial stronghold. A military road, approximately fourteen miles long, had been cut through the thick forests from Fort Edward on the Hudson River to the south end of Lake George. Along this dirt roadway hundreds of bateaux, constructed in bateau "factories" in Schenectady and Albany, were transported on wagons. The October 15, 2008, SCCC class, held outside and near the west parking lot of the community college, was only a few hundred yards from the location of the Schenectady "factories." Thus, in many respects, the class paid homage to the Schenectady bateau boat builders who constructed many of the vessels of the sunken fleet of 1758.[23]

I likewise had the pleasure of teaching other classes and workshops that featured instruction on the history of Lake George's colonial bateaux and underwater archaeological mapping techniques. These included a two-day (eight-hour) workshop on May 14 and 15, 2010, entitled "Intro to Underwater Archaeology for Shipwreck Preserves Development" presented to members of the Finger Lakes Underwater Preserves Association (FLUPA) in Elmira, New York, and a four-hour workshop called "Lake George, New York Submerged Cultural Resources Awareness Workshop for Asian Clam Project 2011" held on April 25, 2011. The latter was given for the Fund for Lake George, Inc., to fulfill cultural awareness sensitivity training mandated by the New York State Historic Preservation Office and U.S. Army Corps of Engineers. On August 12, 2012, I presented a five-hour class that was also given again a week later. That program was entitled "SHIPS" (**S**ubmerged **H**eritage **I**nformation & **P**reservation **S**eminar) and was taught for members of the Volunteer Dive Team of the Biological Field Station-State University of New York-Oneonta (Cooperstown, New York). Another bateau-related educational program entitled "Demonstration of Archaeological Site Mapping of a Colonial Bateau" was presented at Hudson Crossing Park's 12th Annual Cardboard Boat Races in Schuylerville, New York, on August 20, 2016. During these instructional classes, a twenty-five-foot model of a replica bateau shipwreck was featured to engage participants in a simulated archaeological mapping exercise.

Boat and Shipwreck Scale Models

Boat and shipwreck scale models date back to the very beginning of water transportation. Today these likenesses are generally fashioned of wood, but also of plastic, metal, and paper. These scale models, if based on the archaeological record, can be quite valuable for interpreting and depicting historic vessels. Bateaux Below was indeed very fortunate to have a ship modeler on our staff.

John Farrell, an experienced underwater and terrestrial archaeologist, was also an accomplished scale boat modeler. He constructed eighteen vessel models from several different types of material, but mainly used various types of wood as his creative medium. However, Farrell also favored plastic, metal, foam board, and paper. The very first scale model ever made of the 1758 *Land Tortoise* radeau shipwreck, crafted for use by the archaeological team directed by Dr. D.K. (Kathy) Abbass from 1991 to 1993, was of foam board construction. That scale model of the radeau proved extremely helpful in aiding Abbass when assigning scuba divers their archaeological tasks during the mapping of that sunken warship in the early 1990s.

Farrell's boat and shipwreck models and dioramas, too, were each a representation based upon the archaeological record. His exemplary creations were exhibited at the Lake George Historical Association's museum, the Fort William Henry Museum, the Caldwell-Lake George Library in the Town of Lake George, the Lake George Arts Project in the Town of Lake George, the Rogers Island Visitor Center in Fort Edward, New York, and elsewhere. Farrell had many different nautical subjects, too. These included British colonial bateaux as boat models and also

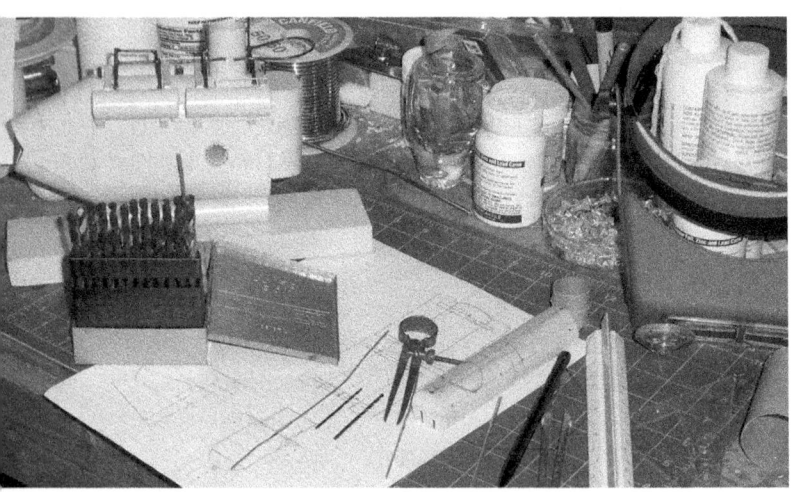

Figure 19.6
The work station of Bateaux Below's John Farrell, not only an accomplished archaeologist but a superb boat modeler, too. Farrell's scale model of the 1960 *Baby Whale* research submarine is in the background of this photograph. (Credit: Bateaux Below Collection)

as a shipwreck diorama, a research submarine constructed in 1960 to photograph Lake George's sunken bateaux, and the 1758 *Land Tortoise* radeau. Animator John Whitesel employed these boat and shipwreck models to produce realistic animation featured in Pepe Productions' Lake George shipwreck documentaries. John Farrell's scale models were likewise displayed at several public lectures, thus enriching the experience for attendees.[24]

Paintings and Other Art

Lake George's colonial bateaux have been portrayed in several excellent paintings. Mark L. Peckham, an historic preservationist and accomplished artist, has produced both ink and watercolor illustrations depicting colonial-era bateaux. His classic ink drawings of bateaux have been featured in numerous reports, articles, documentaries, and books (including this one). He sketched two ink drawings of bateaux that he later colorized that appeared in the DVD documentary "Wooden Bones: The Sunken Fleet of 1758."[25]

Peckham described these two paintings:

The illustrations were done on 11 inch x 14 inch paper using pen and ink and watercolor. The first one [used as this book cover's art] illustrates bateaux being ballasted and sunk on the lake's east shore late in the [1758] season; some of the boats are swamped and a crew is going around distributing more ballast; lines have been attached to shore in order to facilitate recovery in the spring. The second one shows them regimented on the lake bottom in winter with lines leading to shore and crude lobster pot type buoys [cut logs, each with a hole through it] as suggested by [archaeological diver] Terry Crandall. One boat is drawn with a stem broken during the sinking process and all show a mound of mud piled up at the stern; [in 1997 when Bateaux Below deliberately sank a replica bateau] we saw the replica [when it was sunk] bulldoze into deeper water once it lost buoyancy.[26]

Peckham drew another fine representative piece of art of a bateau, a "field notes" ink drawing dated August 5, 1999, depicting a bateau-class shipwreck he examined on the shores of Cumberland Bay on Lake Champlain at Plattsburgh, New York. There had been a summer drought in 1999 that dramatically lowered the lake level, exposing a bateau watercraft identified as being from the War of 1812.[27] Later that month, another War of 1812 bateau shipwreck was revealed nearby.[28] Though these bateaux were from another waterway, Lake Champlain, and another era, the War of 1812 (1812–1815), they deserve mention here because

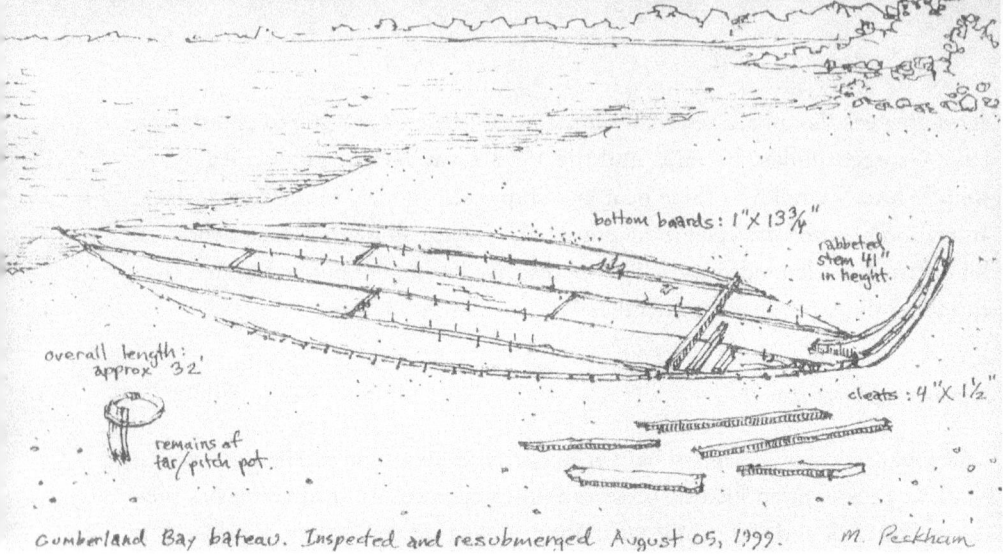

Figure 19.7 Mark L. Peckham's sketch of a War of 1812 bateau found in Cumberland Bay (Plattsburgh, New York), Lake Champlain. Peckham inspected the remarkably well-preserved bateau on August 5, 1999, during a drought that exposed the historic watercraft. Field illustrations like this provide unique insight into archaeological sites. (Credit: Mark L. Peckham)

Figure 19.8 Tim Cordell's "Sinking of the Radeau" depicts the *Land Tortoise* radeau on October 22, 1758. Cordell's artwork also shows the role of bateaux that were undoubtedly used for this event during the French & Indian War. (Credit: Tim Cordell and Lake George Historical Association)

they were somewhat similar to the traditional British bateaux of the eighteenth century and contained some unique artifacts.

The first-discovered Cumberland Bay bateau was thirty-two feet long, similar in length to many of Lake George's sunken bateaux. However, it had five bottom boards that Peckham measured at one inch thick and 13-3/4 inches wide. The sunken colonial bateaux found in Lake George were either three or four bottom boards wide. The Plattsburgh bateaux's battens (cleats) were of varying lengths, but they were 1-1/2 inches thick and 4 inches wide, quite different in size to the wider battens found on the 1758 Lake George bateaux.[29]

As mentioned, Peckham observed some unique artifacts associated with one of the War of 1812 vessels: "The most interesting discovery for me was the pitch pot. There was a circle of tar/pitch in the bow [of the bateau] where it glued itself to the bottom boards and I recall that we found a tar-laden brush at the site. I'll bet pots like this were in common use."[30]

Tim Cordell is a professional artist from Queensbury, New York, who for years has painted Lake George colonial scenes, including watercraft, soldiers, and forts, as well as other Adirondack-themed subjects. Cordell has painted a variety of French and Indian War-era vessels, including a Ranger whaleboat (water color), Ed Bethel's French and Indian War re-enactor boat on the Hudson River off Rogers Island (oil), the 1759 radeau *Invincible* on Lake George (oil), and possibly his most famous watercraft oil painting, "Sinking of the Radeau."

For a quarter-century, "Sinking of the Radeau" has been on exhibit at the Lake George Historical Association museum in the Town of Lake George. It is well worth a visit to the historical society building to peruse Cordell's art, as well as to view the facility's other displays. The Cordell painting depicts the October 22, 1758, deliberate sinking of the 1758 *Land Tortoise* radeau, a type of floating battery. This interpretive artwork, painted in the early 1990s, also shows three bateaux used by the British regulars and provincials as they tried to sink the radeau in shallow water, a type of "wet storage" (aka "cold storage") for recovery in the spring 1759.[31] Historically, British soldiers had difficulty getting the radeau down, and the odd-shaped battle craft floated out into the middle of the lake and sank deeper than a hundred feet. Cordell wrote of the role of the bateaux in his painting:

> The bateaux [and bateaumen] are trying to keep the vessel from gaining deep water which would (and did) make it impossible to recover [the radeau] in the spring [1759]. Since "they" worked the chief of the night to sink it, it makes sense that there would have been bateaux or whale boats

to help with the sinking and to save the men involved on board when it [the radeau] went under.[32]

Cordell's "Sinking of the Radeau" is one of my favorite pieces of maritime art. The painting not only realistically depicts that historic event, the 1758 *Land Tortoise* radeau being deliberately sunk in Lake George by British forces on October 22, 1758, it likewise shows the versatility of the colonial bateau as a workhorse watercraft.

Conclusion

I am now in my late sixties and age has finally caught up to this maritime archaeologist. So, several years ago I retired from Lake George fieldwork on underwater archaeology and cultural resources management projects. Nonetheless, I do have some final thoughts on the 1758 sunken bateaux of Lake George.

The cultural resources management of these colonial warships will continue to be a difficult challenge in the decades ahead. Safeguarding these icons of the eighteenth century will not come from a single program. The shipwrecks are British warships in an American waterway, and Americans, both from officialdom and the general public, will play integral roles in deciding their ultimate fate. Possibly one day more sunken bateaux in Lake George will be nominated to the National Register of Historic Places, thus according them a greater degree of protection. Furthermore, the State of New York and local government agencies and non-government organizations will hopefully accelerate efforts to educate the local populace and visitors to Lake George about the bountiful history of these French and Indian War shipwrecks. If historic preservation

Figure C.1 Signage like this installed at one of Lake George's shipwreck sites reminds scuba enthusiasts to "Dive into History" and to be good stewards of the waterways' submerged cultural resources. (Credit: Bateaux Below Collection)

strategies are successful, scuba divers are more likely to "Dive into History" using nondisturbance visitations, thus contributing to the cultural well-being of the waterway and the area's efforts to successfully promote cultural tourism.

Over 1988 to 2016, I paid Terry Crandall numerous visits to his residence in the Mohawk Valley. We spent hours telling diver tales, drinking coffee, and discussing the sunken bateaux of 1758. That dialogue began in earnest when we first met in 1988. Crandall said that by the time he began fieldwork for the Adirondack Museum in 1963, many of the sunken bateaux that had been discovered in 1960 had regrettably already been vandalized. Nevertheless, Crandall related that he had inspected one sunken bateau that amazingly had three strakes (side boards), a two-hundred-year-old wooden vessel that still maintained much of its structural integrity.

Public education programs such as innovative museum exhibits, history tours for the public, lectures, documentary-style video programs, and Internet websites devoted to the sunken bateaux will certainly aid preservation efforts. For best results, regional scuba instructors, dive shops, and dive clubs must be proactive. Some scuba shop owners and dive instructors already articulate an historic preservation stance toward submerged cultural resources. Those scuba enthusiasts that have explored the depths of Lake George and who have been good stewards of the lake's cultural and natural resources deserve our thanks and praise. I believe that dive shop owners and employees and scuba instructors can play a leading role in advocating a historic preservation stance toward Lake George's historic shipwrecks.

Moreover, these historic shipwrecks and other sunken vessels in Lake George could one day be affected by the colonization of zebra mussels (*Dreissena polymorpha*), a small freshwater mussel, into the lake. Bateaux Below's Bob Benway and I, while scuba diving in Lake George conducting a benthic clean-up on December 18, 1999, found the very first zebra mussels in the waterway.[1] Because zebra mussels attach to sunken vessels, these pesky mollusks, if they fully colonize in the waterway, could certainly damage and degrade shipwrecks. Fragile eighteenth-century bateaux could literally collapse under the weight of thousands of zebra mussels. Zebra mussel infestation on sunken vessels would also partially conceal shipwrecks, minimizing divers' enjoyment when visiting these iconic cultural sites.

Furthermore, there are no informational road signs along Interstate 87 ("Adirondack Northway"), running near Lake George, to "proclaim" that the waterway is the home of the Sunken Fleet of 1758. Such highway signage would greatly cultivate public awareness about this historical treasure and encourage a heartier heritage preservation mentality. Bateaux Below personnel tried over a decade and a half ago to get the state government to erect highway signage notifying the public about the 1758 *Land Tortoise* radeau, a National Historic Landmark and major component of the shipwreck preserves. However, state government officials promptly denied that request, a decision I still find hard to believe. Because historic shipwrecks and sunken artifacts are for the most part "out of sight, out of mind," over the past few decades minimal attention has been exerted to protect these shipwrecks.

My hope is that the experiment with shipwreck preserves to facilitate controlled public access for diver visitation to these sunken vessels, begun by the State of New York in 1993, will continue at Lake George. Possibly we are beginning to see some positive steps. In September 2018, the State of New York opened an upgraded and remodeled visitor center on Interstate 87. The structure, only ten miles from the south end of Lake George, is a gateway stop for people coming into the region. I was elated to see that inside this building was a touchscreen information panel with a portal entitled "Submerged Heritage Preserves" that gives viewers basic information about Lake George's preserves, including "The Sunken Fleet of 1758."

Also, it is essential for the State of New York to create a "state underwater archaeologist" position. States such as Florida and Maryland, for example, each have a state underwater archaeologist who directs the management of their state's shipwrecks and other submerged heritage resources. The Empire State is bordered by the Atlantic Ocean, Long Island Sound, Lake Ontario, Lake Erie, and the St. Lawrence River, and has numerous interior waterways. A state underwater archaeologist would certainly be kept busy here.

I fear that future generations will not have the opportunities that my colleagues and I have had over the past three and a half decades when we explored the lake's eighteenth-century sunken squadron of bateaux. As a lake stakeholder, I should have been more insistent and clamored with greater fervor to promote the welfare of the Sunken Fleet of 1758. The structural integrity that these historic shipwrecks had back in 1960 has significantly deteriorated. Some sunken bateaux today are nothing more than a pile of disarticulated wooden boards and frames. Thus, today, the term "Ghost Fleet" has a different meaning than it did back in 1960. One day, unless more effective management strategies are implemented by state government, local authorities, the scuba community, historical and environmental groups, and private citizens, these Lake George shipwrecks could be gone, one hull timber at a time, becoming true ghosts.

Appendix I

"Operation Bateaux" Revisited Twenty-Four Years Later — Part 1
Terry Crandall[1]

Back in the early summer of 1963, Dr. Robert Bruce Inverarity (aka RBI), the tall Scotsman who was the director of the Adirondack Museum in Blue Mountain Lake, New York, summoned me to assist him on a scuba diving operation of a reported "Indian canoe" sunk at the south end of the lake not far from Hall's U-Drive It marina on Lake George. He had hired me to represent the museum, the institution that had been granted the license by the State of New York to develop the underwater archaeology program on the early colonial bateaux found in Lake George. To a scuba diver, this was akin to James Bond's 007 badge, as it allowed a certain degree of discretionary freedom in handling known or suspected underwater archaeological sites.

My first exposure was a memorable one . . . accompanied by great splashing and thrashing about by a group of divers, all eagerly competing to wrest a badly rotted canoe free from its muddy grave and brandish said fragments triumphantly to an annoyed RBI aboard a rented pontoon craft. As I recall, RBI terminated the "exercise" shortly after the divers managed to bring up a smelly, muddy, and broken canoe, quite likely of Old Town manufacture, and shove it across the dock of a very irate landowner! Thus, my first official act as a "licensed" diver stuck in my mind as an underwater version of the humorous Keystone Cops from early Hollywood film comedies.

At that time, I was not aware of the certain sensitivities surrounding the bateaux, including the jockeying for jurisdiction by several museums with [State] Education Commissioner James E. Allen, U.S. Navy involvement, and

187

apparently a somewhat hasty raising of three (?) bateaux [in early 1960s] in which one bateau eventually became an exhibit on public display at the fine Adirondack Museum.

RBI provided me with an orientation that consisted of about nineteen sites to investigate and evaluate, some background facts about details of colonial hostilities on Lake George, and the use of and loss of the bateaux.

RBI also facilitated boat use with Sheriff Robert Lilly and the Lake George Park Commission (using Boston Whaler vessels) with their daily patrolling of the lake.

In addition, he recommended a policy of tight security regarding sites, my daily activities, and assistance from others, and charged me not to welcome others to work with me unless properly permitted. Directly, the only ones that bore input into the project, other than those with whom I welcomed, were Howard I. Chapelle, noted antique boat and naval architect at the Smithsonian Institution, and Colonel Edward Hamilton, director of Fort Ticonderoga Museum.

However, since I was on my own and realized the value and safety of competent fellow divers, I felt there was a need to involve others, many who already had on-site experience from their recreational diving. At the risk of slighting some damn fine divers, I generally had to limit my preferred list of dive partners to just four: Lee Couchman, who had been my diving buddy in the past; Charlie Dennis, a businessman and who later became the aquatic director of the United States Coast Guard Academy; Gene Parker, a noted writer-illustrator and designer of underwater systems and procedures; and Jack Sullivan, Gene Parker's dive buddy, who was probably one of the hardest-working divers I have ever known. Of these men, Gene Parker had done much in the area of underwater photography in the early 1960s bateaux recovery program and had indeed gained the respect and support of RBI. Thus, I chose to take my workdays off through the week and reserve weekends for scuba diving with the divers mentioned above if they were available.

July of 1963 found me mostly working alone (talk about breaking your cardinal rule of scuba diving!) on a "drop off-pick up" basis with the Boston Whaler vessels of the Lake George Park Commission marine patrol. Besides spot checking a number of reported bateaux or other shipwreck sites, these scattered from the Village of Lake George in the south all the way north to Howe's Landing [at the north end of the lake], I conducted raw search missions along the eastern shore from Hall's marina (and Wiawaka Holiday House) north.

A typical scuba search pattern had the following components:

1. It roughly followed a lake bottom contour depth of from fifteen to twenty-five feet on average.

2. It held to a **lubber line** major axis predetermined by the general shoreline **azimuth** heading.

3. All body movements were made at 45 degrees east and west of this lubber line, thus, all turns were of 90 degrees.

4. The number of fin "kicks" (right foot) distances was determined by the visibility and underwater topography and might vary from ten to as many as twenty "kicks" or so.

5. My dive compass was wrist-mounted and held directly in line with the median body axis at all times.

6. A search sector was determined by the exhaustion of a single 72 cubic feet steel scuba tank, on average about a 200-yard northerly swim, a 180-degree turn, and then retracing on a crisscross pattern in a southerly direction.

7. All such searches were quickly translated graphically onto the Lake George Power Squadron charts (not the best lake charts, but the only ones available at the time) using a gridded overlay with each grid being divided into a nine-square, then four-square matrix. In this way, a day's search area could be described with six-digit codes: (a) the first digit was the Lake George Power Squadron chart number, (b) the next three digits were the cell number overlay, (c) the fifth digit was within the nine-cell in clockwise rotation, and (d) the sixth digit was within the four-cell in clockwise rotation.

When working with others, and only after the Adirondack Museum purchased a crude, but rugged and ample spaced pontoon barge that was outboard motor-powered, we generally chose tow sled searching, using two divers and a large towed inner tube with a dive flag. Even then you had to be aware that water skiers might try to cut between barge and inner tube! Here the pontoon boat operator or a chart-reading assistant set the boat course pattern, usually a series of back-and-forth passes along a given azimuth, all turns being 180 degrees and courses being about thirty to fifty feet apart using shoreline references. A lot of pattern integrity was lost, however, when someone chose to surface, drop off a marker, or occasionally let free the sled and strike off on his own. As payback for the favors extended to me, I often did some "police" diving for the sheriff or Lake George

Park Commission patrols, more than once spending considerable time on body searches for someone whose Lake George vacation had been tragically terminal.

Two summers of bateau shipwreck searching (1963 and 1964), coupled with actual site fieldwork, did yield a number of new bateaux sites, mostly along the eastern shore of Lake George. Numerous reports of a vast "graveyard" of bateaux, quite likely substantiated by historical support, in or around the mouth of Dunham's Bay, continues to circulate now a quarter of a century later. I cannot personally attest to any such site, although I do not deny its possible existence despite considerable scuba searching by the New York State Police diving squad, as well as myself.[1]

Author's Note

1. Terry Crandall [1932–2016] was a board member of Bateaux Below and in 1963 and 1964 was the chief archaeological diver for Adirondack Museum's "Operation Bateaux" [1960–1965]. This article came out in the July 1988 issue of the *Bateaux Below* newsletter, a publication of the Atlantic Alliance Lake George Bateaux Research Team, a forerunner of the organization that later became known as Bateaux Below. This is an edited version of Crandall's 1988 article.

Figure A.1.1 An undisturbed 1758 sunken bateau, what Terry Crandall called a "raw site." The photo was taken during 1963–1964 fieldwork and several bateau frames (on right) can be seen "standing proud" with the rest of the wooden shipwreck mostly covered with sediment and lake vegetation. (Credit: Terry Crandall)

Appendix II

"Operation Bateaux" Revisited Twenty-Four Years Later—Part 2
Terry Crandall[1]

In the July 1988 issue of the newsletter *Bateaux Below*, published by the Atlantic Alliance Lake George Bateaux Research Team and edited by Joseph W. Zarzynski, I began a recap of the years 1963 and 1964 as an archaeological diver in Lake George charged with the follow-up bateaux research/recovery by the Adirondack Museum begun three summers earlier. Although I had not participated in the early 1960s recovery of sunken bateaux from the lake, one now being exhibited at the Adirondack Museum, I was quite thoroughly briefed on the shipwrecks recovery by Dr. Robert Bruce Inverarity (RBI), the director of the Adirondack Museum.

This article will be devoted to an account of some of the various archaeological handling techniques I employed during "Operation Bateaux." Whenever a bateau shipwreck site was verified, or a new site located through raw search (five or six previously undiscovered sites, to my recollection), my job as directed by RBI was to clean them of mud and debris, possibly photograph them, and make comparisons as far as the condition to the vessels undergoing preservation at the Adirondack Museum. The project was undertaken under a permit granted to the museum from the State Education Department. Part of my mission was to try to locate a bateau craft in better shape, or perhaps one sunk in mud resting on its side that would preserve more detail of the sides and perhaps gunwale (gunnel) sections. Most bateau shipwreck clusters lay in twenty-five feet of water, on average, under nearly three feet of mud and overburden. Some even rested on top of each other. With two hundred plus years of submersion, sometimes any loose timbers would go floating off like a kite in a windstorm. Movement near the bottom had to be carefully measured lest billowing sediments and scattered parts were to be desired. This meant precise buoyancy control, often no use of fins on the lake bottom, "walking" on fingertips, picking up weight to plod to a new location, and a host of other ways to avoid unwanted site and visibility disturbance.

Hand fanning of mud, sometimes augmented by using a common table tennis (ping-pong) paddle, remained the most satisfactory method of "cleaning" and excavating, although an airlift/suction device was once used experimentally. Once an underwater current was established, the direction was kept constant and all material was deposited to the sides and some distance beyond the strakes (side boards) of each sunken vessel.

In the southern regions of the lake, where most sites were located, definite layers of overburden were identifiable. Although I am not sufficiently knowledgeable in Warren County geological history to review the various depositional eras, I can remember visual evidence of many. The bottoms of the sunken bateaux usually lie on primeval white sand and/or rock since they and changes to the countryside were of the same era.

Following the period of colonial hostilities were periods that resulted in forests being cut extensively, followed by erosion and run-off. The results were successive bark chip layers and silt much like a layered drink. Near the top was a pronounced layer of ashes and cinders, the reminders of the days of many steamboats and launches that plied the lake dropping their hot remains (clinker) as the crafts completed their journey from northern trips. Often a richer mud with weeds and algae would provide the icing on the multi-layer cake of deposits over a bateau site.

During excavation, as you neared the bottom boards when fanning sedimentation, care had to be taken not to dislodge timbers or discard small objects. Small artifacts, clay pipe fragments, musket and bird shot of all sizes, even a pair of cufflinks were found lying on the bateau floor boards and were placed in screw top glass bottles for safekeeping to the museum. If certain timbers were to be removed, they were brought to the surface and wrapped in wet newspaper and Saran wrap for temporary preservation while shipping to the Adirondack Museum to be later preserved in a polyethylene glycol (Carbowax 1000) solution.

Many measurements were taken with a metal retractable ruler on a piece of clear plexiglass panel. The panel enabled sight drawings to be made looking through the panel to approximate angles as they existed.

However, artifacts such as the thirteen-inch diameter mortar bombs recovered from the "mortar bateau" were retrieved using a lift bag. When a bateau site was completely excavated, several underwater photographs were taken using 35-mm film, both black-and-white prints and color slides. I also used a Bolex 16-mm movie camera to do some filming over sites.

On one occasion I made a photomosaic of a vessel using a simple plumb-bob arrangement. The "bob" was attached at a known distance from the camera, and then focus was established at three-fourths the distance. Hovering over the site by weight control, a primitive "BC" made from an old surplus "Mae West" flyer's vest, enabled me to shoot a series of slightly overlapped photographs that were later cut and fitted together at the museum.

As previously mentioned, the principle missions were not one of artifact recovery, except for small artifacts found during excavation, but of trying to re-establish certain construction characteristics of the colonial bateau. I was fortunate in locating a section of gunwale (gunnel) with what I called a "thole pin wear block." It was an expendable composite piece that rested below the oars with two holes for the thole pins themselves. This served as a crude oarlock. Along with it were several thole pins, apparently stowed in such a way that they did not float off initially, but later became part of the shipwreck at one site. It was also interesting to note that many of the bateaux showed definite signs of caked mud tracking from the shoes of the troops, soil deposits that could be removed intact from the bottom boards themselves. Often this caked mud is where there were embedded small shot and other tiny artifacts. Samples of the caulking used on the bateaux were also "bottled on the bottom" and later taken to the museum. I was told that this was probably a mixture of (rancid) bear fat or lard and jute, hemp, or some other kind of vegetable fiber. The caulking was found between some of the bottom boards.

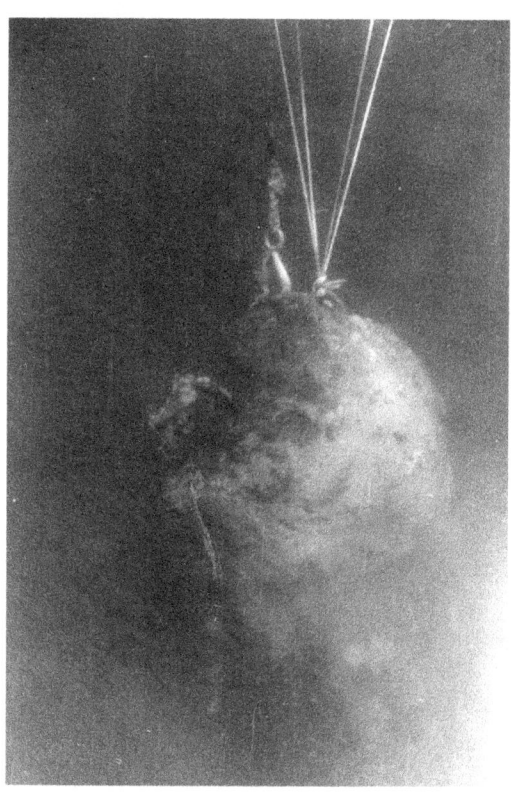

Figure A.2.1 In 1963, archaeological diver Terry Crandall and his team used a lift bag to recover this heavy thirteen-inch diameter iron mortar bomb from a bateau-type shipwreck lying in Lake George. (Credit: Terry Crandall)

Figure A.2.2 During "Operation Bateaux" fieldwork in the 1960s, archaeological diver Terry Crandall (Adirondack Museum) photographed this sunken bateau with one of its thole pin pads (see center of image) that would have received two thole pins. Thus, a thole pin pad with two thole pins became one of the vessel's crude oarlocks (rowlocks) to receive an oar. (Credit: Terry Crandall)

A complete report listing each site, its conditions, and the number of bateaux was prepared by me and submitted to Dr. Inverarity at the close of the 1964 season. In the report, I mentioned that three bateaux were considered suitable for recovery should the museum desire further study, one having evidence of three strakes (side boards) above the vessel's bottom boards.

In retrospect, it is somewhat disturbing to note that the 1965 season ended in an unsuccessful attempt to properly raise any additional bateaux, and that the bateaux project was prematurely scrapped due to political bickering and snarled communications. It matters little now who or what was to blame for the cancellation of the program [in 1965], but what does matter is that the sites have been abandoned to souvenir-hunting divers. A summer 1988 scuba dive made by Dr. Russell P. Bellico, Mark Matucci, Joseph W. Zarzynski, and myself on a nine-vessel bateau cluster indicated extensive scattering and disturbance of this French and Indian War shipwrecks site.[1]

Author's Note

1. This article came out in the December 1988 issue of the *Bateaux Below* newsletter, a publication of the Atlantic Alliance Lake George Bateaux Research Team, a forerunner of the organization that later became known as Bateaux Below. This is an edited version of Crandall's December 1988 article.

Appendix III

Insights Gained from a Replica Lake George Bateau
Mark L. Peckham[1,2]

In 1994, I worked with a group of Boy Scouts (Troop 75, whose members were eleven to seventeen years old and were sponsored by the Delmar United Methodist Church in Delmar, New York) and their parents to build a replica eighteenth-century bateau, similar in design to those used in military campaigns at Lake George. Previously, the troop was very involved in long-distance canoe trips. The bateau was built to increase the capacity and participation in the troop's boating trips while giving new members a sense of pride in the troop's growing "fleet." As often happens with larger replicas, our experience in building the bateau and using it also paid unexpected dividends in understanding its historical antecedents.

Initially, we thought we wanted a thirty-foot bateau capable of carrying an army of scouts and their gear. The problems of trailering and finding storage for a vessel of this length quickly became apparent, and we settled on a twenty-three-foot model similar to that used by educator Ted Caldwell in Bolton Landing, New York, for teaching his gifted and talented public-school students. This proved to be a wise choice, given the sheer weight of these boats and the difficulty in trailering and launching. Caldwell loaned us one of his completed boats for use as a full-scale model, thus saving us the chore of mathematically **lofting** our boat. Although we modified some aspects of the design to reflect our intended uses, the hull was built by laying out our bottom boards on saw horses, placing Caldwell's bateau on top, and scribing the shape of his boat on our boards. These were then cut out and cleated together. The flaring shape of the boat's sides, which changes from station to station, was easily approximated by copying Caldwell's frames one at a time and matching each cut, angle for angle. We added an extra strake (side plank) from Caldwell's bateau design so that it had higher sides and thus more capacity. It became apparent this was probably the identical technique used by British and provincial troops in mass-producing bateaux in the eighteenth century. It requires absolutely no math and no boat-building experience.

In building the bateau's sides, we opted for straight frames, unlike the curved frames seen in the Lake George bateau once exhibited at the Adirondack Museum. We used carvel planking (side planks all flush) instead of lapstrake (side planking overlapping above and below). Again, these choices simplified building and were consistent with our novice skill level. We might have used oak for our frames, as suggested by archaeological evidence from Lake George, but oak can be tough to work with, and considerably more expensive. So, we instead cut our frames from two-inch white pine stock; all the vessel was constructed using local pine. The bottoms of the side frames were connected by transverse floor frames. This system worked fine until we rolled the boat over for the first time without having installed our seats. The sides were not rigid enough by themselves to support the weight of the boat and immediately collapsed, leaving us with a whole range of shattered pine frames. We had now discovered the traditional reason for using oak knees for frames. We found that by permanently installing seats, the boat once again held its intended shape. However, unlike the eighteenth-century examples, we did not have the flexibility of rearranging seats or removing them altogether to accommodate bulky freights.

Another thing we rediscovered is that no matter how carefully planks are dried or how skillfully they are fitted or caulked, a wooden boat will always leak. It will leak less after swelling up for a week or more [in water], but it will still leak and require periodic bailing. In fact, we have found that while the bateau is out of water during the winter, seams often open up wide enough to pass a pencil. We fill these cracks with a wax-like compound in the spring, dump the boat into a nearby river, and a week later, the gaps have all "taken up." I do suspect that lard might have performed almost as well for our eighteenth-century bateaumen.

We designed our bateau with twenty-six-inch sides as compared with Caldwell's twenty-inch sides, anticipating use in rough water with a fully loaded boat. A professional boat builder consulted his tables and warned us against this modification, believing it would make our craft dangerously top heavy. We ignored the advice, but later found that although the boat can be a little "touchy" early in the season, the bottom absorbs considerable weight in water

Figure A.3.1 Mark L. Peckham's drawing of a replica bateau, similar to the one built by Boy Scout Troop 75, Delmar, New York. (Credit: Mark L. Peckham)

over time and automatically ballasts the boat in a few weeks. The boat was not painted, but it was protected by Caldwell's solution of boiled linseed oil, turpentine, and pine tar.

We designed our bateau to be rowed with three pair of seven-foot oars and a twelve-foot steering oar consisting of a pole with a board nailed to it. Longer oars may have worked better, but these were not available commercially within a price range affordable to a scout troop. We also fashioned a fourteen-foot mast from a birch sapling to support a sail rig.

The construction process, an exercise in replica archaeology, taught us that poor workmanship and mistakes are forgiven, and truly, no experience or specialized tools are needed to get a satisfactory product. Assembly goes fast. Once our planks were lengthened with scarf joints, the bateau went together in days with planes, clamps, and handsaws. No need for steam bending. It is now easy for me to imagine a military organization tackling the duty of building hundreds of bateaux by simply breaking the job down into specialized tasks and work groups. Unskilled laborers may have been assigned cutting and hauling timber, while others could be paired and assigned to pits to saw out the thousands of planks necessary. More skilled workers may have been assigned the task of sawing out and roughly shaping thousands of oak knees for later fitting. Parts may have been drawn from stockpiles and carried to each construction site where a single skilled carpenter could have directed the framing and planking of each boat using previously completed boats as templates. Final fitting would be done as each boat came together using saws and planes. Although the effort required in manually sawing out planks and knees seems staggering to those of us used to buying lumber off the shelf, the skills required in building bateaux were easily mastered and represented an important factor in selecting this craft for military uses.

During the first two years of our bateau's existence, we used our bateau on numerous outings. Our experiences provide additional insights into the uses and limitations of this unusually versatile craft.

Handling the bateau on land can be described as miserable. The boat is heavier than imaginable when wet and requires at least six strong individuals to pick it up and carry it. We found that rollers were invaluable for moving it. The bateau's flat bottom helps in drawing the boat up onto a beach. I would encourage anyone interested in the logistics of moving these vessels to read *Arundel*, Kenneth Roberts's novel, to get a feeling for Benedict Arnold's soldiers struggling to carry a fleet of bateaux through the Maine woods during his 1775 Quebec campaign in the American Revolution. Troop 75 can certainly certify the authenticity of Roberts's account. On one excursion we needed twenty men and a pickup truck to get our bateau up the muddy banks of the Susquehanna River. A thirty-foot bateau of the kind found sunken in Lake George would have been almost impossible to carry overland without the use of a special carriage and reasonably passable roads. Perhaps that is why many sunken bateaux were never recovered!

By contrast, the colonial military bateau's design makes it extremely maneuverable in the water and its rugged construction seems immune to damage from grounding, hidden obstructions, or rough use. We designed our bateau with a three-inch rocker, that is, the bottom of the boat is three inches higher at each end than it is in the center. This improves the ability of the boat to spin around its center and adds greatly to its ability to steer. Our twenty-three-foot vessel has a carrying capacity of eleven scouts. When I dived at "The Sunken Fleet of 1758" shipwreck preserve at Lake George, I noticed that surviving frames and garboards of the best-preserved bateaux show evidence of considerable flair in the amidships area suggesting great carrying capacity.

Our bateau rows well, although it is slower than our troop's twenty-six-foot cedar canoe. Our bateau steers easily with a long steering oar lashed to the sternpost.

We have experimented with the use of two traditional sail rigs—a rectangular twelve-foot canvas spritsail with a diagonal boom and an eight-by-eight-foot square sail. Our bateau's top speed under sail is approximately five knots [5.75 mph]. Two saplings and some tent cloth or even a wool blanket would have served equally well in the eighteenth century for mast and sail.

Another experience that may bear our understanding of the submerged bateaux in Lake George is that of the boat's natural buoyancy. Heavy rains associated with tropical storm Bertha (summer 1996), turned our bateau's ordinarily calm berth in a Hudson River tributary into a raging torrent. A waterlogged tree trunk lodged on top of our mooring line and prevented the bateau from rising as the tide came in from the river. The bateau flooded and filled with mud and stones. We found it on the bottom the next day. As soon as the tree trunk was cleared from the mooring line, the boat floated right to the top, rocks, mud, eels, fish, and all. It occurred to me that it would take some serious ballast to keep the boat down, even if one augured a hole in the bottom. Evidence of ballast rocks can be seen throughout the Wiawaka bateaux site and on other Lake George bateaux. I'll wager every rock was needed to keep these unsinkable boats down.[1]

Author's Notes

1. This is a reprint of an article that originally appeared in volume 5, number 2 [1996] of *The Lake George Nautical Newsletter* published by Zarzynski Consulting & Underwater Survey [Wilton, New York] for Bateaux Below, Inc. Mark L. Peckham was an historic preservation manager from the Albany area with a keen interest in regional maritime history. His 1996 article has been edited for inclusion in this book.

2. When Troop 75 was no longer using the replica bateau they donated the boat to Herkimer Home State Historic Site, where it was used interpreting both eighteenth-century travel on the Mohawk River and Nicholas Herkimer's role in operating one of the carries around Little Falls, New York.

Appendix IV

A List of Some of the Dive Teams, Underwater Archaeology Teams, and Scuba Divers Who Dived Lake George's Sunken Bateaux of 1758 During Rediscovery and Study

Some of the Divers (1950s, 1960s, 1970s, 1980s) Who Reportedly Participated in Bateau Research Diving at Lake George

Guy Atkinson, Linda Atkinson, Allen Bassett, Richard Boileau, Fred Bolt, Michael Burnelle, Bernie Campoli, Charles Diehl, Carl Dunn, Bill Gordon, Gerry Hamilton, Bernard J. Kolenberg, Peter LaVoy, Robert LaVoy, Leonard Maimone, New York State Police Scuba Divers, Nick Pallassino, Suzanne Potts, Don Robillard, Bruce M. Smith, Dr. Lewis L. Smith, Walter Stroup, Fred Tarrant, Newman Wait, John Wheeldon, Stan Zeccolo

"Operation Bateaux," 1960-1965

Department of the Navy – U.S. Navy Experimental Diving Unit, Darold Cerrone, Daniel Donnelly, Charles Jefts, and Terry Crandall. Among the divers who helped Crandall's archaeological diving fieldwork for the Adirondack Museum in 1963 and 1964 were Lee Couchman, Charlie Dennis, Robert Drose, Tony George, Ronald Higgins, Lorraine J. Kelleher, Gene Parker, and Jack Sullivan.

Atlantic Alliance Lake George Bateaux Research Team, 1987

Sandy Arnold, Dr. Russell P. Bellico, Bob Benway, Vince Capone, Norm Channing, John Earl, John Farrell, Bill LaBarge, R. Duncan Mathewson III, Jeff P. Mauro, Julien L. McCall Jr., Mary Patram Meaney, Alan Melia, Les (Wit) Richmond,

Brian Silverman, Jack Sullivan, David Van Aken, Joe Van Cook, Steven Whitney, Joseph W. Zarzynski

Bateaux Below Board Members

Dr. Russell P. Bellico, Bob Benway, Vincent J. Capone, Terry Crandall, John Farrell, Joseph W. Zarzynski

Scuba Divers, Archaeologists, Boat Support, Shore Personnel, and Others Who Worked with the Lake George Bateaux Research Team and Bateaux Below During Lake George Sunken Bateaux Projects (1987-2011 and Afterward)

Dr. D.K. (Kathy) Abbass, Amanda Andreas, Bill Appling, Dr. Russell P. Bellico, Bob Benway, Peter Benway, Dr. Samuel Bowser, Vince Capone, Carolynn Raven Carpenter, Steve Cernak, Charlie Chiodo, Paul Cornell, Steve Corrie, Tom Cousino, Terry Crandall, Dale Currier, Department of Environmental Conservation (Lake George-based staff), Bob Doheny, John Earl, John Farrell, Chris Fox, Dr. Warren Gemmell, John & Peter Howell, Dr. Alexey Khodjakov, Dr. Ron Kingsley, Dr. Mike Koonce, Lake George Volunteer Fire Department Scuba Divers, Lake George Historical Association (Staff), Bob Leombruno, Don Leu, Shannon Leu, Maria Macri, Mark Matucci, Don Mayland, Chris McGuirk, Scott Padeni, Gary Paine, Denny Pajak, Mark L. Peckham, Joe Pepe, Peter Pepe, Jerry Pepper, Walt Powell, Tom Rasbeck, Steve Resler, Les (Wit) Richmond, Dr. Megan Springate, Jack Sullivan, Bruce Terrell, Jeff Tingle, Charles Vandrei, Scott Waldman, John Whitesel, Wiawaka Holiday House (staff), Susan Winchell-Sweeney, Joseph W. Zarzynski, Liz Zieschang.

Author's Note

1. Although much time was spent trying to be inclusive, it is quite possible that some individuals are not recognized in these lists. Also, some names might be misspelled, primarily due to spelling errors in newspaper articles and other publications. My apologies to anyone left out or for any incorrect spellings.

Glossary

Abandoned Shipwreck Act of 1987 (ASA)—This act was enacted into law in 1988. Among other things, the ASA affirmed that state governments had the right to claim and manage shipwrecks on their respective state submerged lands and gave the federal government title to sunken U.S. warships. The ASA also stated that the laws of finds and salvage did not apply to abandoned shipwrecks claimed by the government.

American Academy of Underwater Sciences (AAUS)—This organization was formed to develop scientific divers by the advancement of standards for scientific diving and their safety.

apron—A piece of curved wood attached to the after side of the stem on a bateau to support that bow timber; sometimes the apron is referred to as the "inner stem."

assemblage—A collection of things, such as artifacts.

autonomous underwater vehicle (AUV)—This is a robotic instrument programmed to drive underwater such as on a mission to collect data and is directed without real-time human control.

azimuth—In this case, this is the horizontal angle of a scuba diver measured clockwise from a standard direction, such as north.

bateau—In the plural, bateaux. A flat-bottomed colonial watercraft, pointed at bow and stern, that was asymmetrical, fuller in the bow and slender in the stern. These wooden vessels were generally built of pine planks with oak frames, stem, and sternpost. They were either carvel- or clinker-planked. Bateaux were generally rowed, but could be poled in shallow water, and sometimes were rigged with a crude mast and sail. This type of vessel had no rudder, so an oar or paddle was used off the stern for steering. In the literature, a bateau was sometimes spelled batteau, batoe, or battoe.

bateau "factories"—An expression to describe boatyards and areas where bateau vessels were constructed by many carpenters and laborers to mass produce these boats.

battens—Planks of wood used as transverse cleats nailed down across a bateau's bottom boards to hold the boards in place.

bomb ketch—A naval vessel whose main artillery was a mortar, the heavy ordnance generally employed for bombarding a fort or city.

butt joint—A joinery technique in which two planks are fashioned together end to end without overlapping.

carvel—A vessel with its outer planking affixed side by side rather than overlapping like clinker-built or lapstrake-built vessels.

caulked—During the colonial era, to make boats and ships watertight, a fibrous material, known as caulking, was inserted between the seams of wooden planks.

classical archaeology—The study of the material remains of the Greek and Roman civilizations and their immediate forebears.

clinker—A watercraft in which its outer hull planking overlaps; also called lapstrake.

colonial wars—A series of military conflicts fought between the English, later known as the British, and the French in colonial North America. These military conflicts were principally known as King William's War (1689–1697), Queen Anne's War (1702–1713), King George's War (1744–1748), and the French and Indian War (1755–1763).

craft-of-opportunity—Using any vessel that is available for a project, but generally a watercraft that is not specifically designed for the type of work in which it will be employed.

cultural resources managers—These are people whose jobs are to regulate and protect heritage locations such as archaeological sites and historic structures.

dory—A small narrow, flat-bottomed boat with flaring sides, a high and sharp bow, and a narrow transom.

experimental archaeology—A field of archaeology where one tests a hypothesis by replicating artifacts, methods, or techniques from the past to determine the feasibility of a previous people's lifestyle. *See* replica archaeology.

falconet—A light cannon that fired a cannonball about one pound in weight. The falconet became popular on naval vessels as antiboarding artillery.

floating gun batteries—Developmental and often improvised armed vessels that carried heavy artillery. They sometimes had little resemblance to traditional warships.

floor timbers—The central parts of frame timbers that lay across the keel and on which the floor of the vessel is laid.

frames (aka ribs)—A transverse boat or ship timber or an assembly of timbers to which hull planking is fastened.

frogmen—A frequently used term from the past to describe scuba divers dating to the 1950s and 1960s; frogman in the singular.

futtocks—Pieces of hull timber, the top sections that form the compound frames of a larger vessel.

garboard strakes—The lowest hull planking on the outside of a boat or ship.

German auxiliary—German auxiliary troops during the American Revolution (1775–1783) were non-British mercenary soldiers; today they are sometimes called "Hessians."

"Ghost Fleet"—A term coined by the media in the early 1960s to describe the previously little-known shipwrecks called "Lake George's Sunken Bateaux of 1758."

Global Positioning System (GPS)—This is a satellite-based navigation array that uses a constellation of satellites in outer space to provide accurate geographic location.

gunboat—A small and lightly armed warship used primarily on rivers, lakes, and coastal waters.

gunwale (gunnel)—The upper or top part of a watercraft's hull.

howitzers—Artillery pieces whose barrel was shorter than that of cannons and that fired along a low-angled trajectory, compared to cannons that fired along a rather flat trajectory.

in situ—This Latin phrase means "in its original place." The phrase is popular among archaeologists who desire to study artifacts on site.

knees—Timbers used to support pieces of hull structure, roughly at right angles.

Lake George's Sunken Bateaux of 1758—In 1758, the British deliberately sank 260 bateaux at Lake George in the colony of New York to protect their warships over the winter of 1758–1759 from their enemy, the French and their Native American allies. The British recovered many of these 260 sunken bateaux in 1759, but a few dozen warships were not raised from the waterway and today are shipwrecks.

lapstrake—A watercraft in which its outer hull planking overlaps; also called clinker.

lofting—Drawing full-sized patterns in boat building.

LORAN (long range navigation)—A long-range navigation system that used radio signals from land-based towers to affix position. The system was not that accurate and was replaced by GPS.

lubber line—A fixed line on a compass that points straight ahead.

mortars—Muzzle-loaded, smooth bore artillery pieces. These had a short tube compared to the artillery piece's large caliber. This ordnance threw a heavy projectile in a high trajectory over a relatively shorter range than did a cannon or howitzer.

Museum of Underwater Archaeology (MUA)—Incorporated in 2004, the MUA is an Internet-based museum that presents the research of underwater archaeologists.

National Historic Landmark (NHL)—A structure, site, ship, or shipwreck recognized by the federal government of the United States as being of national historic significance. Of the 90,000 properties, representing 1.4 million individual resources on the National Register of Historic Places, only about 2,500 are NHLs.

National Register of Historic Places—This is the official registry of historic and archaeological sites, structures, buildings, ships, shipwrecks, and other cultural objects determined to be significant because they meet at least one of four criteria established by the U.S. Department of the Interior and National Park Service. This listing program was established in 1966 after Congress passed the National Historic Preservation Act.

National Science Foundation (NSF)—A U.S. government agency that supports and funds research in the field of nonmedical sciences and engineering.

NOAA—National Oceanic and Atmospheric Administration, a federal scientific agency under the Department of Commerce, whose focus is on the oceans and atmosphere.

North American Society for Oceanic History—NASOH is a not-for-profit organization of maritime historians, underwater archaeologists, retired naval personnel, and others interested in the maritime and naval history and heritage of North America's oceanic and inland waterways.

ordnance—Military weapons and ammunition, especially related to artillery.

polyethylene glycol (PEG)—A synthetic resin with many applications. PEG is sometimes used to conserve wooden objects that have been in water. PEG replaces the water in wooden objects and helps make the wood more dimensionally stable and also reduces shrinking and warping.

portage—To carry a boat overland, generally to move from one body of water to another waterway or to transport the vessel around waterfalls.

prams—Small, snub-nosed, flat-bottomed boats.

Principal Investigator (PI)—The Principal Investigator or PI in an archaeology project is a professional archaeologist with at least a master's degree in archaeology, anthropology, or related field. This person is the overall director of the project and thus formulates plans, analyzes data collected during the project, and writes reports.

provincial—A soldier, generally of a militia, from one of the thirteen British colonies in America.

public outreach—Activities designed to give information to the populace to educate and inform them about a mission and programs.

radeaux—The French term "radeau" (radeaux, plural) means *raft* but was a type of floating gun battery.

raked—To slant from the perpendicular.

redoubt—A temporary enclosed defensive works generally made of logs and earthworks. A redoubt was sometimes positioned outside a larger fortification.

remotely-operated-vehicle (ROV)—A tethered underwater vehicle that has video and/or photography capability.

replica archaeology—A field of archaeology where one tests a hypothesis by replicating artifacts, methods, or techniques from the past to determine the feasibility of a previous people's lifestyle. *See* experimental archaeology.

rocker—The amount of curvature of a watercraft along its longitudinal contour.

row galleys—Armed vessels from the "age of sail" that used oars rather than sail as its principal propulsion.

scarf joint—Overlapping joinery used to connect two timbers.

sheathing—A material added to the bottom of a vessel to protect it from the effects of water and marine organisms, the latter sometimes attaching to the bottom of the vessel and affecting its speed. Some bateaux might have been sheathed using tar.

shipwreck preserves—Shipwreck sites protected by government oversight that often permits "controlled public access" for scuba-diving visitation.

sloops—Sailing vessels fore and aft rigged with one mast and a jib.

stem—Sometimes called a stempost, the vertical timber assembly located in the bow of a bateau.

sternpost—The central upright structure at the stern of a vessel that sometimes held a rudder or a steerage oar or paddle.

strakes—The side planking of a vessel's hull from bow to stern.

submerged cultural resources—Physical evidence of people from the past found underwater such as a sunken site, historic structure, object, landscape, and even a shipwreck.

transects—Traversing straight lines where a person or group of people make observations or collect measurements for scientific purposes.

treenails (trunnels)—Hardwood pegs used as fasteners, serving the same function as nails and bolts; for fastening together wooden pieces of vessels.

underwater archaeology—The study of people of the past by examining their material remains in a submerged environment.

Vauban-style earth-and-wooden fortification—A type of colonial American fort generally with four corner bastions. The geometric designs of these forts, conceived by a French military engineer named Vauban for the fortresses in Europe, was later copied by French and English military engineers for their military installations in North America. Vauban's star-pattern design fortification was rather effective as it provided defenders with adequate defense and excellent fields of firing their muskets and artillery.

vernacular watercraft—Vessels that were "common" and built according to specific traditions of a place or culture.

ways—The timber framing and cradle on which a vessel sits as it is being built.

whaleboats—A type of colonial watercraft, similar in length to a small bateau. Little is known about their construction in the eighteenth century as compared to the more modern vessels also known as whaleboats.

Notes

Chapter One Early History of Bateaux

1. Russell P. Bellico, *Sails and Stream in the Mountains: A Maritime and Military History of Lake George and Lake Champlain* (Fleischmanns, NY: Purple Mountain Press, 2001), 13.
2. Howard I. Chapelle, *American Small Sailing Craft: Their Design, Development, and Construction* (New York: W.W. Norton & Company, 1951), 33.
3. E.B. O'Callaghan, *The Documentary History of the State of New York* (Albany, NY: Weed, Parsons & Company, 1849), 68–69.
4. Bellico, *Sails and Stream in the Mountains*, 2001, 23.
5. Ibid., 21–35.
6. Ibid., 39–40.
7. *Schenectady Reflector*, "Attack on Fort William Henry" (Schenectady, NY, April 1, 1842).
8. Bellico, *Sails and Stream in the Mountains*, 2001, 23.
9. Don R. Gerlach, *Philip Schuyler and the American Revolution in New York, 1733–1777* (Lincoln: University of Nebraska Press, 1964), 27–28.
10. Russell P. Bellico, *Sails and Stream in the Mountains: A Maritime and Military History of Lake George and Lake Champlain* (Fleischmanns, NY: Purple Mountain Press, 1992), 77–78.
11. J.W. Bradstreet, *Report of JW Bradstreet to General Amherst* (London, Public Records Office, 1758), 57–58.
12. Bellico, *Sails and Stream in the Mountains*, 1992, 87–114.
13. Gary Zaboly (ed.), "A Royal Artillery Officer with Amherst: The Journal of Captain-Lieutenant Henry Skinner, May 1–July 28, 1759," *The Bulletin of Fort Ticonderoga Museum* (1993), 381.
14. Francis Jennings, *Empire of Fortune: Crowns, Colonies & Tribes in the Seven Years War in America* (New York: W.W. Norton & Company, 1988), 425, 429.
15. John Gardner, "Bateaus Played Key Role in American History," *National Fisherman* (April 1967), 8-A.

16. Chapelle, 34–35.
17. Bellico, *Sails and Stream in the Mountains*, 1992, 121, 131, 165–189.
18. Ibid., 205–235.
19. Ibid., 218.
20. Associated Press, "Historic boat found at Lake Champlain," *The Saratogian* (Saratoga Springs, NY, August 22, 1999).
21. Bruce G. Terrell, "The James River Bateau: Tobacco Transport in Upland Virginia, 1745–1840" (MA Thesis, East Carolina University, Greenville, NC, July 1991).

Chapter Two The Bateau Watercraft

1. John Gardner, "Dutch Influences on American Small Craft During the Colonial Period," *The Log of Mystic Seaport* (Mystic, CT: Mystic Seaport Museum, Summer 1995), 16.
2. Dennis M. Lewis, "Batteaux in the Champlain Waterway 1755–1783," (Plattsburgh, NY: Author, August 1983).
3. Chapelle, 33.
4. Ibid., 34.
5. Ibid.
6. Ibid.
7. Nathan A. Gallagher, "The Lake George Bateaux: British Colonial Utility Craft in The French and Indian War" (MA Thesis, Texas A&M University, College Station, 2015), 4.
8. Chapelle, 34.
9. Robert McG. Thomas Jr. "John Gardner, 90, Boat Curator at Mystic Seaport Museum, Dies," *New York Times* (October 19, 1995).
10. Gardner, April 1967, 28-A.
11. John Gardner, *The Dory Book* (Mystic, CT: Mystic Seaport Museum, 1987), 21.
12. Gardner, April 1967, 8-A, 28-A.
13. Gallagher, 37.
14. Kevin J. Crisman, "Struggle for a Continent: Naval Battles of the French and Indian Wars," *Ships and Shipwrecks of the Americas: A History Based on Underwater Archaeology* (New York: Thames & Hudson, Inc., 1988), 132–133.
15. Gallagher.
16. Ibid., 47, 58–59, 66.
17. Ibid., 76.

18. Adolph B. Benson (ed.), *The America of 1750: Peter Kalm's Travels in North America* (New York: Dover Publications, Inc., 1937, 1964), 333.
19. Ibid.
20. Crisman, 132.
21. Terry Crandall, conversations with author, 1991.
22. Crisman, 132.
23. Gallagher, 83.
24. Caleb Rea, *The Journal of Dr. Caleb Rea, Written During the Expedition Against Ticonderoga in 1758* (Salem, MA: The Essex Institute, 1881), 106.
25. Crisman, 133.
26. Ibid., 133, 137.
27. Gallagher, 55.
28. Crisman, 137.
29. Gallagher, 55.
30. Crisman, 133, 137.
31. Ibid.
32. Ibid, 137.
33. John Gardner, "Famous Boat Type in Transitional Stage," *National Fisherman* (May 1967), 8-A.
34. Crisman, 137.
35. Robert E. Hager, *Mohawk River Boats and Navigation Before 1820* (Syracuse, NY: Canal Society of New York State, 1987), 32.
36. Crisman, 133, 137.
37. Gardner, May 1967, 8-A.
38. Crandall, 1991.
39. Crisman, 137.
40. Hager, 45.
41. Stan Zeccolo, Letter to Dr. Robert Bruce Inverarity, on file at Adirondack Museum (Blue Mountain Lake, NY, August 1, 1961).
42. Lemuel Wood, "A Journal of the Canada Expedition in the Year 1759." *Chronicles of Lake George: Journeys in War and Peace*, edited by Russell P. Bellico (Fleischmanns, NY: Purple Mountain Press, 1995), 130.
43. Jeffery Amherst, *The Journal of Jeffery Amherst: Recording the Military Career of General Amherst in America from 1758–1763*, edited by Clarence Webster (Toronto: The Ryerson Press, 1931), 165.
44. Gallagher, 22.
45. Alexander Moneypenny, "Moneypenny Orderly Book," *The Bulletin of the Fort Ticonderoga Museum* (Ticonderoga, NY, Fort Ticonderoga, October 1970), 434–461.

46. Lewis, 1983.
47. Gallagher, 97.
48. Gallagher, 5.
49. Joseph F. Meany Jr., "Bateaux and 'Battoe Men': An American Colonial Response to the Problem of Logistics in Mountain Warfare," Website (Saratoga Springs, NY, New York State Military Museum, September 26, 2003).
50. Nathaniel Bouton, D.D. *Documents and Records Relating to the Province of New-Hampshire from 1749 to 1763* (Manchester, James M. Campbell, State Printer, 1872), n.p.
51. Meany.
52. Lewis, 1983.

Chapter Three Building Techniques

1. Gallagher, 47, 59, 67.
2. Hager, 29.
3. John Gardner, "Construction Details of Old Bateaux Show Basic Design with Variations," *National Fisherman* (June 1967), 8-A.
4. Ibid., 9-A.
5. Hager, 28–32.
6. Gardner, *National Fisherman*, June 1967, 9–A.
7. Crisman, 137.
8. Hager, 32, 35.
9. Ibid., 37–39.
10. Ibid., 28–45.

Chapter Four Discovery of Lake George's Sunken Bateaux of 1758

1. *Lake George Mirror*, "The Sunken Batteaux of Lake George" (June 10, 1893).
2. *Lake George Mirror*, "Along the Shore," July 8, 1893.
3. *Lake George Mirror*, "A Relic of By-Gone Days: A Forty-foot Plank from the Hull of a Sunken Batteaux," August 3, 1895.
4. Mark L. Peckham, conversation with author, 1997.
5. *Lake George Mirror*, "The Sunken Batteaux of Lake George," September 10, 1898.
6. *Lake George Mirror*, "French and Indian War: Timbers from the Colonial Batteaux in the Caldwell Station," June 24, 1899.

7. *Lake George Mirror* June 9, 1900. This article was on a piece of a colonial boat raised.
8. Russell P. Bellico, conversation with author, 1990.
9. Terry Crandall, "Questions to Ask Terry Crandall" (Richfield Springs, NY, n.d.).
10. Joseph W. Zarzynski, personal dive logs and notes (Wilton, NY, October 10, 1993).
11. Bellico, 1992, 78–79.
12. *Brooklyn Daily Standard Union*, "A Relic of the French and Indian Wars Raised from the Bottom of Lake George" (November 22, 1903).
13. Ibid.
14. Ibid.
15. *The Chatham Courier* (July 29, 1891). This article was on colonial history at Lake George.
16. *Brooklyn Daily Standard Union*, "A Relic."
17. Joseph W. Zarzynski, "French and Indian War Artifacts at Warrensburgh Museum of Local History," *The French and Indian War Society Newsletter* (Lake George, NY, The French and Indian War Society, December 2014), 4–6.
18. Artec, "Eva Scanner," Website (accessed December 1, 2017).
19. *The Warrensburgh News*, "Improvement of Beach at Lake George (Warrensburg, NY, June 24, 1920).
20. *Glens Falls Post-Star*, "Relic Hunters Are Numerous, (Glens Falls, NY, July 24, 1915).
21. *The Saratogian*, "Clock Case of Old Timbers," April 10, 1919.
22. *Lake George Mirror*, "Preserve Historical Relics," August 18, 1934.

Chapter Five The 1950s and Early 1960s: "Rediscovery"

1. Carl Dunn, conversations with author, 1995.
2. Bernard E. Empleton (ed.), *The New Science of Skin and Scuba Diving* (Chicago: Follett Publishing Company, 1957, 1980).
3. Stanley M. Gifford, *Fort William Henry: A History* (Glens Falls, NY: The Bullard Press, 1955), 57–59.
4. *The Knickerbocker News*, "Watch for Relics. Kiwanians Urged" (Albany, NY, April 21, 1954).
5. *Ticonderoga Sentinel*, "Skin Diving Booming in State" (Ticonderoga, NY, August 21, 1958).
6. *The Troy Times Record*, "Rare Find" (Troy, NY, August 13, 1959).

7. Ibid.
8. *The Troy Record*, "Skindivers Find Old Cannon" (Troy, NY, August 12, 1959).
9. Ibid.
10. *The Troy Times Record*, "Rare Find."
11. *The Saratogian*, "38 Present at Adult Club Meeting Despite Cold" (Saratoga Springs, NY, January 24, 1961).
12. Dan Barr, "Teenage Scuba Divers Discovered Lake George Relics: Historical Boat Finds Authenticated," *Albany Times-Union* (Albany, NY, July 25, 1960).
13. *The Saratogian*, "$20,000 Price Tag Put on Fort Clinton Restoration" (Saratoga Springs, NY, April 25, 1961).
14. Barr, "Teenage Scuba Divers."
15. *The Citizen Register*, "French-Indian War Batteaux Believed Lake George Find" (Ossining, NY, July 29, 1960).
16. *Glens Falls Times*, "Smithsonian Institution Experts Will Make Study of Lake George Artifacts" (Glens Falls, NY, July 26, 1960).
17. Ibid.
18. *New York Times*, "Sunken 1758 Boat Believed British" (July 30, 1960).
19. *Amsterdam Evening Recorder*, "Find Naval Relics at Bottom of Lake" (Amsterdam, NY, July 28, 1960).
20. Joseph W. Zarzynski, "Lake George Profiles: Robert LaVoy," *The Lake George Nautical Newsletter* (Wilton, NY, vol. 2, no. 1, 1993), 3.
21. Sean Ryan, "Bottom of Lake George: Divers Find Craft With 40 Mortars," *Albany Times-Union* (Albany, NY, July 31, 1960).

Chapter Six Toward Better Management

1. *Glens Falls Times*, "Legal Battle Develops on Artifacts" (Glens Falls, NY, July 29, 1960).
2. *New York Times*, "Sunken 1758 Boat Believed British."
3. *The Knickerbocker News*, "Study of Sunken Boats in Lake George OKd" (Albany, NY, August 2, 1960).
4. *Glens Falls Times*, "Historic Assoc. to Direct Work of Recovering Boats," August 2, 1960.
5. Kenneth J. Vrana and Edward M. Mahoney (eds.), *Great Lakes Underwater Cultural Resources: Important Information for Shaping our Future* (East Lansing, MI: Michigan State University, Department of Park, Recreation and Tourism Resources, 1993).
6. National Park Service, "American Antiquities Act of 1906," *Links to the Past*, Website (accessed December 5, 2000).

7. Shirley Armstrong, "Historical Unit Raps Bateaux Policy Critics," *Albany Times-Union*, August 25, 1960.

8. *Lake George Mirror*, "Shall Historic Objects Found in Lake George Go to Museums Elsewhere?" August 12, 1960.

9. *Lake George Mirror*, "Fortune Beneath the Waves!" August 12, 1960.

10. *Albany Times-Union*, "Ticonderoga Opposes State Action: 2 Forts Join in Bateau Battle," August 20, 1960.

11. *Lake George Mirror*, "Mirror Gets Support on Stand Taken on Historic Items Recovered in Lake," August 26, 1960.

12. *Lake George Mirror*, "Forts May Get Bateaux If Enough Are Raised Intact from Depths of the Lake," July 21, 1961.

13. R.B. Inverarity, *Manual of Puppetry* (Portland, OR, 1936).

14. Elinor Mahoney, "The Federal Art Project in Washington State. From 'The Great Depression in Washington State.'" Website (accessed May 9, 2016).

15. *Watertown Daily Times*, "Dr. Robert Inverarity Resigns Museum Post" (Watertown, NY, July 22, 1965).

16. Archives of American Art-Smithsonian Institution, "Robert Bruce Inverarity papers," Website (accessed November 6, 2014).

17. Ibid.

18. Paul A.F. Walter and Arthur J. O. Anderson (eds.), "Dedication." *El Palacio* (Santa Fe, NM, Archaeological Society of New Mexico, September 1953), 309–314.

19. Archives of American Art-Smithsonian Institution.

20. *Ottawa Citizen*, "Works to U.K" (Ottawa, QC, June 8, 1976).

21. *Watertown Daily Times*, July 22, 1965.

22. Dr. Robin K. Wright, "Searching for what inspired the Seattle Seahawks logo," Website (accessed November 19, 2014).

23. *Albany Times-Union*, "Hunt Called Off at Lake George," August 23, 1960.

24. *Glens Falls Times*, Historical Assoc. Asks Skin Divers to Report Artifacts," August 30, 1960.

25. Michele Aubry, "Abandoned Shipwreck Act (U.S.)," *Encyclopedia of Underwater and Maritime Archaeology*, edited by James P. Delgado (London, British Museum Press, 1997), 16.

26. Alan Bauder, e-mail communication (December 15, 2000).

27. Ibid.

28. Anne G. Giesecke, "The Abandoned Shipwreck Act 1988 to 1998," *Underwater Archaeology* (Atlanta, Society for Historical Archaeology, 1998), 114.

29. National Park Service, "Archeology Program—New York," Website (accessed November 3, 2016).

Chapter Seven Underwater Archaeology

1. *Watertown Times*, "Raising of Ship Being Planned" (Watertown, NY, September 22, 1960).
2. George F. Bass, *Archaeology Under Water* (Middlesex, England, Penguin Books Ltd., 1970, revised edition), 54.
3. George F. Bass (ed.), *Beneath the Seven Seas: Adventures with the Institute of Nautical Archaeology* (London: Thames & Hudson Ltd., 2005), 13–14.
4. Bass, *Archaeology Under Water* (New York, Frederick A. Praeger, 1966), 57–58.
5. *Schenectady Union Star*, "TV to Aid in Charting Sunken Ships" (Schenectady, NY, September 22, 1960).
6. Dan Barr, "Bateau Raised in Lake George," *Albany Times-Union* (Albany, NY, September 24, 1960).
7. Commander Norval E. Nickerson, "Diving Assistance to the Adirondack Museum," (Washington, DC, U.S. Navy, September 28, 1960).
8. Ibid.
9. *Schenectady Union Star*, September 22, 1960.
10. *Albany Times Union*, "TV Eye Will Pry For Lake Relics," October 28, 1960.
11. Barr, "Bateau Raised in Lake George."
12. Ibid.
13. Nickerson.
14. Ibid.
15. *Glens Falls Times*, "First of Ancient Boats Raised from Bottom of Lake George by Divers," September 24, 1960.
16. *Plattsburgh Press-Republican*, "Bateau Raised from Lake" (Plattsburgh, NY, September 24, 1960).
17. *Ticonderoga Sentinel*, " 'Aqua Vandals' Wreck Bateau," October 27, 1960.
18. *Utica Daily Press*, "Aquanaughties Wreck Bateau" (Utica, NY, October 29, 1960).
19. Howard Lewis, "Calls for Skin Diver Licensing—Destruction of Relics Deplored," *The Knickerbocker News* (Albany, NY, January 12, 1961).
20. Ibid.
21. Tony Hillerman, *A Thief of Time* (New York: Harper & Row, 1988).
22. *Lake George Mirror*, "Forts May Get Bateaux If Enough Are Raised Intact from Depths of the Lake," July 21, 1961.

23. Lars Åke Kvarning "*Vasa*," *Encyclopedia of Underwater and Maritime Archaeology*, edited by James P. Delgado (London, British Museum Press, 1997), 454–456.

24. Dr. Margaret Rule, "*Mary Rose*," *Encyclopedia of Underwater and Maritime Archaeology*, edited by James P. Delgado (London, British Museum Press, 1997), 264–266.

25. *Utica Observer-Dispatch*, "18th Century Boat Found" (Utica, NY, August 25, 1963).

26. June Drenning Holmquist and Ardis Hillman Wheeler (eds.), *Diving into the Past: Theories, Techniques, and Applications of Underwater Archaeology, The Proceedings of a Conference on Underwater Archaeology* (St. Paul: The Minnesota Historical Society, 1964), iii.

27. Robert Bruce Inverarity, "The Conservation of Wood from Fresh Water." In *Diving into The Past: Theories, Techniques, and Applications of Underwater Archaeology*, 68–70.

28. Inverarity, "New York Report" In *Diving into the Past: Theories, Techniques, and Applications of Underwater Archaeology*, 80–81.

29. Holmquist and Wheeler, 1964.

30. Jerry Pepper, letter to author (January 26, 1999).

31. Gallagher, 34.

32. Ibid.

33. *Lake George Mirror*, "Fort Ticonderoga Builds a Replica of Old Bateau," July 7, 1961.

34. Joseph W. Zarzynski, "Fort Ticonderoga's Bateau," *The Lake George Nautical Newsletter* (vol. 2, no. 1, 1993), 3.

35. *Lake George Mirror*, "Divers Will Form Salvage Body But Won't Receive Pay," July 14, 1961.

36. *Schenectady Gazette*, "Skindivers to Safe Guard Artifacts in Lake George" (Schenectady, NY, February 7, 1962).

37. *The Saratogian*, "Scouts Learn About Turkey," November 16, 1961.

38. *Lake George Mirror*, "Scuba Diving in Lake George," June 29, 1962.

39. Terry Crandall, "Lake George: Time Capsule in Controversy" (Richfield Springs, NY, n.d.).

40. Dr. Robert Bruce Inverarity, letter to Colonel Edward P. Hamilton (October 3, 1960).

41. Terry Crandall, conversations with author, 2014.

42. *Sarasota Herald-Tribune*, "Scolded For Water Raids" (Sarasota, Florida, April 29, 1963).

43. Holmquist and Wheeler, 1964.

44. Matthew A. Russell, "Integrating Underwater and Terrestrial Archaeology." The Underwater Blogger, Museum of Underwater Archaeology (2010), Website (accessed December 30, 2014).
45. *New York State Divers Association, Inc. Information Booklet* (Ava, NY, n.d.).
46. Mendel Peterson, *History Under the Sea: A Handbook for Underwater Exploration*, (Washington, DC: Smithsonian Institution Press, 1965), 5–9.
47. Marion Clayton Link, *Sea Diver: A Quest for History Under the Sea* (Coral Gables, FL: University of Miami Press, 1958), 1–26.
48. Susan Van Hoek and Marion Clayton Link, *From Sky to Sea: A Story of Edwin A. Link* (Flagstaff, AZ: Best Publishing Company, 2003), 39–60.
49. Bass, 2005, 14–15.
50. Crandall, "Lake George: Time Capsule in Controversy" (n.d.)
51. Crandall, 2014.
52. Terry Crandall, "Operation Bateaux Revisited . . . Twenty-Four Years Later (Part 1)," *Bateaux Below* (Wilton, NY, Atlantic Alliance Lake George Bateaux Research Team, July 1988), 2–4.
53. Terry Crandall, "Operation Bateaux" (Richfield Springs, NY, 1964).
54. Terry Crandall, "Untitled Map of Sunken Bateaux at Lake George" (Richfield Springs, NY, n.d.).
55. Crandall, 1964.
56. Peter Pepe (director and video editor) and Joseph W. Zarzynski (writer), "Wooden Bones: The Sunken Fleet of 1758," DVD (Glens Falls, NY, Pepe Productions and Bateaux Below, Inc., 2010).
57. *Richfield Springs Mercury*, "Terry Crandall at Archeology Conference" (Richfield Springs, NY, April 22, 1965).
58. Russell, 2010.
59. Terry Crandall, conversations with author (1991).
60. Richard J.H. Johnston, *New York Times*, "Lake George Divers Find 1758 Battle Craft," (June 27, 1965).
61. Robert Bruce Inverarity, letter to Dr. Hugh M. Flick (Albany, NY, June 28, 1965).
62. Crandall, "Operation Bateaux Revisited . . . Twenty-Four Years Later (Part 1)," *Bateaux Below*, July 1988, 2–4.
63. *Watertown Daily Times*, "Dr. Robert Inverarity Resigns Museum Post," July 22, 1965.
64. *The Otsego Farmer*, "Swinney Is Named Museum Director" (Cooperstown, NY, September 23, 1965).
65. Jerry Pepper, conversation with author (October 25, 2016).

66. Celia Hahn, *The Knickerbocker News*, "Historians, Divers Collide on Treasures" (Albany, NY, November 9, 1967).
67. Ibid.
68. Paul Scudiere, *Diving into History: A Manual of Underwater Archeology for Divers in New York State* (Albany: The University of the State of New York, State Education Department, 1969), 19.
69. Lud Wolf, "Lake George," *Skin Diver Magazine* (July 1969), 56–59.
70. M. Timothy O'Keefe (ed.), *Erving's World Wide Skindiver's Guide* (Winter Park, FL: Erving Publishing Company, 1973).
71. Philip Lord Jr., correspondence with Diving Discovery (Albany, NY, 1978 and 1982).
72. Schenectady Urban Cultural Park, "The Batteau Project" (Schenectady, NY, 1992).
73. *New York Times*, "Museum, with Just a Relic to Go On, Tries to Rebuild Lost Piece of History" (August 16, 1987).

Chapter Eight A Renaissance of Interest

1. Philip Lord Jr., conversations with author (1987).
2. Joseph W. Zarzynski, "October 1988 Side-Scan Sonar Expedition at Lake George," *Bateaux Below* (Wilton, NY, Atlantic Alliance Lake George Bateaux Research Team, December 1988), 7.
3. Martin Klein, "Side scan sonar," *Encyclopedia of Underwater and Maritime Archaeology*, edited by James P. Delgado (London, British Museum Press, 1997), 384–385.
4. Martin Klein, conversation with author (2017).
5. The Explorers Club, "Side Scan Sonar Explorers for Lake George, New York Shipwrecks," *The Explorers Newsletter* (March–May 1989).
6. Joseph W. Zarzynski and John Farrell, "Recent Underwater Archaeological Surveys at Lake George, New York," *Archaeology of the French and Indian War: Military Sites of the Hudson River, Lake George, and Lake Champlain Corridor*, edited by David R. Starbuck (Queensbury, NY: Adirondack Community College, 1994), 6.
7. Ibid.
8. Kvarning, 1997, 455.
9. Terry Crandall, e-mail to author, July 27, 2000.
10. Terry Crandall, e-mail to author, October 22, 1999.
11. Bateaux Below, Inc., "Bateaux Below, Inc. Draft, National Register of Historic Places Registration Form-shipwreck site and remains, bateaux c. 1758 [Wiawaka Bateaux Site]" (Wilton, NY, November 17, 1991).

12. Zarzynski and Farrell, 6–7.
13. Joseph W. Zarzynski, personal dive logs and notes, July 27, 1988.
14. Bellico, *Sails and Stream in the Mountains*, 1992, 77.
15. Joseph W. Zarzynski, "35 Years Later—Lake George's Lost Submarine Found by Bateaux Below, Inc.," *The Lake George Nautical Newsletter* (Albany, NY, Zarzynski Consulting & Underwater Survey and Bateaux Below, Inc., vol. 4, no. 1 1995), 1, 8.
16. Pepe and Zarzynski, "Wooden Bones: The Sunken Fleet of 1758," DVD, 2010.

Chapter Nine The "Mortar Bateau"

1. Ryan, 1960.
2. *Lake George Mirror*, "Saratogians Discover 28-Foot Boat and 40 Mortars in the Lake," August 5, 1960.
3. Dr. Lewis L. Smith, letter to Dr. Robert B. Inverarity with affidavit (August 15, 1960).
4. David Glenn Diehl, "Early SCUBA in Lake George," *Lake George Mirror* (Lake George, NY, August 14, 1998), 15–16.
5. *Lake George Mirror*, "Charles Diehl, Scuba Pioneer, Dies" (Lake George, NY, November 2007).
6. Diehl, 1998, 15–16.
7. Gene Parker (ed.), *Dive: The Complete Book of Skin Diving* (New York: Wilfred Funk, Inc., 1963).
8. Gene Parker, "Report to Dr. R.B. Inverarity on diving/uw photography of September 14, 1962" (Scotia, NY, September 19, 1962).
9. Gene Parker, drawings and map of Lake George "mortar bomb bateau."
10. Terry Crandall, Adirondack Museum-Diving Report (Richfield Springs, NY, September 15, 1963).
11. Crandall, conversations with author, 2014.
12. Terry Crandall, Adirondack Museum-Diving Report (Richfield Springs, NY, October 12, 1963).
13. Crandall, Adirondack Museum-Diving Report, September 15, 1963.
14. Ibid.
15. *Warrensburg-Lake George News*, "James A. Magee" (Warrensburg, NY, December 12, 1979).
16. J.A. Magee, "Bomb Ketch and cargo of bombs" (personal notes) (Lake George, NY, June 30, 1965).
17. Ibid.
18. Ibid.

19. Ibid.
20. Joseph W. Zarzynski, personal dive logs and notes (Wilton, NY, 1987–1998).
21. Crandall, conversations with author, 2014.
22. Ibid.
23. Terry Crandall, Adirondack Museum-Diving Report, October 12, 1963.
24. Zarzynski, e-mail communication with Phil Lord and Mark Peckham (November 26, 1998).
25. *The Saratogian*, "Spa Divers Tell of Lake George 'Battles'" (Saratoga Springs, NY, September 30, 1960).
26. Walter M. Stroup, letter to author, February 24, 1987.
27. *The Bulletin of the Fort Ticonderoga Museum*, "Recent Accessions" (Fort Ticonderoga, NY, volume X, no. 6, 1962).
28. Diehl, 1998, 15–16.
29. Bob Benway, "Mortar Bomb at Lake George Historical Association" (Queensbury, NY, November 2, 1998).
30. Bob Benway, "13 Inch Mortar Bomb from Lake George, NY (Historical Society of the Town of Bolton, Bolton Landing, New York)" (Queensbury, NY, August 31, 2001).
31. Bob Benway, "13 Inch Mortar Bomb from Lake George, NY (Cooper's Cave Ale Co., Glens Falls, New York)" (Queensbury, NY, August 31, 2001).
32. Gallagher, 85–86.

Chapter Ten What Lies Beneath: An Inventory

1. Daniel Lenihan, "Cultural resources management (CRM)," *Encyclopedia of Underwater and Maritime Archaeology*, edited by James P. Delgado (London, British Museum Press, 1997), 119.
2. *The Warrensburg-Lake George News*, "Fort William Henry's 24-Pounder Mounted on a New Field Carriage" (Warrensburg, NY, July 26, 1966).
3. Joseph W. Zarzynski and Amanda Andreas, "Shipwreck Cannons at a Replica 18th Century Fort," *The French and Indian War Society Newsletter* (Lake George, NY, The French and Indian War Society, October 2014), 3–4.
4. *The Warrensburg-Lake George News*, July 26, 1966.

Chapter Eleven Missing Bateau Shipwrecks

1. Johnston, *New York Times*, "Lake George Divers Find 1758 Battle Craft."
2. Joseph W. Zarzynski, D.K. Abbass, and Bob Benway, "*The Sunken Fleet of*

1758" Shipwreck Preserve: 1999 Debris Clean Up and Site Stabilization (Wilton, NY: Bateaux Below, Inc., 2000), 35.

3. *The Troy Record*, "Find Another 'Ghost Fleet' Boat" (Troy, NY, August 15, 1960).

4. Diehl, 1998, 15–16.

5. *The Saratogian*, "New 'Ghost Fleet' Boat Found in Lake George" (Saratoga Springs, NY, August 15, 1960).

6. Crandall, conversations with author, 2014.

7. *Albany Times Union*, "Swimmers Find French-Indian War Cannon, 2 Gunboat Anchors in Waters of Lake George" (Albany, NY, September 5, 1954).

8. *Binghamton Press*, "Glass-Bottomed Boat Provided for Summer Guests at Lake George" (Binghamton, NY, June 25, 1930).

9. Bellico, *Sails and Stream in the Mountains*, 2001, 180.

10. *Albany Times-Union*, "Swimmers Find French-Indian War Cannon, 2 Gunboat Anchors in Waters of Lake George."

11. Ibid.

12. Ibid.

13. *Albany Times-Union*, "Relics Saved in Ft. William Henry Fire" (Albany, NY, September 19, 1967).

14. Dr. Lewis L. Smith, letter to Dr. Robert B. Inverarity, October 14, 1960.

15. John Farrell, conversations with author, 1993.

Chapter Twelve Lake George's *Baby Whale* Submarine

1. National Geographic Society, "Bathyscaphe," (2016) (accessed October 28, 2016).

2. Joseph W. Zarzynski, "35 Years Later—Lake George's Lost Submarine Found by Bateaux Below, Inc.," *The Lake George Nautical Newsletter* (Wilton, NY, vol. 4, no. 1, 1995), 8.

3. *Glens Falls Times*, "Miniature Submarine Is Expected to Help in Lake George Explorations" (Glens Falls, NY, August 4, 1960).

4. Zarzynski, "35 Years Later," 8.

5. Pepe and Zarzynski, "Wooden Bones: The Sunken Fleet of 1758."

6. Alan C. Bauder, letter to author (July 31, 1995).

Chapter Thirteen Wiawaka Bateaux and the National Register of Historic Places

1. Bateaux Below, Inc., "Bateaux Below, Inc. Draft, National Register of Historic Places Registration Form—shipwreck site and remains, bateaux c. 1758 [Wiawaka Bateaux Site]," 1991.

2. Mark L. Peckham, "Lake George Shipwrecks Nominated to National Register," *Preservation League of New York State Newsletter* (Albany, NY, Spring 1992), 12.

Chapter Fourteen Submerged Heritage Preserves

1. Kenneth J. Vrana, "Shipwreck protected areas," *Encyclopedia of Underwater and Maritime Archaeology*, edited by James P. Delgado (London, British Museum Press, 1997), 381.
2. National Park Service, "Abandoned Shipwreck Act Guidelines," Website (accessed December 5, 2000).
3. Ibid.
4. *Lake George Mirror*, "Huletts Man Advocates an Underwater Museum" (Lake George, NY, July 3, 1964).
5. Joseph W. Zarzynski, "Historian Harrison Bird Suggests Underwater Museum," *Lake George Mirror* (Lake George, NY, November 2016), 14.
6. Russell P. Bellico, "The End of the *Sayonara*," *Bateaux Below* (Wilton, NY: Atlantic Alliance Lake George Bateaux Research Team, May 1988), 2–4.
7. Arthur B. Cohn, "Lake Champlain's Underwater Historic Preserve Program: Reasonable Access to Appropriate Sites." In *Submerged Cultural Resource Management: Preserving and Interpreting Our Sunken Maritime Heritage*, edited by James D. Spirek and Della A. Scott-Ireton (New York, Kluwer Academic/Plenum Publishers, 2003), 86.
8. Joseph W. Zarzynski, " 'Submerged Heritage Preserves' Opened at Lake George," *The Lake George Nautical Newsletter* (Wilton, NY, vol. 2, no. 3, 1993), 1.
9. "Submerged Heritage Preserve—The Sunken Fleet of 1758" (New York State Department of Environmental Conservation brochure, Albany, NY, 1993).
10. Cohn, 2003, 85–93.
11. "Submerged Heritage Preserve—The *Forward*" (New York State Department of Environmental Conservation brochure) and "Submerged Heritage Preserve—The Sunken Fleet of 1758" (New York State Department of Environmental Conservation brochure, Albany, NY, 1993).
12. *Glens Falls Post-Star*, "Police charge divers" (Glens Falls, NY, July 30, 1994).
13. Joseph W. Zarzynski, D.K. Abbass, Bob Benway, and John Farrell, " 'Ring-Around-A-Radeau,' or, Fencing in a 1758 Shipwreck for Public Access and Preservation." In *Underwater Archaeology*, edited by Stephen R. James Jr. and Camille Stanley (Cincinnati, OH: Society for Historical Archaeology, 1996), 35–39.

14. Joseph W. Zarzynski, "Bateau Replica Sunk Near 1758 Wiawaka Bateaux," *The Lake George Nautical Newsletter* (Wilton, NY, Zarzynski Consulting & Underwater Survey and Bateaux Below, Inc., vol. 6, no. 2, 1997), 1, 8.

15. Ibid., 1.

16. William Appling, Bob Benway, and Joseph W. Zarzynski, *Lake George's Forward: Historic Vessel, Shipwreck Preserve, and "Underwater Classroom"* (Wilton, NY, Bateaux Below, Inc., August 1998).

17. Joseph W. Zarzynski, Samuel S. Bowser, John Farrell, and Peter Pepe, "Making Shipwrecks Celebrities: Using the National Register, Shipwreck Preserves, Documentary Filmmaking, and Interdisciplinary Projects for Shipwreck Preservation." In *Between the Devil and the Deep: Meeting Challenges in the Public Interpretation of Maritime Cultural Heritage*, edited by Della A. Scott-Ireton (New York: Springer Science+Business Media, 2014), 199–200.

18. Ibid., 197–206.

19. Preserve America, "The Preserve America Initiative," Website (accessed October 28, 2016).

20. Ibid.

21. Michelle Obama, Letter to Volunteers of Bateaux Below, Inc. (Washington, DC, July 29, 2009).

Chapter Fifteen Stabilizing a Bateau Shipwreck Site

1. National Archives and Records Administration, *Federal Register* (Washington, DC, vol. 63, no. 124, June 29, 1998), 35279.

2. Joseph W. Zarzynski, personal dive logs and notes (Wilton, NY, October 1, 2000).

3. Joseph W. Zarzynski, D.K. Abbass, and Bob Benway, "*The Sunken Fleet of 1758" Shipwreck Preserve: 1999 Debris Clean Up and Site Stabilization*, 2000.

4. Ibid.

Chapter Sixteen Students Build Underwater Archaeology Equipment and Replica Bateaux

1. *Schenectady Gazette*, "7th Graders Explore Underwater Archaeology" (Schenectady, NY, January 7, 1988).

2. John F. Coates and Jan Bill, "Experimental archaeology," *Encyclopedia of Underwater and Maritime Archaeology*, edited by James P. Delgado (London, British Museum Press, 1997), 146–148.

3. Ted Caldwell, "Bateaux Building by Tri-District Consortium B.O.C.E.S. and

Adirondack Museum." *The Lake George Nautical Newsletter* (Wilton, NY, Bateaux Below, Inc., vol. 2, no. 1, 1993), 8.

4. Pepe and Zarzynski, "Wooden Bones: The Sunken Fleet of 1758."

5. Terry Crandall, "Operation Bateaux Revisited . . . Twenty-Four Years Later (Part 2)," *Bateaux Below* (Wilton, NY, Atlantic Alliance Lake George Bateaux Research Team, December 1988), 2–4.

6. Joseph W. Zarzynski, "Bateau Replica Sunk Near 1758 Wiawaka Bateaux," *The Lake George Nautical Newsletter* (Wilton, NY, vol. 6, no. 2, 1997), 1, 8.

7. Bateaux Below, Inc., *Lake George's Replica 1758 Bateau "Wreck"* (Wilton, NY & Albany, NY, Bateaux Below, Inc. & Office of General Services, 2008), 1–4.

Chapter Seventeen "Raising the Fleet": An Art/Science Initiative

1. Samuel Bowser, Elinor Mossop, John Farrell, and Joseph W. Zarzynski, "Raising the Fleet: When Archaeology, Art, and Cell Biology Collaborate" Poster (Amelia Island, FL, Society for Historical Archaeology, 2010.)

2. Samuel Bowser, e-mail to author (December 23, 2017).

Chapter Eighteen Documentary Filmmaking, Bateaux, and Archaeologists

1. Peter Pepe and Joseph W. Zarzynski, *Documentary Filmmaking for Archaeologists*. (Walnut Creek, CA: Left Coast Press, 2012), 24.

2. Robert Fulford, "Robert Fulford's column about John Grierson and the Documentary," *The National Post* (October 3, 2000), Website (accessed March 1, 2012).

3. Pepe and Zarzynski, *Documentary Filmmaking for Archaeologists*, 24.

4. Ibid., 25–27.

5. Joseph W. Zarzynski, "Lake George, New York: Making Shipwrecks Speak," *Out of the Blue: Public Interpretation of Maritime Cultural Resources* (New York: Springer Science+Business Media, LLC, 2007), 123.

6. Pepe and Zarzynski, *Documentary Filmmaking for Archaeologists*, 60–61.

7. Ibid., 62.

8. Zarzynski, Bowser, Farrell, and Pepe, "Making Shipwrecks Celebrities: Using the National Register, Shipwreck Preserves, Documentary Filmmaking, and Interdisciplinary Projects for Shipwreck Preservation," 203.

9. Pepe and Zarzynski, *Documentary Filmmaking for Archaeologists*, back cover.

10. Zarzynski, Bowser, Farrell, and Pepe, "Making Shipwrecks Celebrities: Using the National Register, Shipwreck Preserves, Documentary Filmmaking, and Interdisciplinary Projects for Shipwreck Preservation," 203.

Chapter Nineteen Public Education Programs

1. Scudiere, *Diving into History.*
2. Joseph W. Zarzynski, "Bateau Bulletin—Your Editor's Comments," *Bateaux Below* (Wilton, NY, Atlantic Alliance Lake George Bateaux Research Team, December 1988), 1.
3. Joseph W. Zarzynski, "The Third Annual Shipwreck Weekend at the LGHA," *The Lake George Nautical Newsletter* (Wilton, NY, Bateaux Below, Inc., vol. 1, no. 3, 1992), 3.
4. Joseph W. Zarzynski, "Preserving Eighteenth Century Shipwrecks at Lake George, New York, USA Through Underwater Archaeology, Shipwreck Preserves, and Museum Exhibits," *Bermuda Journal of Archaeology and Maritime History*, edited by Dr. J.C. Arnell (Mangrove Bay, BER, vol. 5, 1993), 169–170.
5. Zarzynski, Bowser, Farrell, and Pepe, "Making Shipwrecks Celebrities: Using the National Register, Shipwreck Preserves, Documentary Filmmaking, and Interdisciplinary Projects for Shipwreck Preservation," 201.
6. Joseph W. Zarzynski, "Calendar of Special Events," *The Lake George Nautical Newsletter* (Wilton, NY, Bateaux Below, Inc., vol. 1, no. 2, 1992), 7.
7. Joseph W. Zarzynski, "Drop Anchor Newsbriefs," *The Lake George Nautical Newsletter.* Bateaux Below, Inc. (Wilton, NY, Bateaux Below, Inc., vol. 1, no. 2, 1992), 5.
8. Joseph W. Zarzynski and Bob Benway, *Lake George Shipwrecks and Sunken History*, (Charleston, SC: The History Press, 2011), 37.
9. Catskill Castings (Bloomville, NY), Website (accessed December 1, 2013).
10. New York State Museum, "Outreach-State Historic Markers-How Do I get a New York State Historic Marker?" Website (accessed September 27, 2012).
11. Zarzynski, Bowser, Farrell, and Pepe, "Making Shipwrecks Celebrities: Using the National Register, Shipwreck Preserves, Documentary Filmmaking, and Interdisciplinary Projects for Shipwreck Preservation," 201.
12. Ibid.
13. Zarzynski and Benway, *Lake George Shipwrecks and Sunken History*, 37.
14. Joseph W. Zarzynski, "Bateaux Below, Inc. to Erect Wiawaka Bateaux Historic Marker," *The Lake George Nautical Newsletter* (Wilton, NY, Zarzynski Consulting & Underwater Survey and Bateaux Below, Inc., vol. 4, no. 3, 1995), 3.
15. Russell P. Bellico, Bob Benway, Tim Cordell, John Farrell, Scott Padeni, and Joseph W. Zarzynski, *Colonial Wars of Lake George: Self-Guided Tour* (Wilton, NY, Bateaux Below, Inc., 1996).

16. R.T. Green (ed.), *"Land Tortoise* Dedication Among the Highlights at Lake George Conference," *NASOH Newsletter* (Greenville, NC, North American Society for Oceanic History, Fall 1999), 1.
17. Zarzynski, personal dive logs and notes, May 22, 1996.
18. Peter D. Shaver, *The National Register of Historic Places in New York State* (New York, Rizzoli International Publications, Inc., 1993), 187.
19. Zarzynski, Bowser, Farrell, and Pepe, "Making Shipwrecks Celebrities: Using the National Register, Shipwreck Preserves, Documentary Filmmaking, and Interdisciplinary Projects for Shipwreck Preservation," 199.
20. Joseph W. Zarzynski, "Lake George Hosts 1997 NYSAA Conference," *The Lake George Nautical Newsletter* (Wilton, NY, Zarzynski Consulting & Underwater Survey and Bateaux Below, Inc., vol. 6, no. 1, 1997), 1.
21. Zarzynski and Benway, *Lake George Shipwrecks and Sunken History*, 134.
22. T. Kurt Knoerl, e-mail to author (July 8, 2014).
23. Zarzynski and Benway, *Lake George Shipwrecks and Sunken History*, 34–36.
24. Zarzynski, Bowser, Farrell, and Pepe, "Making Shipwrecks Celebrities: Using the National Register, Shipwreck Preserves, Documentary Filmmaking, and Interdisciplinary Projects for Shipwreck Preservation," 202.
25. Pepe and Zarzynski, "Wooden Bones: The Sunken Fleet of 1758."
26. Mark L. Peckham, e-mail to author (December 3, 2013).
27. Shannon Casey, "Wooden planks possibly from historic War of 1812 bateau," *Plattsburgh Press-Republican* (Plattsburgh, NY, August 6, 1999).
28. *The Saratogian*, "Historic boat found at Lake Champlain" (Saratoga Springs, NY, August 22, 1999).
29. Mark L. Peckham, "Cumberland Bay bateau 'field notes' drawing" (Albany, NY, August 5, 1999).
30. Peckham, e-mail to author (December 4, 2013).
31. Tim Cordell, e-mail to author, December 3, 2013.
32. Ibid, December 4, 2013.

Conclusion

1. John Wimbush, Marc E. Frischer, Joseph W. Zarzynski, and Sandra A. Nierzwicki-Bauer, "Eradication of colonizing populations of zebra mussels (*Dreissena polymorpha*) by early detection and SCUBA removal: Lake George, NY," *Aquatic Conservation: Marine and Freshwater Ecosystems* (Hoboken, NJ, Wiley InterScience, 2009), 703.

Appendix I "Operation Bateaux" Revisited Twenty-Four Years Later (Part 1)

1. Crandall, "Operation Bateaux Revisited . . . Twenty-Four Years Later (Part 1)," *Bateaux Below*, Wilton, NY, July 1988, 2–4.

Appendix II "Operation Bateaux" Revisited Twenty-Four Years Later (Part 2)

1. Crandall, "Operation Bateaux Revisited . . . Twenty-Four Years Later (Part 2)," *Bateaux Below*, Wilton, NY, December 1988, 2–4.

Appendix III Insights Gained from a Replica Lake George Bateau

1. Mark L. Peckham, "Insights Gained from a Replica Lake George Bateau," *The Lake George Nautical Newsletter* (Wilton, NY, Zarzynski Consulting & Underwater Survey and Bateaux Below, Inc., vol. 5, no. 2., 1996), 1, 7, 8.

Bibliography

Albany Times-Union (Albany, NY). "Bateau Raised in Lake George," September 24, 1960.

———. "Hunt Called Off at Lake George," August 23, 1960.

———. "Relics Saved in Ft. William Henry Fire," September 19, 1967.

———. "Swimmers Find French-Indian War Cannon, 2 Gunboat Anchors in Waters of Lake George," September 5, 1954.

———. "Ticonderoga Opposes State Action: 2 Forts Join in Bateau Battle," August 20, 1960.

———. "TV Eye Will Pry For Lake Relics," October 28, 1960.

Amherst, Jeffery. *The Journal of Jeffery Amherst: Recording the Military Career of General Amherst in America from 1758–1763*. Edited by J. Clarence Webster. Toronto: The Ryerson Press, 1931.

Amsterdam Evening Recorder (Amsterdam, NY). "Find Naval Relics at Bottom of Lake," July 28, 1960.

Appling, William, Bob Benway, and Joseph W. Zarzynski. *Lake George's Forward: Historic Vessel, Shipwreck Preserve, and "Underwater Classroom."* Wilton, NY: Bateaux Below, Inc., August 1998.

Archives of American Art-Smithsonian Institution, Smithsonian Institution. "Robert Bruce Inverarity papers." www.aaa.si.edu/collections/robert-bruce-inverarity-papers-6796/more#biohist. Accessed November 6, 2014.

Armstrong, Shirley. "Historical Unit Raps Bateaux Policy Critics." *Albany Times-Union* (Albany, NY), August 25, 1960.

Artec. "Eva Scanner." www.artec3d.com/portable-3d-scanners/artec-eva?keyword=artec%20eva%20%2Bscanner&gclid=CjwKCAjw0JfdBRACEiwAiDTALkMpfdTKgAhsi9yUuutiH7y3JKUfbba3Lswdj4bWuOI7maNi-5nLABoCUYIQAvD_BwE. Accessed December 1, 2017.

Aubry, Michele. "Abandoned Shipwreck Act (US)." *Encyclopedia of Underwater and Maritime Archaeology*. Edited by James P. Delgado. 16–17. London: British Museum Press, 1997.

Barr, Dan. "Bateau Raised In Lake George." *Albany Times-Union* (Albany, NY), September 24, 1960.

———. "Teenage Scuba Divers Discovered Lake George Relics: Historical Boat Finds Authenticated." *Albany Times-Union* (Albany, NY), July 25, 1960.

Bass, George F. *Archaeology Under Water*. New York: Frederick A. Praeger, 1966.

———. *Archaeology Under Water*. Revised ed. Middlesex, England: Penguin Books Ltd., 1970.

Bass, George F. (Ed.). *Beneath the Seven Seas: Adventures with the Institute of Nautical Archaeology*. London: Thames & Hudson Ltd., 2005.

Bateaux Below, Inc. Draft, National Register of Historic Places Registration Form–Shipwreck site and remains, bateaux c. 1758 [Wiawaka Bateaux Site]. Wilton, NY: Bateaux Below, Inc., November 17, 1991.

———. *Lake George's Replica 1758 Bateau "Wreck."* Wilton, NY: Bateaux Below, Inc. & Albany, NY: Office of General Services, 2008.

Bauder, Alan C. E-mail to author, December 15, 2000.

———. Letter to author, July 31, 1995.

Bellico, Russell P. Conversation with author, 1990.

———. *Chronicles of Lake George: Journeys in War and Peace*. Fleischmanns, NY: Purple Mountain Press, 1995.

———. Empires in the Mountains: French and Indian War Campaigns and Forts in the Lake Champlain, Lake George, and Hudson River Corridor. Fleischmanns, NY: Purple Mountain Press, 2010.

———. "The End of the *Sayonara*." *Bateaux Below* 2–4. Wilton, NY: Atlantic Alliance Lake George Research Team, May 1988.

———. *Sails and Steam in the Mountains: A Maritime and Military History of Lake George and Lake Champlain*. Fleischmanns, NY: Purple Mountain Press, 1992.

———. *Sails and Steam in the Mountains: A Maritime and Military History of Lake George and Lake Champlain*. Revised ed. Fleischmanns, NY: Purple Mountain Press, 2001.

Bellico, Russell P., Bob Benway, Tim Cordell, John Farrell, Scott Padeni, and Joseph W. Zarzynski. *Colonial Wars of Lake George: Self-Guided Tour*. Wilton, NY: Bateaux Below, Inc., 1996.

Benson, Adolph B. (Ed.). *The America of 1750: Peter Kalm's Travels in North America*. Vol. 1. New York: Dover Publications, Inc., 1937, 1964.

Benway, Bob. "Mortar Bomb at Lake George Historical Association." Queensbury, NY: Author, November 2, 1998.

———. "13 Inch Mortar Bomb from Lake George, NY (Cooper's Cave Ale Co., Glens Falls, New York)." Queensbury, NY: Author, August 31, 2001.

———. "13 Inch Mortar Bomb from Lake George, NY (Historical Society of the

Town of Bolton, Bolton Landing, New York)." Queensbury, NY: Author, August 31, 2001.

Binghamton Press (Binghamton, NY). "Glass-Bottomed Boat Provided for Summer Guests at Lake George," June 25, 1930.

Bird, Harrison. *March to Saratoga: General Burgoyne and the American Campaign, 1777.* Oxford: Oxford University Press, 1963.

———. *Navies in the Mountains: The Battles on the Waters of Lake Champlain and Lake George, 1609–1814.* Oxford: Oxford University Press, 1962.

Bouton, Nathaniel, D.D. *Documents and Records Relating to the Province of New-Hampshire from 1749 to 1763.* Vol. VI. Manchester, NH: James M. Campbell, State Printer, 1872.

Bowser, Samuel, Elinor Mossop, John Farrell, and Joseph W. Zarzynski. "Raising the Fleet: When Archaeology, Art, and Cell Biology Collaborate." Poster. Amelia Island, FL: Society for Historical Archaeology, 2010.

Bradstreet, J.W. *Report of JW Bradstreet to General Amherst.* Public Records Office 160, 34/57–58, fol. 17, London: Public Records Office, December 31, 1758.

Brooklyn Daily Standard Union (Brooklyn, NY). "A Relic of the French and Indian Wars Raised from the Bottom of Lake George," November 22, 1903.

The Bulletin of the Fort Ticonderoga Museum. "Recent Accessions." Vol. X, No. 6. Ticonderoga, NY: Fort Ticonderoga Museum, 1962.

Caldwell, Ted. "Bateaux Building by Tri-District Consortium B.O.C.E.S. and Adirondack Museum." *The Lake George Nautical Newsletter.* Vol. 2, No. 1. p. 8. Wilton, NY: Bateaux Below, Inc., 1993.

Casey, Shannon. "Wooden planks possibly from historic War of 1812 bateau." *Plattsburgh Press-Republican* (Plattsburgh, NY), August 6, 1999.

Catskill Castings. Bloomville, NY. www.catskillcastings.com/markers.htm. Accessed December 1, 2013.

Chapelle, Howard I. *American Small Sailing Craft: Their Design, Development, and Construction.* New York: W.W. Norton & Company, Inc., 1951.

The Chatham Courier (Chatham, NY). [article on colonial history at Lake George], July 29, 1891.

Christofferson, David J. *Volume Two, Batteau, Battoe.* St. Paul, MN: Fox in Circle Productions, 1987.

The Citizen Register (Ossining, NY). "French-Indian War Batteaux Believed Lake George Find," July 29, 1960.

Coates, John F., and Jan Bill. "Experimental archaeology." *Encyclopedia of Underwater and Maritime Archaeology*, pp. 146–148. Edited by James P. Delgado. London: British Museum Press, 1997.

Cohn, Arthur B. "Lake Champlain's Underwater Historic Preserve Program:

Reasonable Access to Appropriate Sites." *Submerged Cultural Resource Management: Preserving and Interpreting Our Sunken Maritime Heritage*, pp. 85–93. Edited by James D. Spirek and Della A. Scott-Ireton. New York: Kluwer Academic/Plenum Publishers, 2003.

Cooper, James Fenimore. *The Last of the Mohicans*. New York: Charles Scribner's Sons, 1826, 1947.

Crandall, Terry. "Adirondack Museum-Diving Report." Richfield Springs, NY: Terry Crandall, September 15, 1963.

———. "Adirondack Museum-Diving Report." Richfield Springs, NY: Terry Crandall, October 12, 1963.

———. "Lake George: Time Capsule in Controversy." Richfield Springs, NY: Terry Crandall, n.d.

———. "Operation Bateaux." Richfield Springs, NY: Terry Crandall, 1964.

———. "Operation Bateaux Revisited . . . Twenty-Four Years Later (Part 1)." *Bateaux Below*, pp. 2–4. Wilton, NY: Atlantic Alliance Lake George Bateaux Research Team, July 1988.

———. "Operation Bateaux Revisited . . . Twenty-Four Years Later (Part 2)." *Bateaux Below*, pp. 2–4. Wilton, NY: Atlantic Alliance Lake George Bateaux Research Team, December 1988.

———. "Questions to Ask Terry Crandall." Richfield Springs, NY: Terry Crandall. n.d.

———. "Untitled Map of Sunken Bateaux at Lake George." Richfield Springs, NY: Terry Crandall, n.d.

Crisman, Kevin J. "Struggle for a Continent: Naval Battles of the French and Indian Wars." *Ships and Shipwrecks of the Americas: A History Based on Underwater Archaeology*, pp. 129–148. Edited by George F. Bass. New York: Thames and Hudson Inc., 1988.

Delgado, James P., and A National Park Service Task Force. *National Register Bulletin 20* [*Nominating Historic Vessels and Shipwrecks to the National Register of Historic Places.*] Washington, DC: U.S. Department of the Interior-National Park Service, 1992.

Diehl, David Glenn. "Early SCUBA in Lake George." *The Lake George Mirror*, August 14, 1998, pp. 15–16.

Dunnigan, Brian Leigh. *Siege 1759: The Campaign Against Niagara*. Youngstown, NY: Old Fort Niagara Association, Inc., 1996.

Empleton, Bernard E. (Ed.). *The New Science of Skin and Scuba Diving*. Chicago: Follett Publishing Company, 1957, 1980.

The Explorers Club. "Side Scan Sonar Explorers for Lake George, New York Shipwrecks." *The Explorers Newsletter*. New York: The Explorers Club, March–May 1989.

Fulford, Robert. "Robert Fulford's column about John Grierson and the Documentary." *The National Post*, October 3, 2000. www.robertfulford.com/JohnGrierson.html. Accessed March 1, 2012.

Gallagher, Nathan A. "The Lake George Bateaux: British Colonial Utility Craft in The French and Indian War." Master of Arts Thesis (Anthropology). Texas A&M University, College Station, 2015.

Gardner, John. "Bateaus Played Key Role in American History." *National Fisherman*, pp. 8-A, 9-A, 19-A, April 1967.

———. "Construction Details of Old Bateaux Show Basic Design with Variations." *National Fisherman*, pp. 8-A, 9-A, June 1967.

———. *The Dory Book*. Mystic, CT: Mystic Seaport Museum, Inc., 1987.

———. "Dutch Influences on American Small Craft During the Colonial Period." *The Log of Mystic Seaport*. Mystic, CT: Mystic Seaport, Summer 1995.

———. "Famous Boat Type in Transitional Stage." *National Fisherman*, pp. 8-A, 9-A, 28-A, May 1967.

Gerlach, Don R. *Philip Schuyler and the American Revolution in New York, 1733–1777*. Lincoln: University of Nebraska Press, 1964.

Giesecke, Anne G. "The Abandoned Shipwreck Act 1988 to 1998." *Underwater Archaeology*, pp. 111–114. Edited by Lawrence E. Babits, Catherine Fachs, and Ryan Harris. Atlanta: Society for Historical Archaeology, 1988.

Gifford, Stanley M. *Fort William Henry: A History*. Glens Falls, NY: The Bullard Press, 1955.

Glens Falls Post-Star (Glens Falls, NY). "Police charge divers," July 30, 1994.

———. "Relic Hunters Are Numerous," July 24, 1915.

Glens Falls Times (Glens Falls, NY). "First of Ancient Boats Raised from Bottom of Lake George by Divers," September 24, 1960.

———. "Historic Assoc. to Direct Work of Recovering Boats," August 2, 1960.

———. "Historical Assoc. Asks Skin Divers to Report Artifacts," August 30, 1960.

———. "Legal Battle Develops on Artifacts," July 29, 1960.

———. "Miniature Submarine Is Expected to Help in Lake George Explorations," August 4, 1960.

———. "Smithsonian Institution Experts Will Make Study of Lake George Artifacts," July 26, 1960.

Green, R.T. (Ed.). "*Land Tortoise* Dedication among the Highlights at Lake George Conference." *NASOH Newsletter*. Greenville, NC: North American Society for Oceanic History, Inc., Fall 1999.

Hager, Robert E. *Mohawk River Boats and Navigation Before 1820*. Syracuse, NY: Canal Society of New York State, 1987.

Hahn, Celia. "Historians, Divers Collide on Treasures." *The Knickerbocker News* (Albany, NY), November 9, 1967.

Hillerman, Tony. *A Thief of Time*. New York: Harper & Row, 1988.

Holmquist, June Drenning, and Ardis Hillman Wheeler (Eds.). *Diving into the Past: Theories, Techniques, and Applications of Underwater Archaeology (The Proceedings of a Conference on Underwater Archaeology)*. St. Paul: The Minnesota Historical Society, 1964.

Inverarity, R.B. *Manual of Puppetry*. Portland, OR: Binsford & Mort., 1936.

Inverarity, Robert Bruce. *Art of the Northwest Coast Indians*. Berkeley: University of California Press, 1950.

———. "The Conservation of Wood from Fresh Water." *Diving into the Past: Theories, Techniques, and Applications of Underwater Archaeology (The Proceedings of a Conference on Underwater Archaeology)*, pp. 68–70. Edited by June Drenning Holmquist and Ardis Hillman Wheeler. St. Paul: The Minnesota Historical Society, 1964.

———. "New York Report." *Diving into the Past: Theories, Techniques, and Applications of Underwater Archaeology (The Proceedings of a Conference on Underwater Archaeology)*, pp. 80–81. Edited by June Drenning Holmquist and Ardis Hillman Wheeler. St. Paul: The Minnesota Historical Society, 1964.

Jennings, Francis. *Empire of Fortune: Crowns, Colonies & Tribes in the Seven Years War in America*. New York: W.W. Norton & Company, 1988.

Johnston, Richard J.H. "Lake George Divers Find 1758 Battle Craft." *New York Times*, June 27, 1965.

Klein, Martin. "Side scan sonar." *Encyclopedia of Underwater and Maritime Archaeology*, pp. 384–385. Edited by James P. Delgado. London: British Museum Press, 1997.

The Knickerbocker News (Albany, NY). "Study of Sunken Boats in Lake George OKd," August 2, 1960.

———. "Watch for Relics. Kiwanians Urged," April 21, 1954.

Kvarning, Lars Åke. "*Vasa*." *Encyclopedia of Underwater and Maritime Archaeology*, pp. 454–456. Edited by James P. Delgado. London: British Museum Press, 1997.

Lake George Mirror (Lake George, NY). "A Relic of By-Gone Days: A Forty-foot Plank from the Hull of a Sunken Batteaux," August 3, 1895.

———. "Along The Shore," July 8, 1893.

———. [article on piece of colonial boat raised], June 9, 1900.

———. "Charles Diehl, Scuba Pioneer, Dies," November 2007.

———. "Divers Will Form Salvage Body But Won't Receive Pay," July 14, 1961.

―――. "Fort Ticonderoga Builds a Replica of Old Bateau," July 7, 1961.

―――. "Fort William Henry's 24-Pounder Mounted on New Field Carriage," July 21, 1966.

―――. "Forts May Get Bateaux If Enough Are Raised Intact from Depths of the Lake," July 21, 1961.

―――. "Fortune Beneath the Waves!" August 12, 1960.

―――. "French and Indian War: Timbers from the Colonial Batteaux in the Caldwell Station," June 24, 1899.

―――. "Huletts Man Advocates an Underwater Museum," July 3, 1964.

―――. "Mirror Gets Support on Stand Taken on Historic Items Recovered in Lake," August 26, 1960.

―――. "Preserve Historical Relics," August 18, 1934.

―――. "Saratogians Discover 28-Foot Boat and 40 Mortars in The Lake," August 5, 1960.

―――. "Scuba Diving in Lake George," June 29, 1962.

―――. "Shall Historic Objects Found in Lake George Go to Museums Elsewhere?" August 12, 1960.

―――. "The Sunken Batteaux of Lake George," June 10, 1893.

―――. "The Sunken Batteaux of Lake George," September 10, 1898.

Lenihan, Daniel. "Cultural resources management (CRM)." *Encyclopedia of Underwater and Maritime Archaeology*, pp. 119–120. Edited by James P. Delgado. London: British Museum Press, 1997.

Lewis, Dennis M. "Batteaux in the Champlain Waterway 1755–1783." Plattsburgh, NY: Author, August 1983.

Lewis, Howard. "Calls for Skin Diver Licensing—Destruction of Relics Deplored." *The Knickerbocker News* (Albany, NY), January 12, 1961.

Link, Marion Clayton. *Sea Diver: A Quest for History Under the Sea*. Coral Gables, FL: The University of Miami Press, 1958.

Lorenzini, M., and R. Clark. *MA Archaeology and Heritage: Study Guide*. Edited by R. Sunley and A. McWhirr. Leicester, United Kingdom: School of Archaeological Studies, University of Leicester, n.d.

Magee, J.A. "Bomb Ketch and cargo of bombs" [personal notes]. Lake George, NY: Fort William Henry, June 30, 1965.

Mahoney, Eleanor. "The Federal Art Project in Washington State. From 'The Great Depression in Washington State.' " Seattle: University of Washington. depts.washington.edu/depress/FAP.shtml. Accessed May 9, 2016.

Meany, Joseph F., Jr. "Bateaux and 'Battoe Men': An American Colonial Response to the Problem of Logistics in Mountain Warfare." Saratoga Springs, NY: New

York State Military Museum. www.dmna.stat.ny.us/historic/articles/bateau. htm. Accessed September 26, 2003.

Moneypenny, Alexander. "Moneypenny Orderly Book." *The Bulletin of the Fort Ticonderoga Museum*, pp. 434–461. Ticonderoga, NY: Fort Ticonderoga Museum, October 1970.

National Archives and Records Administration. *Federal Register*. Vol. 63, No. 124. 35279. Washington, DC: National Archives and Records Administration, June 29, 1998.

National Geographic Society. 2016. "Bathyscaphe." nationalgeographic.org/encyclopedia/bathyscaphe/. Accessed October 28, 2016.

National Park Service. "Abandoned Shipwreck Act Guidelines." www.cr.nps.gov/aad/submerged/Intro.htm. Accessed December 5, 2000.

———. "American Antiquities Act of 1906." *Links to the Past*. www.cr.nps.gov/local-law/anti1906.htm. Accessed December 5, 2000.

———. "Archeology Program-New York." www.nps.gov/archeology/SITES/statesubmerged/newyork.htm. Accessed November 3, 2016.

New York State Department of Environmental Conservation. "Submerged Heritage Preserve-The *Forward*" [brochure]. Albany, NY, 1993.

———. "Submerged Heritage Preserve—The Sunken Fleet of 1758" [brochure]. Albany, NY, 1993.

———. "Submerged Heritage Preserves Program." www.dec.ny.gov/lands/315.html. Accessed April 11, 2013.

New York State Divers Association. *New York State Divers Association, Inc. Information Booklet*. Ava, NY: New York State Divers Association. n.d.

New York State Museum. "Outreach-State Historic Markers-How Do I get a New York State Historic Marker? www.nysm.nysed.gov/service/marker/srvmarkers.html. Accessed September 27, 2012.

New York Times. "Museum, With Just a Relic to Go On, Tries to Rebuild Lost Piece of History," August 16, 1987.

———. "Sunken 1758 Boat Believed British," July 30, 1960.

Nickerson, Commander Norval E. "Diving Assistance to the Adirondack Museum." Washington, DC: U.S. Navy, September 28, 1960.

O'Callaghan, E.B. *The Documentary History of the State of New York*. Vol. 1. Albany, NY: Weed, Parsons & Company, 1849.

O'Keefe, M. Timothy (Ed.). *Erving's World Wide Skindiver's Guide*. Winter Park, FL: Erving Publishing Company, 1973.

The Otsego Farmer (Cooperstown, NY) "Swinney Is Named Museum Director," September 23, 1965.

Ottawa Citizen (Ottawa, QC). "Works to U.K." June 8, 1976.

Oxley, Ian. "The Investigation of the Factors Which Affect the Preservation of Underwater Archaeological Sites." *Underwater Archaeology Proceedings from the Society for Historical Archaeology Conference*, pp. 105–110. Edited by Donald H. Keith and Toni L. Carrell. Kingston, JA: Society for Historical Archaeology, 1992.

Parker, Gene. "Report to Dr. R.B. Inverarity on diving/uw photography of September 14, 1962." Scotia, NY: Gene Parker, September 19, 1962.

Parker, Gene (Ed.). *Dive: The Complete Book of Skin Diving*. New York: Wilfred Funk, Inc., 1963.

Peckham, Mark L. "Insights Gained from a Replica Lake George Bateau." *The Lake George Nautical Newsletter*. Vol. 5, No. 2, pp. 1, 7, 8. Wilton, NY: Zarzynski Consulting & Underwater Survey and Bateaux Below, Inc., 1996.

———. "Lake George Shipwrecks Nominated to National Register." *Preservation League of New York State Newsletter*. Albany, NY: Preservation League of New York State, Spring 1992.

Pepe, Peter (Director and Video Editor), Dr. Samuel Turner (Writer), and Joseph W. Zarzynski (Writer). "Search for the *Jefferson Davis*: Trader, Slaver, Raider" (DVD). Glens Falls, NY: Pepe Productions, Lighthouse Archaeological Maritime Program, St. Augustine Lighthouse & Museum, and First Light Maritime Society, 2011.

Pepe, Peter (Director and Video Editor), John Whitesel (Writer), and Joseph W. Zarzynski (Writer). "The Lost Radeau: North America's Oldest Intact Warship" (DVD). Glens Falls, NY: Pepe Productions, Bateaux Below, Inc., Whitesel Graphics, and Black Laser Learning, 2005.

Pepe, Peter (Director and Video Editor) and Joseph W. Zarzynski (Writer). "Wooden Bones: The Sunken Fleet of 1758" (DVD). Glens Falls, NY: Pepe Productions and Bateaux Below, Inc., 2010.

Pepe, Peter, and Joseph W. Zarzynski. *Documentary Filmmaking for Archaeologists*. Walnut Creek, CA: Left Coast Press, 2012.

Peterson, Mendel. *History Under the Sea: A Handbook for Underwater Exploration*. Washington, DC: Smithsonian Institution Press, 1965.

Plattsburgh Press-Republican (Plattsburgh, NY). "Bateau Raised From Lake," September 24, 1960.

Preserve America. "The Preserve America Initiative." www.preserveamerica.gov/overview.html. Accessed October 28, 2016.

Rea, Caleb. *The Journal of Dr. Caleb Rea, Written During the Expedition Against Ticonderoga in 1758*. Vol. XVIII, pp. 81–120, 177–205. Salem, MA: The Essex Institute, 1881.

Richfield Springs Mercury (Richfield Springs, NY). "Terry Crandall at Archeology Conference," April 22, 1965.

Roberts, Kenneth. *Arundel.* New York: Doubleday, 1930.

Rule, Dr. Margaret. *"Mary Rose."* *Encyclopedia of Underwater and Maritime Archaeology*, pp. 264–266. Edited by James P. Delgado. London: British Museum Press, 1997.

Russell, Matthew A. "Integrating Underwater and Terrestrial Archaeology." The Underwater Blogger. Museum of Underwater Archaeology. muablog.wordpress.com/2010/05/17/the-advisory-council-on-underwater-archaeology-by-matthew-a-russell. Accessed December 30, 2014.

Ryan, Sean. "Bottom of Lake George: Divers Find Craft with 40 Mortars." *Albany Times-Union* (Albany, NY), July 31, 1960.

Sarasota Herald-Tribune (Sarasota, FL). "Scolded For Water Raids," April 29, 1963.

The Saratogian (Saratoga Springs, NY). "$20,000 Price Tag Put on Fort Clinton Restoration," April 25, 1961.

———. "Clock Case of Old Timbers," April 10, 1919.

———. "Historic Boat Found at Lake Champlain," August 22, 1999.

———. "New 'Ghost Fleet' Boat Found in Lake George," August 15, 1960.

———. "Scouts Learn About Turkey," November 16, 1961.

———. "Spa Divers Tell of Lake George 'Battles,'" September 30, 1960.

———. "38 Present at Adult Club Meeting Despite Cold," January 24, 1961.

Schenectady Gazette (Schenectady, NY). "7th Graders Explore Underwater Archaeology," January 7, 1988.

———. "Skindivers to Safe Guard Artifacts in Lake George," February 7, 1962.

Schenectady Reflector (Schenectady, NY). "Attack on Fort William Henry," April 1, 1842.

Schenectady Union Star (Schenectady, NY), "TV to Aid in Charting Sunken Ships." September 22, 1960.

Schenectady Urban Cultural Park. "The Batteau Project." Schenectady, NY: Schenectady Urban Cultural Park, 1992.

School of Archaeological Studies. *MA Archaeology and Heritage: Dissertation Guidelines*. Leicester, UK: School of Archaeological Studies, University of Leicester, n.d.

Scudiere, Paul. *Diving into History: A Manual of Underwater Archeology for Divers in New York State.* Albany, NY: The University of the State of New York, State Education Department, 1969.

Shaver, Peter D. *The National Register of Historic Places in New York State.* New York: Rizzoli International Publications, Inc., 1993.

Starbuck, David R. *The Great Warpath: British Military Sites from Albany to Crown Point*. Hanover, NH: University Press of New England, 1999.

Steele, Ian K. *Betrayals: Fort William Henry & The "Massacre."* New York: Oxford University Press, 1990.

Terrell, Bruce G. *The James River Bateau: Tobacco Transport in Upland Virginia, 1745–1840*. Master of Arts Thesis (Program in Maritime History and Underwater Research). East Carolina University, Greenville, NC: July 1991.

Thomas, Robert McG. Jr. "John Gardner, 90, Boat Curator at Mystic Seaport Museum, Dies." *New York Times*, October 19, 1990.

Ticonderoga Sentinel (Ticonderoga, NY). "'Aqua Vandals' Wreck Bateau," October 27, 1960.

———. "Skin Diving Booming in State," August 21, 1958.

The Troy Record (Troy, NY). "Find Another 'Ghost Fleet' Boat," August 15, 1960.

———. "Skindivers Find Old Cannon," August 12, 1959.

The Troy Times Record (Troy, NY). "Rare Find," August 13, 1959.

Utica Daily Press (Utica, NY). "Aquanaughties Wreck Bateau," October 29, 1960.

Utica Observer-Dispatch (Utica, NY). "18th Century Boat Found," August 25, 1963.

Van Hoek, Susan, and Marion Clayton Link. *From Sky to Sea: A Story of Edwin A. Link*. Flagstaff, AZ: Best Publishing Company, 2003.

Village of Lake George. "Lake George Village Walking Tour of August 1757." Lake George, NY: Village of Lake George, 2007.

Vrana, Kenneth J. "Shipwreck protected areas." *Encyclopedia of Underwater and Maritime Archaeology*, pp. 380–382. Edited by James P. Delgado. London: British Museum Press, 1997.

Vrana, Kenneth J., and Edward M. Mahoney (Eds.). *Great Lakes Underwater Cultural Resources: Important Information for Shaping our Future*. East Lansing: Michigan State University, Department of Park, Recreation and Tourism Resources, 1993.

Walter, Paul A.F., and Arthur J.O. Anderson (Eds.). "Dedication." *El Palacio*, pp. 306–336. Santa Fe, New Mexico: Archaeological Society of New Mexico, September 1953.

The Warrensburgh-Lake George News (Warrensburg, NY). "Fort William Henry's 24-Pounder Mounted on a New Field Carriage," July 26, 1966.

———. "James A. Magee," December 12, 1979.

The Warrensburg News (Warrensburg, NY). "Improvement of Beach at Lake George," June 24, 1920.

Watertown Daily Times (Watertown, NY). "Dr. Robert Inverarity Resigns Museum Post," July 22, 1965.

Watertown Times (Watertown, NY). "Raising of Ship Being Planned," September 22, 1960.

Wheeler, Ardis Hillman. *Diving into the Past: Theories, Techniques, and Applications of Underwater Archaeology*. The Proceedings of a Conference on Underwater Archaeology. Edited by June Drenning Holmquist and Ardis Hillman Wheeler. St. Paul: The Minnesota Historical Society, 1964.

Wimbush, John, Marc E. Frischer, Joseph W. Zarzynski, and Sandra A. Nierzwicki-Bauer. "Eradication of colonizing populations of zebra mussels (*Dreissena polymorpha*) by early detection and SCUBA removal: Lake George, NY." *Aquatic Conservation: Marine and Freshwater Ecosystems*, pp. 703–713. Hoboken, NJ: Wiley InterScience, 2009.

Wittman, Robert K., and John Shiffman. *Priceless: How I Went Undercover to Rescue the World's Stolen Treasures*. New York: Broadway Paperbacks, 2010.

Wolf, Lud. "Lake George." *Skin Diver Magazine*, pp. 56–59. Los Angeles, CA: Peterson Publishing Company, July 1969.

Wood, Lemuel. "A Journal of the Canada Expedition in the Year 1759." *Chronicles of Lake George: Journeys in War and Peace*, pp. 129–145. Edited by Russell P. Bellico. Fleischmanns, NY: Purple Mountain Press, 1995.

Wright, Dr. Robin K. "Searching for what inspired the Seattle Seahawks logo." Seattle, WA: Burke Museum of Natural History and Culture. burkemuseum.blogspot.com/2014/01/in-search-of-true-inspiration-for.html#.VGzq3L6QZSV. Accessed November 19, 2014.

Zaboly, Gary (Ed.). "A Royal Artillery Officer with Amherst: The Journal of Captain-Lieutenant Henry Skinner. May 1–July 28, 1759." *The Bulletin of Fort Ticonderoga Museum*, pp. 362–387. Ticonderoga, NY: Fort Ticonderoga, 1993.

Zarzynski, Joseph W. "Bateau Bulletin—Your Editor's Comments." *Bateaux Below*. Wilton, NY: Atlantic Alliance Lake George Bateaux Research Team, December. 1, 1988.

———. "Bateau Replica Sunk Near 1758 Wiawaka Bateaux." *The Lake George Nautical Newsletter*. Vol. 6, No. 2, pp. 1, 8. Wilton, NY: Zarzynski Consulting & Underwater Survey and Bateaux Below, Inc., 1997.

———. "Bateaux Below, Inc. to Erect Wiawaka Bateaux Historic Marker." *The Lake George Nautical Newsletter*. Vol. 4, No. 3, p. 3. Wilton, NY: Zarzynski Consulting & Underwater Survey and Bateaux Below, Inc., 1995.

———. "Calendar of Special Events." *The Lake George Nautical Newsletter*. Vol. 1, No. 2, p. 7. Wilton, NY: Bateaux Below, Inc., 1992.

———. "Cultural Resource Management of Lake George's Sunken Bateaux of 1758: How History, Underwater Archaeology, Public Education Programs, and Shipwreck Preserves Promote Site Protection." Master of Arts Thesis (Archaeology). Leicester, UK: School of Archaeological Studies, University of Leicester, January 2001.

———. "Drop Anchor Newsbriefs." *The Lake George Nautical Newsletter.* Vol. 1, No. 2, p. 5. Wilton, NY: Bateaux Below, Inc., 1992.

———. "Fort Ticonderoga's Bateau." *The Lake George Nautical Newsletter.* Vol. 2, No. 1, p. 3. Wilton, NY: Bateaux Below, Inc., 1993.

———. "French and Indian War Artifacts at Warrensburgh Museum of Local History." *The French and Indian War Society Newsletter*, pp. 4–6. Lake George, NY: The French and Indian War Society, December 2014.

———. "Historian Harrison Bird Suggests Underwater Museum." *Lake George Mirror* (Lake George, NY), November 2016.

———. "Lake George Hosts 1997 NYSAA Conference." *The Lake George Nautical Newsletter.* Vol. 6, No. 1, p. 1. Wilton, NY: Zarzynski Consulting & Underwater Survey and Bateaux Below, Inc., 1997.

———. "Lake George, New York: Making Shipwrecks Speak." *Out of the Blue: Public Interpretation of Maritime Cultural Resources*, pp. 112–126. Edited by John H. Jameson Jr. and Della A. Scott-Ireton. New York: Springer Science+Business Media, LLC, 2007.

———. "Lake George Profiles: Robert LaVoy." *The Lake George Nautical Newsletter.* Vol. 2, No. 1, p. 3. Wilton, NY: Bateaux Below, Inc., 1993.

———. "October 1988 Side-Scan Sonar Expedition at Lake George." *Bateaux Below.* Wilton, NY: Atlantic Alliance Lake George Bateaux Research Team, December 7, 1988.

———. "Preserving Eighteenth Century Shipwrecks at Lake George, New York, USA through Underwater Archaeology, Shipwreck Preserves, and Museum Exhibits." *Bermuda Journal of Archaeology and Maritime History.* Vol. 5, pp. 166–171. Edited by Dr. J.C. Arnell. Mangrove Bay, BER: Bermuda Maritime Museum Association, 1993.

———. "'Submerged Heritage Preserves' Opened at Lake George." *The Lake George Nautical Newsletter.* Vol. 2, No. 3, pp. 1, 7. Wilton, NY: Bateaux Below, Inc., 1993.

———. "The Third Annual Shipwreck Weekend at the LGHA." *The Lake George Nautical Newsletter.* Vol. 1, No. 3, p. 3. Wilton, NY: Bateaux Below, Inc., 1992.

———. "35 Years Later—Lake George's Lost Submarine Found by Bateaux Below, Inc." *The Lake George Nautical Newsletter.* Vol. 4, No. 1, p. 8. Wilton, NY: Zarzynski Consulting & Underwater Survey and Bateaux Below, Inc., 1995.

Zarzynski, Joseph W. (Ed.). "Terry Crandall, Renowned Lake George Archaeological Diver, Dies." *The French and Indian War Society Newsletter.* Lake George, NY: The French and Indian War Society, September 2016.

Zarzynski, Joseph W., and Amanda Andreas. "Shipwreck Cannons at a Replica 18th Century Fort." *The French and Indian War Society Newsletter.* Lake George, NY: The French and Indian War Society, October 2014.

Zarzynski, Joseph W., D.K. Abbass, and Bob Benway. *"The Sunken Fleet of 1758" Shipwreck Preserve: 1999 Debris Clean Up and Site Stabilization.* Wilton, NY: Bateaux Below, Inc., 2000.

Zarzynski, Joseph W., D.K. Abbass, Bob Benway, and John Farrell. " 'Ring-Around-A-Radeau,' or, Fencing in a 1758 Shipwreck for Public Access and Preservation." *Underwater Archaeology*, pp. 35–39. Edited by Stephen R. James, Jr. and Camille Stanley. Cincinnati, OH: Society for Historical Archaeology, 1996.

Zarzynski, Joseph W., D.K. Abbass, and Russell P. Bellico. "Strange Bedfellows: Research and Politics of the *Land Tortoise*, Lake George's 1758 Radeau Shipwreck." *Underwater Archaeology Proceedings from the Society for Historical Archaeology Conference*, pp. 74–79. Edited by Robyn P. Woodward and Charles D. Moore. Vancouver, BC: Society for Historical Archaeology, 1994.

Zarzynski, Joseph W., and Bob Benway. *Lake George Shipwrecks and Sunken History.* Charleston, SC: The History Press, 2011.

Zarzynski, Joseph W., and John Farrell. "Recent Underwater Archaeological Surveys at Lake George, New York." *Archaeology of the French and Indian War: Military Sites of the Hudson River, Lake George, and Lake Champlain. Corridor*, pp. 5–9. Edited by David R. Starbuck. Queensbury, NY: Adirondack Community College, 1994.

Zarzynski, Joseph W., Samuel S. Bowser, John Farrell, and Peter Pepe. "Making Shipwrecks Celebrities: Using the National Register, Shipwreck Preserves, Documentary Filmmaking, and Interdisciplinary Projects for Shipwreck Preservation." *Between the Devil and the Deep: Meeting Challenges in the Public Interpretation of Maritime Cultural Heritage*, pp. 197–206. Edited by Della A. Scott-Ireton. New York: Springer Science+Business Media, 2014.

Index

Note: Entries in *italics* reference figures; entries in **bold** reference glossary terms.

Abandoned Shipwreck Act of 1987 (ASA), 48–49, 129, 131, 133, 203
Abbass, D. "Kathy," 90, 107, *128*, 133, 138, 178
Abercromby, James, 6
Abercromby military campaign, 6, *7*, 15, 36, 97–98, *136*
ad-hoc Committee for Submerged Cultural Resources, 48–50, 143–44
Adirondack Historical Association, 43
Adirondack Museum
  Caldwell's students visit to, 148
  CCTV camera system used by, *52*, 53–54
  conservation of raised bateaux at, 57–60, 192
  establishment of, 46
  Gardner's consultation with, 163
  Lake George's Sunken Bateaux exhibit at, 13, 60, 176
  liaison with Lake George Chamber of Commerce, 48
  location of, 43
  "Mortar Bateau" studies of, 94–97, 106
  mortar bombs exhibited at, 102–4
  Operation Bateaux. *See* Operation Bateaux
  pontoon barge purchased by, 189
  public information campaign by, 47–48
  raised bateaux reassembled at, *59*
  shipwreck inventories by, 105–11
  underwater archaeology permit assigned to, 41–44, 62
Advisory Council on Underwater Archaeology (ACUA), 64. *See also* Council of Underwater Archaeology (CUA)

Albany
  bateau "factories" in, 6, 12, 19, 177
  Burgoyne's campaign against, 9, 109, 115
  in colonial wars, 3, 5
  dimensions of bateaux from, 19
  map of, *2*
Albany Times Union, 43, 47, 53–54, 93–94
Allen, James E., 187
American Academy of Underwater Sciences (AAUS), 155, 203
American Antiquities Act of 1906, 42–43
American Revolution
  Arnold's Quebec campaign in, 198
  Burgoyne campaign in, 9, 109, 115
  Durham boats in, 176
  Franklin's diplomatic mission to Canada during, 9, 148
  German auxiliary in, 9, 176, 205
  military bateaux in, 7–9
  shipwrecks from, 109, 115, 117
  submerged wharf from, 91
Amherst, Jeffery, 6, 19
Amherst military campaign, 6–7, 18–19, 111, 155, 176
Amsterdam Evening Recorder, 39
anchors
  at Bateau(x) Site VIII, 110
  damage to shipwrecks from, 84
  grapnel, 54, *116*, 117–19
  souvenir collecting of, 71
anti-boarding artillery, falconet, 36–38, 204
Appling, Bill, *128*, *139*, 149–151
apron, 25, 203

243

"Archaeological Research Assistant Workshop," xiii–xv, 73–75, 78, 164
Arnold's Quebec campaign, 198
Artillery Cove, 115
Arundel (Roberts), 198
Atlantic Alliance for Maritime Heritage Conservation, xiii, 164
Atlantic Alliance Lake George Bateaux Research Team. *See also* Bateaux Below; Lake George Bateaux Research Team
  assessment of, xviii
  divers participating in, 201–2
  founding of, 73, 164
  lectures by members of, 175
  "Mortar Bateau" studies by, 99
Atocha (galleon), xiii
Attorney General, NYS Office of, 50
Aubrey (Captain), 117
autonomous underwater vehicle (AUV), 76, 77, 203
Axel Wenner-Gren Foundation for Anthropological Research, 46
azimuth, 189, 203

Baby Whale, 90, 121–25, *166*, 171, *178*, 179
bailing scoops, 18–19, 21, 25, 196
Bartlett, Florence Dibell, 46
Basin Harbor Maritime Museum, 13–14, 71–72, 135
Bass, George F., 51, 53, 64–65
Bateau 2626 (NYS Museum), 12–14, *16*, 17–18, 21, *24*, 60. See also *Perseverance*
Bateau 4560 (NYS Museum), 14, 21, 60
Bateau 4566 (NYS Museum), 14, 21, 60
Bateau A (Wiawaka), 78, *80*, 85–86
Bateau B (Wiawaka)
  assessment of, 146
  description of, 78, 86
  drawing of, *80*
  inventory of disarticulated pieces in area of, 145
  vandalization of, 84, 86, 88, 143
Bateau C (Wiawaka), *78*, *79*, *81*, 86
Bateau D (Wiawaka), 78, 79, *82*, 87–88, 151

Bateau E (Wiawaka), 78, *82*, 87
Bateau F (Wiawaka), 78, *83*, 87
Bateau G (Wiawaka), 78, *83*, 87
bateaux. *See also* military bateaux; *individual boats*
  ballast rocks to sink, 149–51, 199
  British standard for, 7
  building techniques, 21–25
  buoyancy of replica, 199
  carrying capacity of, 198
  construction analysis, 11–19
  defined, 1–3, 11, 203
  drawing of, *3*, *197*
  hull form, 62
  Kalm description of, 14–15
  life span of, 9
  origins of, 11–15
  in "Sinking of the Radeau" painting, 181–82
  speed under sail, 198
  steering of, 15, 25, 148, *149*, 197–98, 203
  weight of replica, 149
Bateaux Below. *See also* Lake George Bateaux Research Team
  Baby Whale discovery by, 90
  board members of, 202
  "Colonial Walking Tour of Lake George" by, 170
  dock for, 29, 137, 149
  formation of, 75
  Forward park remodeling by, 139–40
  grants for, xviii–xvix
  historic markers by, 168–70
  "Historic Vessels and Shipwrecks of Lake George" exhibit, 168
  Land Tortoise radeau studies by, 90
  lectures by members of, 175
  in Maple Ave. students' project, 153
  mission of, 75
  MOU with NYS, 136
  in National Register nomination process, 127–29
  newsletter, 39, *166*, 167, 195–99
  Pepe Productions and, 159–61
  Preserve America Steward award for, 141–42
  in "Raising the Fleet: An Art/Science Initiative," 155–58

replica bateaux sunk by, 138–39, 149–51
Schenectady's exhibit on colonial bateaux allied with, 167
shipwreck surveys by, 19, 105–11, 114
"Shipwreck Weekend at Lake George," 164–65
side-scan sonar surveys by, 99
stabilizing Wiawaka bateaux, 143–46
in Submerged Heritage Preserves program, 133–42
"Sunken Fleet of 1758" park cleanup by, 143–44
"Underwater Archaeology" exhibit, collaboration with, 174
Wiawaka bateaux studies by, 113–14
Bateaux Below newsletter, 164, 167, 187–194
Bateaux Collection 4530 (NYS Museum), 14, 15
bateau "factories," 3, 6, 12, 19, 176–77, 203
"bateaux plats," 11
Bateau(x) Site I, 38–39, 41, 47, 106, 115. *See also* Operation Bateaux
Bateau(x) Site II. *See* "Mortar Bateau"
Bateau(x) Site III, 106. *See also* English Brook bateau
Bateau(x) Site IV. *See* Wiawaka bateaux
Bateau(x) Site V, 107
Bateau(x) Site VI, 107, *108*
Bateau(x) Site VII, 107–9, 113, 115, 117–19
Bateau(x) Site VIII, *108*, 109–10
Bateau(x) Site IX, 35, 110, 172
Bateau(x) Site X, 110
Bateau(x) Site XI, 66–67, 110
Bateau(x) Site XII, 110–11
bathyscaphe, 121–22, 124
"Batteau Project, The," 72, 167ni
battens. *See also* cleats
of Bateau 2626, 13, 17
bottom board planks and, 17, 23
defined, 17, 204
dimensions of, 17
fasteners for, 17
photograph of recovered, 24
in "Sunken Fleet of 1758" park, 145
of Wiawaka bateaux, 79, 84, 86

wood used for, 17, 21
Battle of Lake George, 3–5
Battle of Plattsburgh, 9
Battoe Service, 6
Bauder, Alan, 48–49, 150, 153–54, 174
Beaver, 117–18
Bellico, Russell
"Archaeological Research Assistant Workshop," xiii, 73, 98, 164
on Bateau(x) Site VIII, 109
"Colonial Walking Tour of Lake George" brochure by, 170
on Floating Battery Island shipwrecks, 29
Fort George Battlefield Park signs by, 171
on *Land Tortoise* radeau, 90
lectures by, 175
in National Register nomination process, 127
photographs from
of Adirondack Museum exhibit, *13*, 102
in "Historic Vessels and Shipwrecks of Lake George" exhibit, 168
in situ Bateaux Site VI, *108*
in situ floating gun battery hull timbers, 29
in situ Land Tortoise radeau, *48*
in situ Wiawaka bateau, *78*, *79*
Preserve America Steward award for, 142
Sails and Steam in the Mountains, xix, 177
on "Save the *Sayonara* Committee," 133
"Underwater Archaeology" exhibit, collaboration with, 174
Benthos Mini-Rover MkII, xiv, 78, 89
Benway, Bob
Baby Whale discovery by, 90, 122–24, *125*
"Colonial Walking Tour of Lake George" brochure by, 170
on English Brook dive, 114
Floating Battery Island studies by, 29
in "Historic Vessels and Shipwrecks of Lake George" exhibit, 168
Land Tortoise radeau find by, 90

Benway, Bob (*cont'd*)
in Maple Ave. students project, 153
"Mortar Bateau" studies by, 100–3
NYS Underwater Blueway Trail display at Visitor Center by, 173
Preserve America Steward award for, 142
replica bateau studies by, *139*, 151
on side-scan sonar survey of Onondaga Lake, 167–68
"Video Virtual Reality Tour of a Sunken Colonial Bateau Site" by, 172
"Wit's Bateaux" find by, 110–11
zebra mussels find by, 184
Bethel, Ed, 181
Binghamton Press, 117
Bird, Harrison K., Jr., 61, 131–32
Black Laser Learning, 89, 159, 161
Blais, Bob, 153–54
Bolt, Fred, 38, 41, 106
Bolton, Historical Society of, 102–3
bomb ketch, 93, 204. *See also* "Mortar Bateau"
Boston Tea Party Ship Museum, 102
bottom board planks
of Bateau 2626, 13, 17, 21
battens and, 17, 23
with caulked seams, 18, 193
"cross-beams" to reinforce, 97
of Cumberland Bay bateau, *180*, 181
in Delmar Boy Scout Troop's replica bateau, 195–96
edges of, 17
frames and, 17
joints for, 23
knees and, 17, 25
length of, 21
on "Mortar Bateau," 97
from Operation Bateaux, 54
photograph of *in situ*, *14*
photograph of recovered, *16*
rocker curve of, 23
sheathing for, 21
stem and, 17
sternpost and, 17, 25
strakes and, 17
in "Sunken Fleet of 1758" park, 145

thickness of, 17, 23
on ways, 23
of Wiawaka bateaux, 78–79, 84, 86–87
width of, 23
wood used for, 14, 17, 19, 21, 203
Bowser, Samuel, 142, 155, 158
Bradstreet, John, 6
British
in colonial wars. *See* **colonial wars**
holes drilled in bateaux by, 84
orientation of bateaux by, 79, 88, 151
recovery of boats in "wet storage," 6, 54
Broadwater, John, 172
Brown's attack on Diamond Island, 117
Bulletin of the Fort Ticonderoga Museum, 102
buoys, 68, 135–36, 179
Burgoyne campaign, 9, 109, 115
butt joint, 23, 204

Cadet ex *Olive* shipwreck, 129, 170
Caldwell, James, 28ni
Caldwell, Ted
Delmar Boy Scout Troop, full-scale model for, 195
mortar bombs studies facilitated by, 103
photograph of replica bateau, *84*
pitch solution of, 197
replica bateaux built by students of, *84*, *85*, 138–39, 148–51, 154, 172
Campoli, Bernie, 71, 97
Canada
Arnold's Quebec campaign against, 198
in colonial wars. *See* **colonial wars**
Franklin's diplomatic mission to, 9, 148
map of, *2*
Canal Corp./Thruway Authority, 49
cannonballs, 31, 110
cannons
conservation of, 119
of Diamond Island shipwrecks, 109, 117–19
in French and Indian War, 7, 19
vs. howitzers, 205
from July 1903-raised 1757 sloop, 31
on *Land Tortoise* radeau, 90
on military bateaux, 19

vs. mortars, 93, 206
1954-raised 18-pound French, 109, 117–19
1959-raised falconet, 36–38, 204
trunnions for, 37
Cape Gelidonya shipwreck, 51
Capone, Vince
"Archaeological Research Assistant Workshop," xiii, xiv, 73, *74*, 164
Baby Whale studies by, 124
Black Laser Learning, 89, 159, 161
expert advice from, xix
Land Tortoise radeau find by, 90
photograph of, *74, 89*
Preserve America Steward award for, 142
on side-scan sonar survey of Onondaga Lake, 167–68
sonar technician and ROV operator, 75, 78, 89–90, 99
Carney, Jim, *116*, 117–19
Carpenter, Carolynn Raven, *150*, 151
carvel planking, 18, 196, 204
caulked seams, 18, 25, 193, 196, 204
Cavotta, Karen, 153
Cerrone, Darold, 106, 114
Champlain Maritime Society, 135
Champlain Valley
in French and Indian War, 5–7, 9, 15, 18–19, 96, 111, 155, 176
in War of 1812, 9
Chapelle, Howard I., 1, 3, 11, 19, 188
Chatham Courier, 31
checking, 59
classical archaeology, 51, 204
cleats, 9, 43, 101, *180*, 181. *See also* **battens**
clinker planking, 18, 203, 204, 205. *See also* **lapstrake** planking
closed-circuit television (CCTV) camera system, *52*, 53–54
Cohn, Arthur, 12–13, 72
"Colonial Walking Tour of Lake George," 170
colonial wars
defined, 204
French and Indian War. *See* French and Indian War

King George's War, 1, 204
King William's War, 1, 204
Lake George wharf from, 91
military bateaux in, 1–9, 15, 18–20
Queen Anne's War, 1, 3, 204
"Colonial Wars of Lake George" walking tour, 172
computer-generated images (CGI), 8, *12*
Conference on Underwater Archaeology, 59, 63–64
Coolidge's Diamond Point House, 28
Cooper, Bill, 153
Cooper, Dexter, 13
Cooper, James Fenimore, 5
Cooper's Cave Ale Company, 103
Cordell, Tim, 7, 151, 170, 172, *180*, 181–82
Corey, Albert B., 55, 61
Cornell, Paul, *135*, 142, 151
Couchman, Lee, 67, 188
Council of Underwater Archaeology (CUA), 59, 63–64, 68
craft-of-opportunity, 77, 90, 204
Crandall, Terry
on buoys for sunken bateaux, 68, 179
on carvel planking on bateaux, 18
death of, xviii, 68
drawing of bateau, *20*
on Floating Battery Island dives, 29
on Lake George Bateaux Research Team, 88, 99
in Maple Ave. students project, 154
"Mortar Bateau" studies by, 96–97, 99–102, 106, 192, *193*
in Operation Bateaux, 62–64, 66–68, 90, 105–11, 187–94
photograph of, *63, 67, 96*
"police" diving by, 189–90
Preserve America Steward award for, 142
in "Shipwreck Weekend at Lake George," 165
thole pins and pin pads find by, 15, 193, *194*
"Underwater Archaeology" exhibit, collaboration with, 174
on vandalization of bateaux, 88, 107, 184, 194

Crandall, Terry (*cont'd*)
  Wiawaka bateaux studies of, 87–88, 106, 113
Crisman, Kevin J., 12–17, *18*, 25, 103–4, 176
Crosbyside Hotel bateau, 27. *See also* Wiawaka bateaux
Crown Point. *See* Fort St. Frédéric
Cucuteanu, Maddy, *80–83*
cultural resources managers
  challenges facing, 183
  defined, 204
  after July 1960 bateaux discovery, 39
  newsletters to, 167
  recommendations for, 119–20
  on souvenir collecting, 70
  strategies for, 145–46
Cumberland Bay bateau, 179–81

decks, 25, 93, 95, 97, 101, 106
Delgado, James P., 127
Delmar Boy Scout Troop, 195–99
"Demonstration of Archaeological Site Mapping of a Colonial Bateau" program, 177
Dennis, Charlie, 188
Diamond Island, 115, 117, *137*
Diamond Island shipwrecks, 107–9, 113, 115–19, 129, 134, 140
Diehl, Charles, 94, 97, 102, 103, 115
Diehl, David, 102
Differential Global Positioning System (DGPS), 100
Discovery bateau, 72, 167ni
Dive (Parker), 94
dive shops, 49, 120, 140, 184
Diving into History (NYS), 70–71, 163
docks. *See also* piers; wharfs
  Baby Whale stolen from, 90, 121–23
  Bateaux Below's, 29, 137, 149
  July 1903-raised 1757 sloop near old steamboat, 31
  Wiawaka Holiday House's, 84–85
documentaries, 159–161. *See also individual works*
Documentary Filmmaking for Archaeologists (Pepe and Zarzynski), 161
Dome Island, 66

Donnelly, Daniel, 106, 114
Dow, Bill, 172
Drose, Robert, 94–95
Dunham's Bay, 190
Dunn, Carl, xviii, 35, *36*, 110
Durham boats, 72, 167–68, 176. *See also* "Schenectady boat"

Earl of Halifax (sloop), 6, *91*, 170
Education Department, NYS. *See also* New York State Museum
  on ad-hoc Committee for Submerged Cultural Resources, 50
  at "Archaeological Research Assistant Workshop," 73
  correspondence with dive shop, 71
  Diving into History, 70–71, 163
  duties of, 50
  order to seal off area around sunken bateaux, 41, 47
  permits for underwater archeology from, 41–44, 62, 95, 106
  reports to, from Lake George Bateaux Research Team, 75
Eggleston, Richard, 9
Ellsworth, Marie, 151
Engelke, Karen, 167
English Brook bateau, 61, 114–15. *See also* Bateau(x) Site III
Environmental Conservation, NYS Department of
  on ad-hoc Committee for Submerged Cultural Resources, 49
  brochures from, *136*, 138, 140
  duties of, 50
  at Fort George Battlefield Park, 138, 171
  Green Island facilities, 138
  Internet address for, 138
  in Maple Ave. students project, 153
  monitoring of preserves for, 140–41
  Submerged Heritage Preserves program oversight, 50, 119, 133, 138
  at Wiawaka bateaux site cleanup, 144
Erving's World Wide Skindiver's Guide, 71
experimental archaeology. *See also* **replica archaeology**
  defined, 204

goals of, 148
by Maple Ave. students, 151–54
in "Sunken Fleet of 1758" park, *84*, 85, *114*, *134*, 138–39, 149–51

falconet, 36–38, 204
Farrell, John
Baby Whale studies by, 124
cartographic map of Wiawaka bateaux by, *86*
"Colonial Walking Tour of Lake George" brochure by, 170
death of, xviii, 174
drawings of Wiawaka bateaux by, *80–83*
illustrations and models by, xix
Land Tortoise radeau find by, 90
in Maple Ave. students project, 153
models from, in "Historic Vessels and Shipwrecks of Lake George" exhibit, 168
NYS Underwater Blueway Trail display at Visitor Center by, 173
Preserve America Steward award for, 142
in "Raising the Fleet: An Art/Science Initiative," 156
replica bateaux sunk by, 151
scale boat models by, 178–79
shipwreck dioramas by, 178–79
"Underwater Archaeology" exhibit, collaboration with, 174
"Wit's Bateaux" find by, 110–11
Finger Lakes Underwater Preserves Association (FLUPA), 177
Flacke, Robert, 38, 70
Flaherty, Robert J., 159–60
float, tire inner tubes for, *52*, 68
Floating Battery Island shipwrecks, 29
floating gun batteries
Bateau(x) Site XI as, 110
defined, 204
photograph of *in situ*, *29*
purpose of, 23
radeaux. *See* **radeaux**
treenails used in, 23
floor timbers, 31, 204
foraminifera, 155

Fort Carillion, 2, 7, 43–44, 91, *136*. *See also* Fort Ticonderoga
Fort Edward, 2, 177, 178. *See also* Fort Lyman
Fort George Battlefield Park, 138, 171
Fortin, Will, 153
Fort Lyman, 3. *See also* Fort Edward
Fort Orange, 12. *See also* Albany
Fort St. Frédéric, 2, 7, 19, 91
Fort Ticonderoga. *See* Fort Carillion
Fort Ticonderoga Museum, 43–44, 60–61, 102
Fort William Henry, 2, 5, 35, 44, *137*, 174
Fort William Henry Corporation
authentication of Bolt-LaVoy find by, 38
Diamond Island shipwrecks, Veeder on, 107, 119
Dunn working for, xviii, *36*
Gifford's archaeological dig funded by, 35
Hamilton on raising of bateaux by, 44
Lake George survey, Flacke on, 70
military bateaux, Veeder list of, 66
museum administration by, 66, 173
1954-raised cannon sold to, 118
"skin diving treasure hunt" sponsored by, 47
Fort William Henry Hotel bateaux, 27, 28, 110
Fort William Henry Museum
arson fire at, 119
artillery at, inventory of, 109, 118
bateau frame in collection of, 24
colonial bateau pieces from, for replica archeology, *152*, 153
construction of, 35
grapnel anchors at, 118
July 1903-raised 1757 sloop remnants in, 31, 32
location of, 173
mortar bombs donated to, 102
1954-raised cannon at, 118
opening of, 173
photograph of, *4*
reaction to Adirondack Museum's underwater archaeology permit, 44

Fort William Henry Museum (*cont'd*)
  scale boat models exhibited by, 178
  "Underwater Archaeology of 'The
    Sunken Fleet of 1758'" exhibit by,
    173–74
Forward shipwreck, 129, 134, 140
"*Forward* Underwater Classroom, The,"
  132, 134–40
frames. *See also* **knees**
  of Bateau 2626, 13–14, 17
  in bateaux construction, 18, 25
  bottom board planks and, 17
  construction of, 25
  defined, 205
  in Delmar Boy Scout Troop's replica
    bateau, 195–96
  fasteners for, 17
  for floating gun batteries, 29
  futtocks, 31, 205
  in Lake George Historical Association's
    collection, 167
  on "Mortar Bateau," 95, 97, 101
  photograph of *in situ*, 14, *190*
  photograph of recovered, *24*
  in "Sunken Fleet of 1758" park, 145,
    198
  thickness of, 25, 97
  of Wiawaka bateaux, 79, 84, 86–87
  width of, 17
  wood used for, 13, 17, 21, 196, 203
Franklin, Benjamin, 9, 148
French and Indian War
  Abercromby military campaign in, 6, *7*,
    15, 36, 97–98, *136*
  Amherst military campaign in, 6–7,
    18–19, 111, 155, 176
  bateaux "factories" in, 177
  Battle of Lake George, 3–5
  Battoe Service in, 6
  duration of, 1, 1nii, 204
  Fort Carillon in, 7, 43–44, 91, *136*
  Fort St. Frédéric in, 7, 19, 91
  Fort William Henry in, 5
  military bateaux in, 3–9, 15, 18–20
  Speakman's Rangers re-enactors group,
    151
  submerged wharf from, 91
  Treaty of Paris on, 7

"wet storage" of warships during, 6, *8*,
  54, 111, 155, 176
French and Indian War Society, 109, 173
frogmen, xiii, 53–54, 205
Fund for Lake George, Inc., The, xviii–
  xix, 139, 143, 177
futtocks, 31, 205

Gallagher, Nathan A., 11, 14, 19, 60
garboard strakes
  attachment of, 25
  of Bateau 2626, 13, 17
  in bateaux construction, 18
  bottom board planks and, 17
  defined, 205
  on "Mortar Bateau," 101
  from Operation Bateaux, 54
  photograph of *in situ*, *14*
  in "Sunken Fleet of 1758" park, 198
  of Wiawaka bateaux, 79, 84, 86–87
Gardner, John
  on bottom board planks, 23
  on carvel vs. clinker planking on
    bateaux, 18
  on French and Indian War, 7
  National Fisherman articles by, 163
  on origin of bateaux, 12
  replica bateaux by, 12, 61
  on rocker, 23
  on stems, 17, 25
General Electric CCTV camera system,
  52, 53–54
General Services, NYS Office of, 49–50,
  124, 133, 138, 150, 153–54
George, Tony, 67
German auxiliary, 9, 176, 205
"**Ghost Fleet,**" xviii, 70, 90, 114, 131,
  164, 185, 205. *See also* **Lake
  George's Sunken Bateaux of
  1758**
Giesecke, Anne G., 49
Gifford, Stanley M., 35–36, *37*
Glens Falls Post-Star, 32–33
Glens Falls Times, 38, 41, 47, 54–55, 123
Global Positioning System (GPS), 100,
  205
Gottschalk, Elinor Mossop, 142, 156,
  157

grapnel anchors, 54, *116*, 117–18
Great Britain, 1ni, 7, 48, 57. *See also*
    British
Green Island, 138
Grierson, John, 159
gunboat, 117, 205
gunwales (gunnels), 25, 191, 193, 205

Hager, Robert E., *22*, 23, *26*
Hamilton, Edward P., 44, 62, 188
Haudenosaunee, 3
Herkimer Home State Historic Site, 199n2
Hessians. *See* **German auxiliary**
Higgins, Ronald, 94–95
Hill View bateau, 27
historic preservation ethic, 57, 64
Hochschild, Harold K., 69
Hood, James, 174
howitzers, 7, 93, 205, 206
Hudson River
    in American Revolution, 9
    bateau "factories" along, 3, 19
    in colonial wars, 1
    Cordell painting of Bethel's re-enactor boat on, 181
    in French and Indian War, 177
    map of, *2*
    hull timbers, 14, *29*, 31, *32*, 60, 205

"inner stem." *See* **apron**
in situ, 21, 53, 205
"Intro to Underwater Archaeology for Shipwreck Preserves Development" workshop, 177
Inverarity, Robert Bruce
    on Adirondack Historical Association's charter, 43
    Bass on, 53
    career of, 44–46
    on CCTV for underwater archaeology, 54
    at Conference on Underwater Archaeology (1963), 59, 63
    conservation treatment chosen by, 57–60
    Crandall and, 62–64, 66–68, 187–88, 191, 194

Diamond Island shipwreck survey of, 107
Floating Battery Island survey of, 29
LaVoy and, 41
list of shipwreck sites in Lake George, 66
meeting with scuba divers, 61
"Mortar Bateau," letter from Smith on, 94
NYS police diver training and, 69
Operation Bateaux director. *See* Operation Bateaux
Parker and, 188
photograph of, *42*
on reconstruction of bateaux "lines," 62
resignation from Adirondack Museum, 68, 69
on sample collection, 87
site security policy of, 188
submarine painting by, *45*
on vandalization of bateaux, 55, 63–64
Invincible radeau, 181
inwales, 25
Iroquois, 3

Jefferson Davis (shipwreck), 159
Jefts, Charles, 48, 61
J. M. Kaplan Fund, 122
Johnson, William, 5
joints, 23, 197, 204, 207
Jones, Art, 121–22
July 1903-raised 1757 sloop, *30*, 31–33

Kalm, Peter, 14–15, 60
keel, 31, 119, *122*, 204
Kelly, Dale R., 150
King George's War, 1, 204
King William's War, 1, 204
Klein, Martin, xix, 77, 89
Klein side-scan sonar, xix, 75–78, 88–90, 99, *108*, 110, *128*, 167–68
knees, 13, 17, 25, 28, 97, 196–98, 205.
    See also **frames**
Knickerbocker News, 41, 69–70
Knoerl, T. Kurt, 156, 174
Kon-Tiki (Heyerdahl's vessel), 148
Kozak, Garry, xix, *76*, 89, 90

Lake Champlain
 in American Revolution, 9
 bateau shipwrecks in, 179–81
 in colonial wars, 1
 in French and Indian War, 2, 5–7, 19, 43–44, 91, *136*
 map of, *2*
 shipwreck preserve program in, 135
 side-scan sonar surveys of, 77, *89*
 in War of 1812, 9, 179–81
Lake Champlain Basin Program, 148, 170
Lake Champlain Maritime Museum, xx, 13–14, 71–72, 135
Lake George
 in American Revolution, 9
 in colonial wars, 1–5, 91
 daily patrols of, 188
 excursion boat tours of, 141
 fieldwork conditions in, 53, 75
 inventory of shipwrecks in, 62, 90, 99, 105–11, 113–14
 map of, *2*
 nickname for, xvii
 side-scan sonar surveys in, 75–78, 88–90, 99
 water level in, 85
"Lake George, NY Submerged Cultural Resources Awareness Workshop," 177
Lake George Arts Project exhibit, *156*, *157*, 178
Lake George Association, 43
Lake George Bateaux Research Team. *See also* Bateaux Below
 accomplishments of, xviii
 Crandall's work with, 88
 divers participating in, 201–2
 fieldwork challenges of, 75
 founding of, 73, 164
 goals of, xv
 Land Tortoise radeau discovery by, 90
 lectures by members of, 175
 "Mortar Bateau" studies by, 99
 new bateaux clusters discovered by, 89–90
 newsletter by, 164, 167, 187–194
 NYS Museum on studies of, 75
 public outreach by, 164
 ROV surveys by, 78

Saratoga Springs JHS students PVC grid for, 147
 shipwreck surveys by, 105
 side-scan sonar surveys by, 75–78, 88–90, 99
 strategy of, 88
 Wiawaka bateaux studies by, 73–88
Lake George Chamber of Commerce, 47, 48
Lake George Historical Association
 colonial bateau frame from collection of, 167
 "Colonial Walking Tour of Lake George" by, 170
 historic markers by, 168, *169*
 "Historic Vessels and Shipwrecks of Lake George" exhibit, 168
 mortar bomb loaned to, 102–4
 1903-raised sloop, pieces donated to, 31
 scale boat models exhibited by, 178
 Schenectady's exhibit on colonial bateaux allied with, 167
 "Shipwreck Weekend at Lake George," 164–65
 "Sinking of the Radeau" painting at, 181
 Submerged Heritage Preserves program and, 133, 138
Lake George Mirror
 on artifacts and relics, 62
 on conservation of raised bateaux, 57
 Diehl's article on diving in Lake George, 102
 on discovery of bateaux, 27–29
 on historic preservation, 33, 44
 on "Mortar Bateau," 94
 on museum, 28
 on replica bateau at Fort Ticonderoga, 60
 on underwater archaeology permit of Adirondack Museum, 43–44
Lake George Nautical Newsletter, 39, *166*, 167, 195–99
Lake George Park Commission, 133, 188, 189–90
Lake George Power Squadron charts, 189
Lake George's *Forward* (Bateaux Below), 140

Lake George Shoreline Cruises, 141
Lake George's Sunken Bateaux of 1758.
  See also *individual boats*
  ballast rocks to sink, 35, 109, 149–51, 199
  Bateaux Below's rediscovery of, 89–90
  as British property, 48
  CGI of, *8*
  conservation of, 57–60
  construction of, 12–19
  vs. Cumberland Bay bateau, 181
  debris deposits on, 192
  decision to sink, 6, 134ni
  defined, 205
  "disappeared," 106–9, 111, 113–20
  drawing of, *8, 20*
  historic markers on, 169–70
  inventory of, 62, 105–11
  Lake George Mirror article on, 27
  LaVoy and Bolt's rediscovery of, 38–39, 41, 88, 106, 115
  "Mortar Bateau," 39, 93–104, 106, 115, 192, *193*
  1960–65 study of. *See* Operation Bateaux
  19th century discovery and salvage of, 27–33
  ownership of, 41
  Peckham on, 28
  photograph of
    Lake George Bateaux Research Team at, *76*
    museum exhibit of, *13, 15, 16*
    raising of, in Operation Bateaux, *52*
    recovered, *56*
    in situ, 14, 67, 108, 190, 194
  public education programs on, 163–79
  rediscovery of (1950s), 35–38
  spatial distribution pattern of, 39
  testate amoebae in sediment near, 155–56
  250th anniversary of raising, 155–58
  vandalization of. *See* vandalization
  off Wiawaka Holiday House. *See* Wiawaka bateaux
Lake George Steamboat Company, 117, 141, 170–72
Lake George Visitor Center, 172–73
Lake Ontario, 2

"*Land Tortoise*—A 1758 Floating Gun Battery," *128*, 137–38, 140–41, 171
Land Tortoise radeau
  discovery of, 90, 99, 137
  documentary on, 142, 159–61
  drawing of, *128*
  historic markers on, 169–70
  mapping of, 99, 178
  on National Register of Historic Places, 90, *128*, 129, 140, 171
  as NHL, 90
  painting of sinking of, *180*, 181–82
  photograph of *in situ*, 48
  request for highway signs about, 185
  scale model of, 178–79
  "wet storage" of, 181–82
lapstrake planking, 18, 196, 204–5
Last of the Mohicans, The (Cooper), 5
LaVoy, Robert "Bob," 38, 39, 41, 51, 88, 93, 97, 106
Law Department, NYS, 49
Lennan, Robert, *116*, 117–19
Lewis, Dennis, 19
Lighthouse Archaeological Maritime Program (LAMP), 159
Lilly, Robert, 188
"lines," 62
Link, Edwin A., 64–65
lofting, 195, 205
Looe, HMS, 64, *65*
LORAN (long range navigation), 100, 205
Lord, Phil, xiv, 73, 167–68
Lord, Robert, 38–39, 41
"Lost Radeau, The" (documentary), 142, 159, 160–61, 174
lubber line, 189, 205

MacDonald, James L., 33
Macdonough, Thomas, 9
Macri, Maria, 151
Magee, James A., 97–98, 109
Maple Ave. Middle School replica bateau, 151–54
Mary Rose, 57
masts, 15, 21, *22*, 197, 198, 203
mast step, 15
Mathewson, R. Duncan, III, xiii–xiv, 73, 127

Index 253

McCoy, Carl K., 47
McMahan, Kendrick, 165
Meany, Joseph, 19
Mediterranean Sea, 51, 64
Memorandum of Understanding (MOU), 136
military bateaux, 1–9, 15, 18–20
"Moana" (documentary), 159–60
Mohawk River, 2, 3, 6, 19, *22*, 23, 167–68, 177
Montcalm (General), 96, 115
Montreal, *2*
mooring lines, 135–36
"Mortar Bateau," 39, 93–104, 106, 115
mortars
  on bateaux, 7, 93
  vs. cannons, 93, 206
  defined, 206
  description of, 93
  in "Historic Vessels and Shipwrecks of Lake George" exhibit, 168
  vs. howitzers, 93, 206
  removed from "Mortar Bateau," 95–97, 101–4, 192, *193*
  weight of, 39, 104
Museum of International Folk Art, 45–46
Museum of Underwater Archaeology (MUA), 156, 174, 206

nails, wrought iron, 17, 23, 60
"Nanook of the North" (documentary), 160
Narrows, Lake George, 66–67, 110, 133
National Fisherman magazine, 163
National Historic Landmark (NHL)
  defined, 206
  Land Tortoise radeau listed as, 90, *128*, 129, 140, 185
National Historic Preservation Act, 206
National Oceanic and Atmospheric Administration (**NOAA**), 9, 161, 172, 206
National Register of Historic Places
  Baby Whale recommendation for, 125
  Cadet ex *Olive* shipwreck on, 129
  defined, 206
  Forward shipwreck on, 129, 140
  Land Tortoise radeau listed on, 90, *128*, 129, 140

NYS overseer for, 50
Wiawaka bateaux on, 100, 119, 127–29, 140
Wiawaka Holiday House on, 143
National Science Foundation (NSF), 155, 206
Native Americans, 5, 48. See also *specific tribes*
Nautical Archaeology Society, 65
Navy scuba divers, 53–54
New France, *2*. See also Canada
New York Sea Grant/Oswego, 164–65
New York State (NYS)
  Bateaux Below's MOU with, 136
  colonial fortification site map, *2*
  Historic Marker Program, 165, 168–69
  request for highway signs near Lake George, 184–85
  state underwater archaeologist position in, 185
New York State Archaeological Association (NYSAA), 172
New York State Divers Association, 133, *135*, 138
New York State Education Law (1958), 41–42, 47
New York State Museum
  bateaux in collection of, 14
  "Batteau Project, The," 72
  July 1903-raised 1757 sloop remnants in, 31, *32*
  on Lake George Bateaux Research Team, 75
  Lake George's Sunken Bateaux exhibit at, *15*, *16*, *24*
  replica bateaux by, 72, 167
  Schenectady's exhibit on colonial bateaux allied with, 72, 167
  shipwreck preserve program and, 133
  storage of bateaux by, 60
New York State Police, 69, 106–7, 113–14, 190
New York State Underwater Blueway Trail, 172–73
New York Sun, 159–60
New York Times, 39, 69, 113
Nickerson, N. E., 53–54
North American Society for Oceanic History (NASOH), 171, 206

Northern Dean construction firm, 153
oarlocks, 15, *16*, 193, *194*
oars
  in Caldwell's replica bateaux, 148, *149*
  creation of, 21, 25
  Crisman on bateaux, 15
  in Delmar Boy Scout Troop's replica bateau, 197, 198
  for steering, 15, 25, 198, 203
Obama, Barack, 32
Obama, Michelle, 141, 142
Old Fort George Hotel bateau, 27
Onondaga Lake, 167–68
Operation Bateaux
  artifacts found during, 192–93
  boats for use in, 188
  duration of, xix, 63
  fieldwork conditions in, 191–92
  LaVoy and, 41
  "Mortar Bateau" studies during, 94–97, 102, 106, 192
  nails found during, 23
  1960 phase of, 51–55, 106
  1961–62 phase of, 44, 57–62
  1963–64 phase of, 62–64, 66–68, 90, 105–11, 187–94
  1965 phase of, 69, 106–7
  permits for, 41–44, 50, 62
  photographs from, 192–93
  pontoon barge purchased for, 189
  security policy for, 188
  shipwreck inventories during, 105–11
  site handling techniques in, 191–94
  thole pins and pin pads found during, 15, *16*, 193
  Wiawaka bateaux studies during, 77, 87
Ord, Thomas, 90
"Ord's Ark," 90. *See also* **radeaux**

paddles, 15, 21, 25. *See also* oars
Padeni, Scott, 124, 151, 170, 171
Pallissino, Nick, 97
Parker, Gene, 61, 67, 71, 94–96, 106, 188
Parks, Recreation and Historic Preservation, NYS Office of
  on ad-hoc Committee for Submerged Cultural Resources, 49

"Mortar Bateau" inspection by, 100
National Register of Historic Places oversight by, 50
Submerged Heritage Preserves program and, 133, 138
Wiawaka bateaux on National Register, case officer for, 100, 127
on Wiawaka site cleanup, 143
parks, underwater. *See* **shipwreck preserves**
Parrott, James, 121–22
Peckham, Mark L.
  Bateaux Below's case officer, 100
  Cumberland Bay bateau drawing by, *180*
  on Delmar Boy Scout Troop's replica bateau, 195–99
  Earl of Halifax at wharf, drawing by, *91*
  Eighteenth-century bateau drawing by, *3, 8, 197*
  ink and watercolor illustrations by, 179
  on Lake George's Sunken Bateaux of 1758, 28, 198
  "Mortar Bateau" studies by, 100–1
  in National Register nomination process, 127
  NYS Underwater Blueway Trail display at Visitor Center by, 173
  replica bateaux sunk by, 151
Pepe, Peter, 2, 4, 60, *137*, 142, 156, 159, 160, 161
Pepe Productions
  Bateaux Below and, 159–61
  CGI by, *8, 12*
  dioramas and scale models used in, 179
  "Lost Radeau, The," 142, 159, 160–61
  NYS Underwater Blueway Trail display at Visitor Center by, 173
  public outreach through documentaries by, 159–61
  in "Raising the Fleet: An Art/Science Initiative," 156
  "Search for the *Jefferson Davis*," 159
  "Underwater Archaeology" exhibit, collaboration with, 174
  "Wooden Bones." *See* "Wooden Bones" (documentary)
Pepper, Jerold "Jerry," 60
Perry-Link *Deep Diver* submarine, 65

Perseverance, 13–14, 71–72
Peterson, Mendel L., 59, 64, 102
Philadelphia Maritime Museum, 46
Piccard, Jacques, 121
piers, 27. *See also* docks; wharfs
pine pitch, 21, 197
pitch pot, *180,* 181
planks
 bottom. *See* bottom board planks
 side. *See* **strakes**
Plattsburgh, 9, 70, 179–81
Plattsburgh Press-Republican, 55
poles, 15, 25, *26*
polyethylene glycol (PEG), 57–60, 192, 206
polyvinyl chloride (PVC) piping, *74,* 147
portage, 20, 177, 198, 206
prams, 11, 206
Preservation League of New York State, 122
Preserve America program, 141–42
Principal Investigator (PI), 90, 206
provincial
 building of bateaux by, 196
 in colonial wars. *See* **colonial wars**
 defined, 207
 holes drilled in bateaux by, 84
 orientation of bateaux by, 79, 88, 151
 recovery of boats in "wet storage," 6, 54
public outreach
 by Adirondack Museum, 47–48
 by Bateaux Below, 164–65
 defined, 207
 through documentaries, 159, 161
 education programs for, 163–79, 184
 by excursion boat operators, 141
 by Lake George Bateaux Research Team, 164
 recommendations for, 119–20
 replica bateaux as, 72
 "Shipwreck Weekend at Lake George," 164–65

Quebec, *2*
Queen Anne's War, 1, 3, 204

radeaux, 6, 90, 207. *See also individual boats*

"Raising the Fleet: An Art/Science Initiative," 155–58
Ranger whaleboat, 181
Rea, Caleb, 15
Reagan, Ronald, 48
recreational dive community
 ad-hoc Committee for Submerged Cultural Resources and, 49
 bateaux research diving by, 201
 vs. historians on artifacts, 69–70
 historic preservation ethic in, 57, 64, 120, 184
 mortar bateau discovered by, 39
 Nautical Archaeology Society's programs for, 65
 in 1950s Lake George, 35–38
 in Operation Bateaux, 44, 51–62, 106, 187, 201
 outreach to, 120
 rediscovery of Lake George bateaux by, 38
 souvenir collecting by, 38–39, 57, 63, 69–71, 75, *108,* 115, 145, 194
redoubt, 5, 207
relic hunting, 27–33, 36, 39, 57, 62, 70. *See also* souvenir collecting
remotely-operated-vehicle (ROV)
 Benthos Mini-Rover MkII, xiv, 78, 89
 defined, 207
 Lake Champlain studies using, 89
 training on using, 73, 89
 underwater fieldwork video shot by, 147
 Wiawaka bateaux studies using, *74,* 78, 147
replica archaeology. *See also* **experimental archaeology**
 by Basin Harbor Maritime Museum, 13–14, 17, 71–72
 by Caldwell's students, *84, 85,* 138–39, 148–49, 172
 at Cardboard Boat Races, 177
 Cohn on, 72
 by colonial re-enactor groups, 148
 defined, 207
 by Delmar Boy Scout Troop, 195–99
 at Fort Ticonderoga, 60–61
 Kon-Tiki, 148

Index

lofting in, 195
  by Maple Ave. Middle School students, 151–54
  by NYS Museum, 72, 167ni
  in "Raising the Fleet: An Art/Science Initiative," 156
  in SCCC class, *175*, 176
Resler, Steve, 31, 142, 153
Rhodes, Hanna, 174
ribs, 9, 21, 25, 29, 54, 62, *95*, 117, 205. *See also* **frames**
Richmond, Les "Wit," 88
Roberts, Kenneth, 198
rocker, 23, 198, 207
Rogers, Michael "Bodhi," 32
Rogers Island, 178, 181. *See also* Fort Edward
Root, Gerald, 121–22
row galleys, 6, 28, 38, 91, 207
rowlocks
  metal, 15
  wooden, *194*. *See* thole pins and pin pads
Rural New York Historic Preservation Grant Program, 122

Sabbath Day Point bateau, 111
sails, 15, 21, *22*, 39, 197, 198
Sails and Steam in the Mountains (Bellico), xix, 177
St. Augustine Lighthouse and Museum, 159
St. Lawrence River, *2*, 3, 11, 185
St. Lawrence River Basin, 19
salvage
  ASA on, 203
  at Bateau(x) Site V, 107, 119
  cost of, vs. preserves, 132
  in French and Indian War, 6, 54, 98
  grapnel anchors for, 118
  in 19th century, 27–33
  in 1954, of French cannon, 109, 117–18
Saratoga, *2*
Saratoga Springs Junior High School students PVC grid, 147
Saratoga Springs Maple Ave. Middle School replica bateau, 151–54

Saratogian, The, 33, 38, 102
Sayonara (launch), 133
scarf joint, 23, 197, 207
Schenectady, 5, 6, 12, 19, *52*, 53, 72, 94, *95*, 110, 167, 176–77
"Schenectady boat," 19, 176. *See also* Durham boats
Schenectady County Community College (SCCC), 175–76
Schenectady Gazette, 61
Schmidt, Linda, *123*, 124, *132*
schooners, 91
Schuyler, Philip, 6, 167–68
scuba diving
  archaeologists, 49, 185
  circle searches during, 99
  historic preservation ethic during, 57, 64, 120, 184
  invention of, 35
  license for, 55
  NY clubs for, 36
  recreational. *See* recreational dive community
  red-and-white dive flag up while, 137
Scudiere, Paul, 70–71, 163
"Search for the *Jefferson Davis*" (documentary), 159
"Search for Underwater Sites from the French and Indian War, The" exhibit, 174
seats, 14, 25, 196
Seven Years' War. *See* French and Indian War
Shaw, Brigid, 32
sheathing, 21, 207
Sheridan, Lauren, 174
Sheriff, Warren County, 47, 62, 95, 188, 189–90
Sherman, Henry L., 27
"Shipwreck Archaeology for Non-Divers" class, 175–76
shipwreck preserves
  ASA on, 131
  creation of, 48, 131
  defined, 131, 207
  goals of, 138
  in Lake George. *See* Submerged Heritage Preserves program

shipwreck preserves (*cont'd*)
recommendations for, 119–20
in Vermont, 133, 135
shipwrecks
Cape Gelidonya, 51
defined, 48
dioramas of, 178–79
Jefferson Davis, 159
plundering of, 57
public access to, 48, 131, 207
Roman, 51
zebra mussels on, 184
"Shipwreck Weekend at Lake George," 164–65
side planks. *See* **strakes**
side-scan sonar surveys, 75–78, 88–90, 99, *108*, 128, 167–68
Simpson, John Boulton, 29
"Sinking of the Radeau" painting, *180*, 181–82
Skin Diver magazine, 71
Skinner, Henry, 7
sloops. *See also individual boats*
in American Revolution, 117
defined, 23, 207
in French and Indian War, 5, 6, *30*, 31–33, 123, 170
treenails used in, 23
wharfs for, *91*
Smith, Bruce M., 94
Smith, Lewis L., 94, 115, 119
Smithsonian Institution, 38, 64, 102
Snyder, Bill, 153
Society for Historical Archaeology, 49, 158
souvenir collecting. *See also* relic hunting
from Bateau(x) Site I, 38–39
from Bateau(x) Site VI, *108*
from Bateau(x) Site X, 110
carvel planking determination and, 18
on Diamond Island shipwrecks, 115–19
from July 1903-raised 1757 sloop, *30*, 31
in nineteenth century, 27
by recreational dive community, 38, 57, 62–63, 194
Skin Diver magazine on, 71

in "Sunken Fleet of 1758" park, 137
on Wiawaka bateaux, 18, 75, 85, 145
Sova, Jeff, 147, 151–53
Speakman's Rangers, 151
spear gun, 137
Stafford, Ronald, 170–71
State, NYS Department of, 49, 50, 173
steamboats, lake debris from, 192
stems
apron and, 25
of Bateau 2626, 13–14, 17
bottom board planks and, 17
of Cumberland Bay bateau, *180*
curvature of, 17
defined, 23, 207
fitted position of, 25
of July 1960-discovered bateaux, 39
knees and, 25
photograph of raised, *24*
raked forward, 25
tracing, for replica bateau, *152*
of Wiawaka bateaux, 79, 85
wood used for, 17, 21, 23, 203
sternpost
attachment point of, 25
of Bateau 2626, 13–14, 17
bottom board planks and, 17, 25
defined, 207
fasteners for, 17
knees and, 17, 25
of Wiawaka bateaux, 85
wood used for, 17, 21, 203
strakes
attachment of, 25
of Bateau 2626, 17, 18
bottom board planks and, 17
with caulked seams, 18
defined, 207
in Delmar Boy Scout Troop's replica bateau, 196
edges of, 18
fasteners for, 17
garboard. *See* **garboard strakes**
on "Mortar Bateau," 95
photograph of *in situ*, *14*
photograph of recovered, *24*
sheathing for, 21
sternpost and, 17

in "Sunken Fleet of 1758" park, 145
of Wiawaka bateaux, 86–87
width of, 18
wood used for, 21, 203
Stroup, Walter, 39, 93, 102, 115
submarines
   painting of Navy, *45*
   Perry-Link *Deep Diver, 65*
   Trieste, 121–22, 124
   yellow. See *Baby Whale*
submerged cultural resources
   defined, 207
   Diving into History on, 70–71
   documentaries on, public outreach through, 159, 161
   Erving's World Wide Skindiver's Guide on, 71
   inspections of, 136
   inventory of, 131–32
   Lake George Mirror on preservation of, 28, 44
   NYS Education Department correspondence on, 71
   protection and management of NYS's, 47–50
   public access to, 48, 131
   public education programs on, 163
   recommendations for, 119–20
   state underwater archaeologist's management of, 185
   strategies for, 145–46
Submerged Heritage Information & Preservation Seminar (SHIPS), 177
Submerged Heritage Preserves program
   administration of, 50, 119, 133, 138
   ASA and, 131, 133, 137–38
   Bateaux Below in, 133–36, 138–42
   Bird on, 131–32
   "*Forward* Underwater Classroom, The," *132,* 134–40
   goals of, 141
   I-87 visitor center display on, 185
   Internet address for, 138
   Lake George Historical Association and, 133, 138
   "*Land Tortoise*—A 1758 Floating Gun Battery," *128,* 137–38, 140–41, 171
   lobbying for, 135
   monitoring of, 140–41
   New York State Divers Association and, 138
   publicity of, 140
   recommendations for, 119–20
   "Save the *Sayonara* Committee" and, 133
   signs for, *183*
   "Sunken Fleet of 1758." *See* "Sunken Fleet of 1758" park
   Vermont underwater park system and, 133, 135
Sullivan, Jack
   "Archaeological Research Assistant Workshop," xiii, 73, 98, 164
   "Mortar Bateau" studies by, 98, 100
   1982 dive to sunken bateaux, xiii
   1983 dive at Floating Battery Island, 29
   1987 dive to find "Mortar Bateau," 98
   in Operation Bateaux, 67, 98, 188
"Sunken Fleet of 1758" park. *See also* Wiawaka bateaux
   access to, 136
   brochures for, 135–36, 138, 140
   buoys in, 135–36
   description of, 134
   "disappeared" bateau in, 113–14
   experimental archaeology in, *84, 85, 114, 134,* 138–39, 149–51
   first underwater preserve in NYS, 119
   location of, 134–35, *137*
   map of, *114, 134, 144, 145*
   in "Raising the Fleet: An Art/Science Initiative," 156–58
   season for, 136
   signs for, *128,* 135–36, 151, 171
   souvenir collecting in, 137
   stabilizing bateaux in, 143–45
   trail lines in, 135–36, 151, 171
Swanton, 9
Sweeney, Preston, 151–53
Swinney, Holman J., 69

tar, 14, 18, 181, 197, 207
Tarrant, Fred, 39, 93, 102, 115
Terrell, Bruce G., 9
testate amoebae, 155–56

thole pins and pin pads, 15, *16*, 25, 193, *194*
Throckmorton, Peter, 51
timbers
  checking along surface of, 59
  floor, 31, 204
  hull, 14, *29*, 31, 60, 205
  laser scanning of July 1903-raised 1757 sloop, 32
Town of Lake George
  dock space in, for Bateaux Below boat, 137
  historic markers along shoreline, 165, 168–70
  Lake George Historical Association exhibit in, 168
  road from Ft. Edward to, 177
  Village of Lake George in, 28*niv*
  walking tours of, 170–71
  Wiawaka Holiday House dock, 27, 84–85, 143–44, *145*
treenails (trunnels), 23, 79, 207
Trieste, 121–22, 124
Troy Record, The, 37, 114
Troy Times Record, The, 37
Tuttle, William H., 31

Underwater Archaeological Research Association, 61
underwater archaeologists, 49, 78, 104, 147, 153, 185
underwater archaeology
  Baby Whale for, 124
  defined, 207
  Diving into History on, 70–71, 163
  first international conference on, 59
  handling techniques in, 191–94
  infancy of (1950s–60s), 51, 64
  NYS permits for, 41–44, 50, 62
  Operation Bateaux. *See* Operation Bateaux
  Peterson's HMS *Looe* excavation, 64
  Saratoga Springs JHS students PVC grid for, 147
  search patterns in, 99, 188–89
  "Shipwreck Weekend at Lake George," 164–65
  standards for, 64
  tenets of, 105

university courses in, 65
workshop for, xiii–xv, 73–75, 78, 164
"Underwater Archaeology of 'The Sunken Fleet of 1758'" exhibit, 173–74
U.S. Forest Products Lab, 57

Van Aken, David, 75, 90, 127
vandalization
  of Bateau(x) Site VI, 107, *108*
  of Bateau(x) Site X, 110
  Inverarity on, 55, 63–64
  in *Land Tortoise* park, 141
  after Operation Bateaux, 88, 184, 194
  by recreational dive community, 55–57, 63–64
  of Wiawaka Bateau B, 84, 86, 88, 143
Vandrei, Charles, 144, 153, 171
Vasa, 57, 79
Vauban-style earth-and-wooden fortification, 5, 90, 208
Veeder, Harold, 66, *66*, 107, 118, 119
Vermont
  Basin Harbor Maritime Museum, 13–14, 71–72, 135
  Swanton, 9
  underwater park system in, 133, 135
vernacular watercraft, 21, 85, 208
"Video Virtual Reality Tour of a Sunken Colonial Bateau Site," 172
Viele, Melodie, 174
Village of Lake George, 28ni, 62, 153–154, 170, 171, 188
Vrana, Kenneth, 131

walking tours, 170, 172
Walsh, James, 121
War of 1812, 9, 179–181
Warrensburgh Museum of Local History, 32
Warrensburgh News, The, 32
warships, 6, 7, 15, 23, 28, 39, 41, 47, 48, 54, 57, 62, 75, 88, 91, 98, *108*, 111, 134, 137, 143, 155, 172, 176, 183, 203, 204, 205. *See also individual vessels*
Washington, George, 176
Washington State's Federal Art Program, 45
Watertown Daily Times, 45

Watertown Times, 51
ways, 23, 208
Wendell, Jacob, 19
Westbrook, Nick, 61
Western Inland Lock Navigation Co., 167–68, 176
"wet storage"
  during French and Indian War, 6, *8*, 54, 111, 155, 176, 181–82
  of *Land Tortoise* radeau, 181–82
whaleboats, 6, *7*, 97, 148, 181, 208
wharfs, 91, 161, 172. *See also* docks; piers
Wheeldon, John, 94
Whitesel, John, *8*, *12*, 159, 160, 173, 179
Wiawaka bateaux. *See also individual bateaux*
  "Archaeological Research Assistant Workshop" dives to, xiii–xv, 73–75, 78, 164
  circular holes in bottom boards, 84
  description of, 78–79, 106–7
  designations (A-G), 78
  "disappeared," 113–14
  drawing of, *80–83*
  Erving's World Wide Skindiver's Guide on, 71
  historic markers on, 169–70
  Lake George Bateaux Research Team studies of, 73–88
  mapping of, 73, 78, 85, 88
  maps of, *86*, *114*
  on National Register of Historic Places, 100, 119, 127–29, 140, 171
  19th century discovery of, 27
  orientation of, 79, 85–88, 151
  photograph of, *xiv*, *xv*, *74*, *78*, *79*
  rediscovery of (1960s), 77
  ROV survey of, *74*, 78
  in "Shipwreck Weekend at Lake George," 165
  side-scan sonar surveys of, 77–78
  signs for, *173*
  site cleanup, 143–45
  stabilizing, 143–46
  strategies for protecting, 145–46
Wiawaka Holiday House, 73, 78, 85, 113, 143, 150, 188
Wiawaka Holiday House dock, 27, 84–85, 143–44, *145*
Winchell-Sweeney, Susan, 151
"Wit's Bateaux," 110–11
Wolf, Lud, 71
Wood, Lemuel, 19
"Wooden Bones" (documentary)
  on *Baby Whale*, 124, 125, 161
  Crandall interview in, 67–68
  DVD cover from, *160*
  Farrell interview in, 124
  on Lake George's 1758 bateaux, 67–68, 161
  length of, 159
  Maple Ave. students' replica bateau in, 153–54
  Maritime Heritage Award for, 161
  Peckham's drawings in, 179
  release of, 161
Works Progress Administration, 45
Wright, Robin K., 46–47

yellow submarine. *See Baby Whale*
Yohn, Frederick Coffay, *4*

Zaboly, Gary, *136*
Zarzynski, Joseph
  aluminum dive boat of, *169*
  dives of, xviii
  Documentary Filmmaking for Archaeologists, 161
  photograph of, *89*, *157*, *175*, *262*
  Preserve America Steward award for, 142
  retirement from underwater archaeology, 183
zebra mussels, 184
Zeccolo, Stan, 18, 61, 106, 114

About the Author

Maritime archaeologist and author Joseph W. Zarzynski repaints a blue-and-yellow metal historic marker entitled WIAWAKA BATEAUX. The signage is located along the shoreline of the Wiawaka Holiday House at Lake George near the site of seven 1758 sunken bateaux. (Credit: M.P. Meaney)

Joseph W. Zarzynski is a maritime archaeologist, retired educator, newspaper columnist, and documentary scriptwriter. A native of Endicott, New York, he now lives in Saratoga County, New York. He has a Bachelor of Arts degree (History) from Ithaca College, a Master of Arts in Teaching degree (Social Sciences) from Binghamton University, and a Master of Arts degree (Archaeology and Heritage) from the University of Leicester (UK). From 1987 to 2011 Zarzynski was executive director of the not-for-profit underwater archaeology group Bateaux Below (previously the Lake George Bateaux Research Team). Some of his other underwater archaeological work includes mapping Revolutionary War shipwrecks and a reputed slave vessel in Rhode Island waters, studying shipwrecks of the eighteenth and nineteenth centuries in the Florida Keys, and excavating an eighteenth-century submerged wharf in Massachusetts. In 1985, as a reporter for a national aviation publication, he covered the recovery of a sunken World War II British Wellington bomber from Loch Ness, Scotland. Recently, Zarzynski and his wife volunteered at the New York State Museum, cataloguing artifacts from an eighteenth-century shipwreck unearthed during 2010 construction of the new World Trade Center building in Manhattan. He was a scriptwriter for four documentaries from Pepe Productions: "The Lost Radeau: North America's Oldest Intact Warship" (2005); "Wooden Bones: The Sunken Fleet of 1758" (2010); "Search for the *Jefferson Davis*: Trader, Slaver, Raider" (2011); and "Iron Sentries: The Mystery Cannons of Fort William Henry" (2016). Zarzynski has published over 450 newspaper, newsletter, and journal articles, encyclopedia entries, and professional reports. A columnist for the *Lake George Mirror* newspaper, he pens articles on local history. This is Zarzynski's sixth book; one of those is a young adult book. Three books he authored, and three were co-authored; four are on maritime archaeology, and two on underwater mysteries. He enjoys jogging, writing, volunteering at museums and on archaeological digs, and visiting historical sites.

www.ingramcontent.com/pod-product-compliance
Lightning Source LLC
Chambersburg PA
CBHW051117160426
43195CB00014B/2250